Table of Contents

Table of Contents

Want to see more?

Via Corsa Car Lover's Guide to Arizona is now in print!

Coming in 2011 - Look for our Guides to California!

Welcome to the Via Corsa Guidebook Series! We are a new publishing company dedicated to writing guidebooks covering the hot spots of car activity in the United States and in Europe. Each book is a comprehensive guide covering every aspect of the automobile - let it be car museums, race tracks, factory tours, car shows, or drives. In other words, this is a book for people who love cars. "Via Corsa Car Lover's Guide to Southern Germany" is our second title, and our next step towards writing and producing guidebooks that will eventually cover most of Europe and the United States. Here at Via Corsa we love cars. We have been around them for decades and want to share our knowledge and insight gained in the process. No matter what your passion, there is something in this book for you, and if you enjoy this guide, please tell us!

About Ron Adams

Ron is the principle author and photographer of *Via Corsa Car Lover's Guide to Southern Germany*. Before graduating from high school in Colorado, Ron Adams had travelled to 6 of the 7 continents; including trips to China, Peru, Zimbabwe, and the Australian Outback. After college, he moved to Munich, Germany to live. He has raced on Mugello, Hungaroring, and Salzburgring in Europe and has raced Road America, Lime Rock, Mazda Raceway Laguna Seca, Infineon Raceway, Road Atlanta, VIR, PIR, and several other race tracks in the United States. He won the 1998-99 Arizona Regional SCCA Championship in Formula Mazda and placed 1st in the 2000 Ferrari Challenge Endurance Series and 4th in the Ferrari Sprint series. Ron currently lives in Paradise Valley, Arizona with his wife and 2 children.

About Oliver Littmann

Oliver is the contributor for the "Via Corsa Car Lover's Guide to Southern Germany". Oliver was born & raised in Munich. In the 1990s, he attended the Pasadena Art Center College of Design in La Tour de Peilz, Switzerland. He received a Bachelor of Science degree in Industrial & Transportation Design. Since then he runs different businesses in design with clients like Audi, BMW, Nissan, TÜV Süddeutschland to name a few. He also gives lectures at the University of Applied Science. His decades of first hand experience as an insider to the world of automotive design and his passion and knowledge of classic European sportscars make him a valuable addition. Oliver currently lives in Munich.

Introduction to Southern Germany

My first trip to Germany was when I was 15 years old. It was a month long summer trip organized by my school in Colorado and my first chance to hunt for "The Autobahn". Just like many teenage boys, I was fascinated with fast cars and the mythical places they lurked. Of course, my 8th grade science teacher /chaperone was more interested in keeping over a dozen of us kids out of trouble, well fed, and hopefully able leave the country with a few history lessons learned. For me, "The Autobahn" would have to wait.

During college I returned to Germany for a semester abroad, but rather than follow my childhood obsession with sports cars, I followed a pretty German girl instead. I dutifully studied my German grammar and spent my weeks commuting between Munich and Augsburg on a train. Of course, as these things sometimes go, the pretty German girl and I parted ways and I returned to the U.S. to finish my studies. Once again, "The Autobahn" would have to wait.

After college graduation I once again went to Germany. I was going to find that pretty German girl and win her back, but as it turned out she had left Germany to study in the United States. Alone and depressed, a funny thing happened. I realized I loved Germany. I loved the culture, the food, the landscape, the beer, and of course the cars. So I did the most rational thing a single male college graduate living in Munich, Germany would do. I bought a BMW M3.

Finally. There it was all before me. Not just a road, but an entire highway system based on the idea that one could drive as fast as the car would go! My first drive in my "new" *Jahreswagen* (see page 52) BMW was a 200+ km/h Sunday morning round trip from Munich to Garmisch-Partenkirchen and back.

This first drive would be the first of many spirited drives on the Autobahn and the seeds of a life long love of a place I call a second home.

Ron Adams

Want to comment?
E-mail: *info@viacorsa.com*

Did we make a mistake?
E-mail: *corrections@viacorsa.com*

Want to submit your business?
E-mail: *submissions@viacorsa.com*

Join us on Facebook at
www.facebook.com/viacorsa
or Twitter at www.twitter.com/viacorsa

Retail Orders -
Our guidebooks are available through Motorbooks International.

Phone orders -
(800) 826-6600 or (715) 294-3345
Internet orders -
www.motorbooks.com
or try
www.amazon.com

There are 8 sections in this book and each section is further broken down into spreads. Each spread includes in depth coverage of that site's history, current events, or exhibitions. This guidebook does not use the tradition guidebook format of listing sites by region.

▶ The 8 sections cover **History**, **Manufacturers**, **Museums**, **Tuners**, **Race Tracks**, **Driving Schools**, **Hot Spots**, and **Road Trips**.

▶ The **Road Trips** section is all about driving your car. We have covered the traditional tourist routes, a classic car rally, one very special event at Kesselberg, 5 of the best Stammtisch lake drives we have taken, and Hans-Joachim Stuck's favorite drive.

▶ The **Appendix** lists a few extra sites to see, a calendar of events, road signs, Autobahn information, and general travel information.

Location Maps, Directions, and Phone Numbers

Description of our directions -

From **Munich:** (*<- starting point*)

▶ Autobahnen are in **BLUE**

▶ Autobahn exit ramps are **WHITE** with a **BLUE** border. All other exit ramps have a **BLACK** border.

▶ Bundes Strasse (*Federal Roads*) are **YELLOW** with **BLACK** border.

▶ Major roads are **BLACK**

▶ The end destination is in **RED**

▶ Some adjacent roads are deleted

▶ The German word for street is "Strasse"or "Straße". In most maps and some directions, we abbreviate "Strasse" as just "..str."

▶ We list most phone numbers as +49 (0) 841/89-37575. To call from the USA, dial 001-49-841/89-37575. Inside Germany, dial 0841/89-37575 (This is Audi's main phone number)

Quick Stats

If you would like a brief overview of a site or topic, refer to our **"Quick Stats"**. These answer the most frequent questions asked.

"Journal Entries"

A Guidebook can be an impersonal place. Usually they seems like it is no more than a collection of facts, figures, and photos. While important, also look for a few of our personal stories from over the years with "Journal Entries".

     ✍   *Ron Adams*

Each Section of our guidebook is denoted by an easy to identify Icon. These Icons are placed at the top of corner of each page. The introduction portion to the guidebook as well as the appendix and index do not have Icons and some pages with photographs will not have an Icon.

History

Explore the dawn of the automobile, racing history, and the birth and development of Autobahn.

Manufacturing

Take a factory tour, visit a forum, or see a museum! Each of the big manufacturers offer the visitor many different options.

Museums

Museums are all over Southern Germany. We cover a total of 22 car related museums in this particular section.

Tuners & Aftermarket

Usually these aftermarket companies are just called "Tuners". This is a generalization as RUF now manufacturers its own sports car.

Race Tracks

There are two main race tracks in Southern Germany. The Hockenheimring and the Nürburgring.

Driving Schools

Some schools teach you skills to improve your driving on the public road while others let you hone your on track racing techniques.

Exclusive Interviews

We have several exclusive interviews and Question and Answer sessions with many notable figures in German Motorsports.

Hot Spots

Anything that doesn't fit into the above categories is listed here. See interesting dealers, restoration shops, restaurants, and more.

Drives

This edition is focusing on drives around Bavaria. Future guides will expand to highlight drives through other German states.

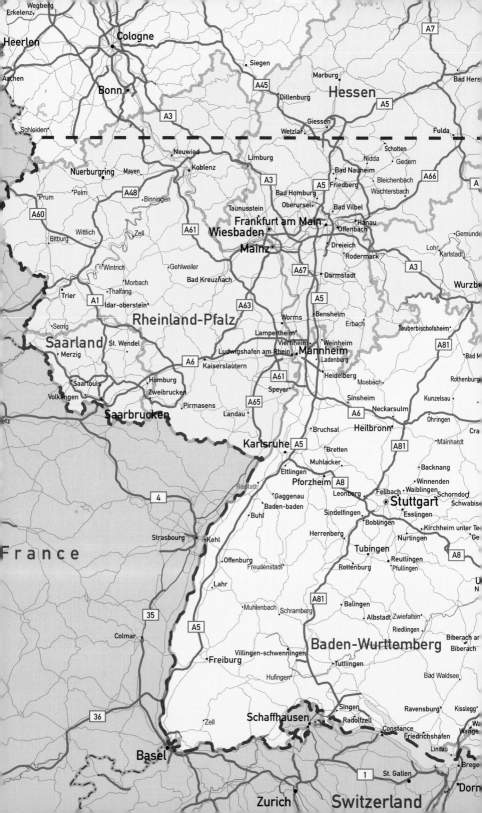

"Via Corsa Car Lover's Guide to Southern Germany" is defined by the dotted line -

0 5 10   20 Miles
0 5 10   20 KM

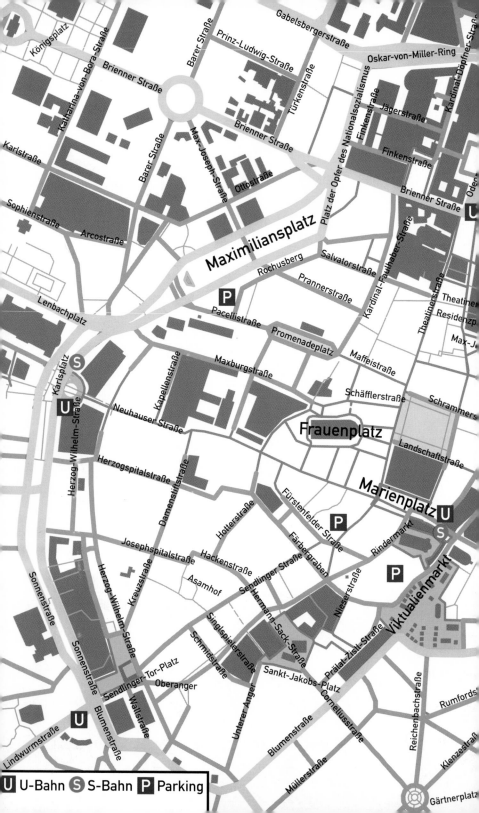

U U-Bahn S S-Bahn P Parking

Introduction to Southern Germany

From the fairy tale castles in the Alps up to the vineyards along the banks of the Rhein (*Rhine*) River, Southern Germany is rich in culture and history, romantic, and simply beautiful. While there are many wonderful sites to visit all around all of Germany, there is also a fascinating and often over looked aspect to Southern Germany - The culture and history of the automobile. This part of the country is home to the best car museums, race tracks, and manufacturers in the world. Southern Germany means many things to different people, but for us, it means "cars" ∎

Via Corsa Car Lover's Guide to Southern Germany

Try Something a Little Different

No visitor should ever pass up the chance to visit **Schloss Neuschwanstein** at the foot of the Alps. After all, thanks to Disney, this is what most U.S. tourists expect to see. Let's go beyond the art museums and Rococo architecture and explore a different part of Germany. Something that most travellers have yearned for, but never before had all the information at their fingertips. Here is Southern Germany from the view of car lovers. We define Southern Germany as everything from the **Nürburgring** in the north to the Alps in the south.

Baden-Württemberg

Located in the southwestern corner of Germany, Baden-Württemberg and the Swabians living there have the lowest rate of unemployment in all of Germany. This is certainly a benefit of living where **Bosch**, **Daimler AG**, **Porsche**, and **SAP** have both factories and their world headquarters. The state is defined by Bodensee (*Lake Constance*) in the south and the Black Forest and Rhein River to the west. Major cities are Stuttgart and Mannheim. The major car factories inside Baden-Württemberg are Audi, Daimler AG (**Mercedes-Benz** is a subsidiary), and Porsche. There are well over a dozen car museums and the tuners including Lorinser and Techart. There is one full time race track - the Hockenheimring in northern part of the state near the Rhein River and the border with Rhineland-Pfalz.

Opposite: The Classic-Gala Schwetzingen International Concours D'Elegance.

Bavaria

The largest state in Germany is also one of its most popular tourist destinations. The Alps form a narrow band in the south with a number of crystal clear mountain lakes in their shadows. The northern part of Bavaria is defined by the Bavarian Forest in the east and the medieval fortresses that dot the Romantic Road in the west. The major cities in Bavaria include Augsburg, Ingolstadt, Munich and Nürnberg (*Nuremberg*). The major car factories inside Bavaria are Audi and BMW with smaller tuners and manufacturers such as Alpina, Novitec Rosso, and RUF located south of Munich. Nürnberg in Northern Bavaria is home to the temporary race track, the Norisring.

Hessen

Only a portion of Hessen is covered in this guide and very few car sites are within its boundaries. Opel's main factory and headquarters are in Rüsselsheim just southwest of Frankfurt and the temporary race track, the Schottenring, is to the northeast of Frankfurt.

Rheinland-Pfalz/Saarland

The wineries and vineyards along the Rhein River are only a short drive to the east from this region's greatest attraction, the **Nürburgring** (and the **Nordschleife**). The major cities are Koblenz, Mainz, Speyer (home to the **Speyer Technical Museum**), and Trier. Rheinland-Pfalz is only covered in part by this guide and Saarland does not have any car related sites covered at all.

Introduction to Munich

What to see

The best way to visit Munich's city center and Fussgängerzone *(pedestrian zone)* is to park your car and take a S-Bahn or U-Bahn to Marienplatz.

City Center

The **Glockenspiel** *(clock that plays)* in the Rathaus chimes at 11:00 AM (12:00 PM and 5:00 PM in the summer) with a show retelling the 16th century wedding of Duke Wilhelm V. The **Viktualienmarkt** is an open air food market with a small, but quaint, biergarten. Additional sites in the center include the **Residenz**, **Hofgarten**, and **Frauenkirche** with its two onion tops.

Englisher Garten

Located to the north of the city center is the Englisher Garten. This massive park has a lake and two biergartens - **Seehaus** and **Chinesischer Turm**.

Surrounding Area

▶ Olympiapark - next to BMW
▶ Dachau Concentration Camp
▶ Tour the Bavaria Filmstadt - See *www.filmstadt.de*

Quick Stats

▶ 1.3 million inhabitants
▶ 089 is the area code
▶ See *www.muenchen-tourist.de* or *www.muenchen.de*

Exploring Munich

The expression "**München ist die nördlichste italienische Stadt**" (*"Munich is the northern most Italian town"*) and term **Gemütlichkeit** (literally defined as *cozy* or *friendly*) is the often used to describe Munich. Munich is an easy going city rich in both tradition and culture. It is also that place in Germany that fulfills all our stereotypes about jolly Germans. Of course Munich is also home to Oktoberfest. Only in Munich would you see a local drink a beer and eat a traditional breakfast of Weisswurst (*white sausage*) while wearing Lederhosen at 11:00 AM. Munich is also home to **Schloss Nymphenburg** and a number of world class art museums most of which are only a U-Bahn stop or two away from the city center.

Above: The Rathaus and Glockenspiel in Marienplatz in the city center of Munich.

Introduction to Stuttgart

Exploring Stuttgart

Stuttgart is an industrial town set in the beautiful Neckar Valley with the city of Stuttgart sitting in a bowl surrounded by rolling green hills. The people in Stuttgart have the reputation of being efficient and conservative. Stuttgart is also the corporate home of Mercedes-Benz, Porsche, and Bosch.

What to see

A good way to begin a tour of Stuttgart is to start at the Hauptbahnhof (*central train station*) and walk along the pedestrian zone to the **Schloss Platz**.

City Center

The 10th century **Altes Schloss** (*Old Castle*) and the 18th century **Neues Schloss** (*New Castle*) are both minutes away by foot. Other sites to see are the new **Kunstmuseum Stuttgart** (see *www.kunstmuseum-stuttgart.de*), **Oberer Schillerplatz**, **Schlossgarten**, **Staatsgalerie** (see *www.staatsgalerie.de*), and the **Carl-Zeiss-Planetarium** (see *www.zeiss.de/planetariums*).

Fehrsehturm

The Fehrsehturm is the world's first television tower. It was completed in 1956 and rises 1,585 feet above sea level. It has an observation deck, restaurant, and shop.
See *www.fernsehturmstuttgart.com*

Surrounding Area

▶ Schloss Solitude is a castle to the southwest of Stuttgart. It is also well known as a former race track (See page 302).
▶ Wilhelma Zoological and Botanical Gardens is a great place to take the kids and it's open all year. See *www.wilhelma.de*

Quick Stats

▶ 600,000 inhabitants
▶ 0711 is the area code
▶ The name Stuttgart has evolved from the word "**Stuotgarten**" (*stud farm*). The black horse that is on the city coat of arms is also part of the Porsche crest.
▶ See *www.stuttgart-tourist.de*

Above: *The Stuttgart Hauptbahnhof.*

German Car Culture

Contrary to popular opinion, not all Germans are lead foot maniacs ever in search of more horsepower and an Autobahn. Most Germans would be content with a sunny day, a convertible, and a casual drive followed by a romantic meal.

The Stereo Typical German

Germans live up to their worldwide stereotype. They are serious, efficient, punctual, organized, and a society of perfectionists. If you ask a German car mechanic about their counterparts around the world, expect a polite scoff that no one could possible match their skill set. Germans are also formal. They shake hands and use the formal "Sie" form even after years of business. Sometimes that barrier may fall with too much Schnapps on the weekend. But without fail, Monday morning brings back that formal "Sie" greeting.

What You Are is What You Drive

Stereotypes about drivers and their owners have existed for decades. For example, Mercedes-Benz drivers "**hat eingebaute Vorfahrt**" ("*have built in right of way*"). As arrogant as that sounds, often that expensive Mercedes-Benz (or BMW or Porsche) is stripped of options. Air-conditioning and power windows are an unnecessary luxury. And while the type of car a German owns helps define their identity, they often take great pains to hide that from the rest of the world. Don't expect to see what version of S-Class that Mercedes-Benz is.

The Environment

Germans care about the environment and they recycle paper, glass, and clothing in giant recycle bins along the sides of roads. But the real conflict for the German car enthusiast is between the Autobahn and the forest. They are in fact torn between their personal freedom to speed and saving the trees. Rest assured, recent reports show the lack of speed limit has little affect on the trees.

The Rules

There is a German parable about a pedestrian that walks across a street and get hits by a car. The driver is let go without a citation while the injured pedestrian is cited for crossing the street against a red light. Rules are everywhere in Germany, and crossing against a red light is one of them. So is insulting another driver in any form. Dare to tap your forehead at another motorist? It's not beyond that insulted motorists to start snapping photos of the offender.

The Opel Manta

Hail to the Opel Manta! The 1980s stereotypical owner of a Manta had a mullet, gold chain, tight jeans, and a blonde hairdresser for a girlfriend. The fiercely proud owner of that Manta lowered it, painted it, and donned it with a large rear spoiler. So of course, there are hundreds of jokes about these owners.

"Why is the Opel Manta only one seat wide? So the Opel Manta driver can hang his arms out both windows".

Opposite: *The wide variety of cars one may see on a sunny summer day.*

Trabants

How do you double the value of a Trabant? Fill up the gas tank.

This little car may be looked at by the rest of the world as a cute, cheap, little collector car and a fascinating piece of history. Germans, on the other hand, hate them. They spewed pollution and are a traffic hazard on the Autobahn. No respectable German car enthusiast would ever want one.

Car Clubs

Over the last few years, enthusiasts around the world have started casual meetings known collectively as *"Cars & Coffee"*. It may be strange to note that there are no *"Cars & Coffee"* in Germany. Germans still prefer the formality of proper car clubs.

Pünktliche Romantics

Everything in Germany is run according to a schedule and everyone is punctual. It's a funny paradox to see someone set their watch to the exact second at one of Germany's many public transportation clocks, only to lose one's self at a candle lit wine bar for hours of conversation.

How Germans See Americans

Germans see us as superficial and culture-less. Of course mainstream media reinforces this idea both in the U.S. and abroad. Although once you talk to a German, more than likely, they will admit they have a secret admiration for their fellow enthusiasts. Ask one about **Route 66** or **Harley-Davidson** and they're aglow in appreciation.

Know Before You Go

When to Visit

There is always something to do all year long, but the best time to go will always be May through October. Many of the smaller museums close in the fall. Avoid travelling to Germany in August at all costs. The major Autobahnen are full with holiday travellers. Factories, their tours, and many businesses are closed.

Where to Fly

Most of the car related sites are centered around Munich and Stuttgart. Both airports have direct flights from the United States.

What to Take

Weather is unpredictable and changes quickly. If you plan to go to the Nürburgring, rain gear is all but mandatory most of the year. We recommend a rain jacket and folding umbrella.

Car versus Train

The advice in this guidebook is aimed at the driver - whether you are renting a car or buying a new car with European Delivery. It is possible to travel around Germany by train to visit the sites in this book, but a number of locations are in rural areas not well served by public transport.

Insurance
When renting a car, the agency will ask if you want optional full coverage (*Vollkaskoversicherung*). Please check your options prior to your departure to see if this best fits your situation.

Visa and Customs
A valid passport is required for all visitors from outside the European Union. Entry visas are not required for U.S. or Canadian citizens. See *www.customs.gov*

Currency and Exchange Rate
The Euro is the currency in Germany and the rest of the European Union. Prices are denoted as either € 5.- or 5 Euro. The exchange rate is roughly $1.40 to € 1.-

German
Most Germans speak English and tours in both factories and larger museums are available in English.

Driver's License
A normal rental car agency doesn't require anything beyond a valid U.S. license, but a number of driving schools require an international permit. Be sure to make photocopies of your license(s) and passport.

Traffic Laws & Signs
German traffic laws and signs are not all that different from laws in North America. However there are some specific road signs and Autobahn laws that visitors should know before departure. See **page 314**.

Opposite: *July in Southern Germany near Schwäbisch Hall.*

Photography
Some museums allow photographers to roam about at will. Other museums have restrictions. Most will not allow the use of a tripod nor commercial photography unless prior arrangements have been made. Some businesses and all factory tours prohibit photography of any kind. Please arrange any permissions you feel you may need well in advance of your trip.

Etiquette
In smaller stores and restaurants, it is customary to greet the staff with a "Guten Tag" and say goodbye with a "Wiedersehen". Hand shakes are customary when saying both hello and goodbye in a business setting.

Money
Credit cards are generally accepted and ATMs by and large use popular networks such as Cirrus. Travellers Checks will never hurt, though.

Phones and Laptops
Germany uses the GSM900/1800 network and AT&T iPhones are compatible. WiFi is standard at most large chain hotels and even some smaller Gasthofs now too.

Electricity and Adapters
Buy a universal plug adapter. German appliances use a 2 prong plug and run at 220V/240V voltage. Most laptops and cell phones today have built in voltage adapters but need plugs.

∗ Please see "German Travel Information" on **page 324** in the appendix for more tips and travel information.

Travel itineraries

Most European Delivery programs allow for 2 weeks of insurance, so it only makes sense for us to organise our travels in one week and two week increments. Please note that some museums are only open certain days of the week.

1 Week Round Trip to Munich

This trip is a casual cruise through the Alps south of Munich on the length of the entire Alpine Road.

Day 1 - Tour BMW Welt, BMW Museum, and BMW Munich Factory. Night in Munich.

Day 2 - Tour either /or both Deutsches Museum and maybe a-workx. Dinner at Alter Wirt or Waldwirtschaft. Night in Munich.

Day 3 - Drive to Chiemsee. Visit C.F. Mirbach and EFA Ammerang Museum. Night at Malerwinkel Hotel at Chiemsee.

Day 4 - Drive to Berchtesgaden and the Alpine Road. Follow the Alpine Road from Berchtesgaden to Leeberghof in Tegernsee. Night at Tegernsee.

Day 5 - Drive to Füssen and over Kesselberg. Stop for lunch at Seehotel/Grauer in Kochel and visit Schloss Neuschwanstein. Night in Füssen.

Day 6 - Detour off the Alpine Road and visit ABT. Drive to Lindau and the end of the Alpine Road. Night in Lindau.

Day 7 - Return to Munich. Stop by Fritz B. Busch Museum and Novitec Rosso along the way. Night in Munich.

1 Week Round Trip to Stuttgart

A loop around Stuttgart visiting sites to the north of the city.

Day 1 - Tour Porsche Museum and Porsche Factory in Zuffenhausen. Night in Stuttgart.

Day 2 - Tour Mercedes-Benz Museum and take a Factory Tour at either Untertürkheim or Sindelfingen. Night in Stuttgart.

Day 3 - Drive to Waiblingen and visit Lorinser. Continue on to Mercedes-AMG in Affalterbach for a tour. Night in Affalterbach.

Day 4 - Drive to Öhringen and visit Motormuseum Öhringen. Continue on to Langenburg and visit the Langenburg Automuseum. Night in Langenburg.

Day 5 - Drive to Neckarsulm to see Audi Forum and Audi factory tour. Continue on to the Technical Museum Sinsheim. Night in Sinsheim.

Day 6 - Visit Technical Museum Sinsheim then drive to Hockenheimring, visit track and museum. Night in Speyer or Hockenheimring.

Day 7 - Visit Technical Museum Speyer and Autovision Museum. Return to Stuttgart.

2 Week Round Trip to Munich

The Nordschleife is the goal of this round trip.

Day 1 - Visit BMW Welt, Museum, and Munich factory. Night in Munich.

Day 2 - See the Deutsches Museums. Night in Munich.

Day 3 - Drive to Ingolstadt and tour Audi and MTM. Night in Ingolstadt.

Day 4 - Drive to either Regensburg or Nürnberg. Visit Maybach Museum and Norisring or BMW Regensburg.

Day 5 - Visit Herpa and Langenburg Museum. Night in Langenburg or Rothenburg o.d.T.

Day 6 - Drive to Sinsheim and visit Technical Museum Sinsheim. Night in Sinsheim.

Day 7 - Drive to Nürburgring. Night at Nürburgring.

Day 8 - Explore Nürburgring and Nordschleife. Night at Nürburgring.

Day 9 - Drive to Speyer to see Hockenheimring, Technical Museum Speyer, and/or Autovision. Night in Speyer.

Day 10 - Drive to Tübingen and visit Marxzell on the way to Boxenstop. Night in Tübingen.

Day 11 - Visit Mercedes-Benz Sindelfingen and Mercedes-Benz Museum. Night in Stuttgart.

Day 12 - Visit Porsche Museum and factory. Night in Stuttgart.

Day 13 - Drive to Friedrichshafen to visit Zeppelin Museum and Dornier Museum. Night in Friedrichshafen.

Day 14 - Return to Munich. Stop by RUF along the way. Night in Munich.

2 Week Round Trip to Stuttgart

Experience a sample of both the Romantic Road and Alpine Road with only a few car related stops.

Day 1 - Tour Porsche Museum and Mercedes-Benz Museum. Night in Stuttgart.

Day 2 - Drive to Würzburg to begin the Romantic Road. Night in Würzburg.

Day 3 - Drive south on the Romantic Road. Night in Rothenburg o.d.T.

Day 4 - Continue south on the Romantic Road. Night in Nördlingen.

Day 5 - Drive to Munich and visit BMW Welt. Night in Munich.

Day 6 - Drive to Chiemsee and visit EFA Museum. Night in Chiemsee.

Day 7 - Start the Alpine Road at Bernau and drive west. Night in Tegernsee.

Day 10 - Continue west on the Alpine Road. Night in Kochel am See.

Day 9 - Continue west on the Alpine Road to Schloss Neuschwanstein. Night in Füssen.

Day 10 - Continue west on Alpine Road. Night in Lindau.

Day 11 - Visit both Zeppelin and Dornier Museums. Night in Friedrichshafen.

Day 12 - Drive to Engstingen and visit both museum and Schloss Lichtenstein. Night in Reutlingen.

Day 13 - Visit Boxenstop Museum. Night in Tübingen.

Day 14 - Return to Stuttgart.

＊ Not all factory tours and museums are open throughout the week.

German Automotive History

For centuries, inventors tried to build a self propelled vehicle with little commercial or technological success. In the 13th century, Guido da Vigevano attempted to use wind to power a vehicle and later in the 15th century, Leonardo da Vinci designed a clockwork driven tricycle. But it was the invention and development of the internal combustion engine that finally moved the world into this new age of transportation ∎

The Engine

The four stroke internal combustion engine was developed in Europe by several different inventors at roughly the same time. Some were granted patents, while others failed to apply. In 1860, Austrian inventor **Christian Reithmann** built a 4 stroke engine in Munich, while concurrently in France, **Alphonse Bear de Rochas** worked on his 4 stroke engine. In 1876, **Nikolaus August Otto** significantly improved the four stroke engine and patented his "**Otto**" cycle engine (patent number DRP 532). He went on to sell over 30,000 of them.

In 1883 **Gottlieb Daimler** together with **Wilhelm Maybach** further developed the Otto engine into the modern high speed and rapid combustion gasoline powered engine. They both continued to develop engines and in 1887 fitted their new "Motor Carriage" (designed from scratch) with their new engine called the "**Grandfather Clock**".

The First Car

Just as with the engine, the automobile slowly developed over several decades. **Karl Benz**, independent of Gottlieb Daimler (see sidebar), is widely accepted as the inventor of the modern day automobile. The **Benz Patent Motor Car** received patent number 37435 in 1885 and debuted in Mannheim on July 3, 1886.

Opposite: *Benz Patent-Motorwagen, Model 3, 1886. The picture shows Karl Benz with his hands on the steering wheel and to the left his employee Josef Brecht.*
Above Right: *Gottlieb Daimler.*

Driven by the success of the patent car, **Benz & Cie.** slowly evolved into a car manufacturer and by 1893 the core of the business was building automobiles. The eventual merger of Benz & Cie. with **Daimler-Motoren-Gesellschaft** to create the Mercedes-Benz brand we see today would not happen for another 3 decades. See"Mercedes-Benz" on page 69.

Who were Gottlieb Daimler & Karl Benz?

"***Daimler***" and "***Benz***". The two words that are both instantly recognized today as the brand names behind the world's leading vehicle manufacturer Daimler AG and its subsidiary Mercedes-Benz. Ironically **Gottlieb Daimler** (1834 - 1900) and **Karl Benz**, sometimes spelled as **Carl Benz**, (1844 - 1929) never met. While Daimler and his partner Wilhelm Maybach (founder of the future Maybach-Motorenbau GmbH and builder of Maybach Automobiles) were building engines outside Stuttgart in Bad Cannstatt, Benz was just over 100 kms away in Mannheim independently working on his 3 wheeled Patent Motor Car. Benz's first car ride was in 1886, a year before Daimler's car (motor carriage) made its 1887 Stuttgart debut.

Race Tracks

Germany is filled with the ghosts of race tracks now gone. Some were not commercial successes, others were closed because of safety issues, and yet more were only temporary tracks, designed to last only a weekend.

Southwest of Stuttgart is one of the more famous ghost tracks, **Solitude Rennen**. Opened in 1903, this track is now trying to make a comeback with events held every few years. Other tracks such as the one in Munich's **Forstenrieder Park** are long gone and barely remembered. The **Schleizer Dreieck** in the state of Thüringen (just north of Bavaria) opened in 1923 and has also had some success in holding revival races.

Some of the post war tracks such as the **Karlsruhe Dreieck** and the **München/Riem Flugplatz Rennen** had short careers in the late 1940s and early 1950s with Formula races, but sadly almost no information about the tracks or races exist today. Not all race tracks are totally forgotten. A track by the name of the **Feldbergring** outside Frankfurt enjoys support by fans with web sites, keeping the memories alive with photos and track maps. Some temporary courses such as **Alemannenring** in Singen were used for a few years for DTM races starting in 1991 but have not made a comeback. Southern Germany is full of (mostly temporary) racing circuits that are now lost in time. Some are worth hunting down in either the small towns that once hosted them or the abandoned alignments of roads now hidden in forests.

The history of **Hockenheimring**, **Nürburgring**, **Norisring**, and **Schottenring** is covered in our Race Track section starting on page 204. For more information about **Solitude Rennen** and other race tracks, see "Additional Sites to see –" on page 302.

Left: Großer Preis von Europa at the Nürburgring, August 1, 1954.

Juan Manuel Fangio in the Mercedes-Benz W 196 R Monoposto leads Froilán González/ Mike Hawthorn in the Ferrari 625.

Schloss Nürburg is in the background.

Opposite: ADAC-Trophy at the Nürburgring, August 20, 1989. Sauber-Mercedes Gruppe-C-Racesportwagen C9.

Start # 61 - the Siegerteam of Jean-Louis Schlesser & Jochen Mass (Race winner).

Start # 62 - teammates Mauro Baldi & Kenneth Acheson in 2nd place.

Motorsports

First Automobile Race

In 1894, the first unofficial automobile race was held in France with the winning car running a Daimler engine. The first proper auto race was held a year later with a Daimler engine once again in the winning car.

Hill Climbs

During the 1930s, the hill climb was a popular type of racing with factory teams drawing the best drivers of the era. In 1930, the European Hill Climb Championship held its German race in Freiburg/Schauinsland with Kesselberg hosting later years. **Hans Stuck** dominated the sport in an Auto Union and aptly earned the title "Bergkönig" (*Mountain King*).

Endurance Racing

It is no mistake that endurance racing is popular in Germany. After all, the Nordschleife is here. Starting in 1953, the ADAC held the first 1000 km Nürburgring race (it lasted about 8 hours) and then in 1970, the **ADAC 24 Hours Nürburgring**.

Formula 1

The Großer Preis von Deutschland (*German Grand Prix*) is the annual FIA Formula 1 race held each year in Germany. Today it alternates between the Hockenheimring and the Nürburgring Grand Prix circuit.

The origins of the race go back to the 1926 Grand Prix that was once organized and sanctioned by the German automobile club the **AvD** (Automobilclub von Deutschland). The debut race was held at **AVUS** in Berlin and won by **Rudolf Caracciola**.

In 1951, Germany rejoined the rest of the world by hosting the German Grand Prix at Nürburgring Nordschleife with **Alberto Ascari** winning the race. (Germany and its drivers were banned from competition until 1951). One significant footnote in history is the near fatal crash of **Niki Lauda** during the 1976 F1 race on the Nordschleife. The crash ended all F1 races on the Nordschleife and the 1977 F1 race was held at the Hockenheimring staying there until 2006 when the circuits began to alternate.

The Autobahn

The Autobahn

The birth of the Autobahn is misunderstood by many. One myth is that the Nazis invented the Autobahn. They did not. The other is that the Autobahn was the first public highway. Also wrong. That honor belongs to the Italians.

But before the Italians built the first Autostrada, there was **AVUS**. Begun in 1912 and opened in Berlin in 1921, AVUS was essentially just a closed race track consisting of 2 lanes separated by a median. Today it is part of the Autobahn A115. In 1923, Italian engineer Piero Puricelli opened the first autostrada as a toll road between

Above: *The Autobahn A95 between Garmisch and Munich. It is one of the nicest sections of Autobahn to drive.*

Milan and Varese. It was this 36 km road that became the model for the German Autobahn.

The Köln to Bonn Autobahn began construction in 1929 at the behest of the mayor of Köln, **Konrad Adenauer** (who also played a key role in the construction of the Nürburgring and became Chancellor of Germany in 1949). The Autobahn opened August 6, 1932, with Adenauer proclaiming "This is how the roads of the future will look." That first Autobahn is part of the Autobahn A555 today.

The Nazi propaganda machine did take a hold of the Autobahn idea, renaming it the "Reichsautobahn", and expanding the system in the 1930s. By 1938, they added an additional 3,000 kilometers.

The 1930s also saw the Autobahn play host to several land speed record attempts. While **Rudolf Caracciola** set the (still unbroken) record in January 1938 of 268.9 mph, it was **Bernd Rosemeyer** who sadly perished. A grave still marks the site on the Autobahn A5.

Construction began again on the Autobahn system in 1953 and in 1959, an aggressive expansion plan expanded the Autobahn in 4 year segments and by 1984, the total was 8,080 kms (5,021 miles). When the Berlin Wall fell in 1989, most expansion plans were put on hold to upgrade the roads in the former East Germany.

The Autobahn Today

Today the system consists of over 12,400 kms (7,705 miles) of roadway.

Quick Stats

- Each Autobahn is 2 to 4 lanes wide with a center median
- Each lane is roughly 11 ½ feet to 12 ⅓ feet wide
- The center median is 10 to 13 feet wide with dual guardrails
- The maximum grade is 4%
- The Autobahn pavement is 27" thick (This is at least twice as thick as a U.S. Interstate)
- There is no Autobahn toll for cars
- There are no billboards
- Proper plural of Autobahn is Autobahnen
- In 1973, there was an Autobahn speed limit of 100 km/h due to the OPEC oil crisis. The speed limit lasted less than 4 months.

The Need for Speed

For those visitors coming from North America to Germany, one of the first things you may notice about Autobahn travel is the lack of sensation when driving fast. Drive a car at 160 km/h (or 100 mph) on an Autobahn and it might seem oddly slow. The reason is the length and distance of the white stripes. In Germany each white strip is almost **20 feet** long separated by a **39 foot** gap, while the white stripes on most U.S. Interstates are **10 feet** long with a **30 feet** gap.

The Autobahn Myth

It is pretty much assumed that everyone with a sports car has heard of the Autobahn. It can also be safely assumed that every car enthusiast outside of Germany has dreamt of a horsepower fueled adrenaline rush of legally speeding along the German Autobahn. Myth #1 is that the Autobahn is just one single epic super highway. It isn't. It is a complicated system of over 140 different highways linking all of Germany together over 12,400 kilometers of roadways. Myth #2 is that there is no speed limit on the Autobahn. This too is not correct. A large part of the Autobahn system has some kind of speed restriction in place. Don't be discouraged. We will tell you when and where to go! See page 314.

Above: *The modern reality of Autobahn travel - A "Stau" on the A8 to Salzburg.*

Southern German Automobile Manufacturers

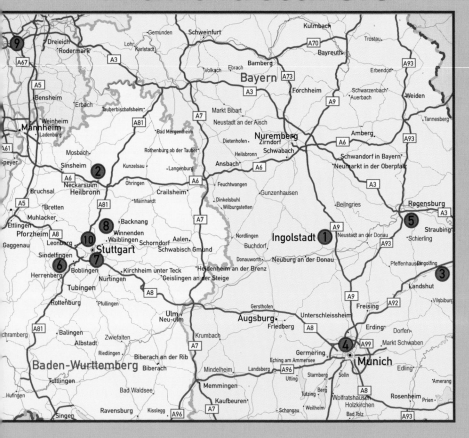

* Opel GmbH is not covered in this guidebook, but the basics and tour information are covered in the appendix in the section - see the Appendix section "Additional Sites" on <u>page 302</u>.

German Manufacturing Plants

Plant	City	Cars	Size
1- Audi	Ingolstadt	A3, A4, A5, Q5	22.6 million square feet
2 - Audi	Neckarsulm	A4 Sedan, A6, A8, R8	10.7 million square feet
3 - BMW	Dingolfing	5,6,7 Series	26.4 million square feet
4 - BMW	Munich	3 Series sedans and wagons	5.4 million square feet
5 - BMW	Regensburg	1 Series,3 Series, Z4	15 million square feet
6 - Mercedes-Benz	Sindelfingen	S, E, SLS	31.2 million square feet
7 - Mercedes-Benz	Untertürkheim	Engines, axles	23 million square feet
8 - Mercedes-AMG	Affalterbach	AMG Engines	Not available
9 - Opel*	Rüsselsheim	Insignia	12.4 million square feet
10 - Porsche	Zuffenhausen	All but Cayenne	484,000 square feet

The first automobile was built and patented in Germany in 1885 followed by the first automobile manufacturer selling cars (*the Benz Patent Motorwagen*) to the public in 1888. Today, the German Automotive industry is the worldwide benchmark for quality craftsmanship, durability, and beautiful designs. There are over a dozen registered manufacturers in Germany, we cover 5 of them ∎

Factory Tours

Every major car manufacturer in Germany offers a factory tour. But just like the cars themselves, each tour is as different as the plant and the cars inside them. Here is our summary of the tours ■

We visited all the factories listed on the opposite page and only reviewed the factory tours we attended as a member of the general public. Every tour has a unique set of rules and regulations and each is discussed in more detail later in the book. Generally speaking, please show up at least 15 to 30 minutes in advance. Most tours are held Monday through Friday and closed for retooling, new model releases, and the entire month of August.

Above: *BMW Welt in Munich is the starting point for tours to the BMW Munich Factory.*

Right: *Look for this "Meeting Point" sign inside the Audi Forum in Neckarsulm to begin your factory tour experience.*

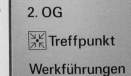

2. OG

Treffpunkt

Werkführungen
Für Besucher-
gruppen und
Einzelbesucher

Factory Tour Summary

Plant	City	Pros	Cons	Rating
Audi	Ingolstadt	Lots of tours available.	Too many tours available. Some tours are expensive.	☆☆☆☆ See page 41
Audi	Neckarsulm	Small groups and was able to see factory areas up close.	A8 & R8 tours are expensive.	☆☆☆☆ See page 47
BMW	Dingolfing	We had a Press tour here, not the regular visitor tour.	No forum or museum.	No rating See page 61
BMW	Munich	Close to city center. Lots to see at BMW Welt & BMW Museum.	Lots of back tracking, very crowded, & tour done from catwalks above factory floor.	☆☆ See page 53
BMW	Regensburg	Longest tour available with very good video presentations.	Lots of walking - almost 5 kilometers.	☆☆☆☆☆ See page 67
Mercedes	Sindelfingen	Interesting E-Class body shell & crash test display.	Tour skips press and paint shops.	☆☆ See page 79
Mercedes	Untertürkheim	Mercedes-Benz Museum.	Engines only - No cars.	Not reviewed
Mercedes/ AMG	Affalterbach	One on one or small group tour and very detailed.	None	☆☆☆☆☆ See page 81
Porsche	Zuffenhausen	Only tour to cover the upholstery department.	Only one type of tour available.	☆☆☆☆ See page 87

Audi

Audi and its history are somewhat unique. Audi didn't have one beginning, it had four beginnings. Each of the rings that make up the Audi emblem represent a different manufacturer, founder, and brand identity. By the time Audi, or Auto Union as it was called back then, merged the four companies into a single entity in 1932, they were assuming decades of history and a legacy. Ring One is Audi, Ring Two is DKW, Ring Three is Horch, and Ring Four is Wanderer. Auto Union AG later merged with NSU and in 1985 and the firm was named Audi AG.

History of Audi

The story begins with August Horch, an automotive pioneer, who founded his car company in 1899.

1902 - Production of Horch cars begins in Reichenbach.

1910 - Due to a dispute with Horchwerke, August Horch names his new automobile company "Audi Automobil-Werke". Audi is based in Zwickau.

1928 - Jorgen Rasmussen and owner of the firm DKW becomes the majority shareholder of Audiwerk AG.

1932 - On June 29, The Rasmussen Group create Auto Union AG with the merger of Audiwerk AG and DKW into the firms Horchwerk AG and the automobile division of Wanderer Werke AG. The four ring emblem is born and the head offices are located in Chemnitz (later to become East Germany).

1938 - Bernd Rosemeyer sadly perishes driving an Auto Union.

Opposite: The Audi Forum in Ingolstadt.

1945 - Offices at Chemnitz are relocated to Ingolstadt and the post World War II rebuilding begins.

1958 - Daimler-Benz acquires a majority stake in Auto Union GmbH.

1964 - Daimler-Benz begins to sell Auto Union to Volkswagen. At the end of 1964, Volkswagen owns 50.3%. By 1966 Auto Union becomes a wholly owned subsidiary.

1969 - NSU and its plant at Neckarsulm merge into Audi. The new name is "Audi NSU Auto-Union AG".

1980 - The four wheel drive Audi quattro debuts at the Geneva Motor Show.

1981 - Audi begins its domination of world rally events around the globe with Michele Mouton at the wheel.

1985 - The company name is shortened to Audi AG.

2000 - Audi begins a winning streak at Le Mans with the Audi LMP R8.

2006 - Audi introduces the Audi R8. This mid engine quattro is available as a street car and endurance race car.

Ingolstadt

Ingolstadt History

Audi came to Ingolstadt by necessity. After the end of World War II, the headquarters of Auto Union was located in Chemnitz and part of East Germany. It was impossible to even return to town. At the end of 1945, a new firm was founded at Schrannenstr. 3 in old army barracks.

At first the new company simply wanted to create a supply depot for cars still on the road, but as years went by, Auto Union, which of course was renamed Audi AG, turned to manufacturing automobiles and motorcycles in Ingolstadt. Today the Ingolstadt factory employs around 32,000 people.

Audi Forum Ingolstadt

The Audi Forum complex was built in 2000, but the core of the forum, the customer center, was built in 1992 as a factory delivery center for customers picking up their new Audis.

Quick Stats
- ▶ Audi Forum opened in 2000
- ▶ Audi Forum renovated in 2008
- ▶ Audi Forum covers 828,500 square feet

Today, over 65,000 new Audis are delivered to customers at the Audi Forum in Ingolstadt each year.

Amenities
- ▶ Central Reception (start here)
- ▶ Museum Mobile
- ▶ Museum Mobile Shop
- ▶ Market Restaurant
- ▶ AVUS Restaurant
- ▶ Bar & Lounge/ Wine Gallery
- ▶ Audi Shop
- ▶ Audi Cinema

Audi Forum
Ingolstadt

Fahrzeugauslieferung

Markt und Kunde

museum mobile

Restaurants Audi For

(H)

Shuttle-Bus

Above: *Entry sign greeting visitors at the Audi Forum in Ingolstadt.*

Below: *New Audis await their owners at the Audi Forum in Ingolstadt.*

Factory Tour - Ingolstadt

Meeting Point: Reception in Audi Forum

Where to book tour:
Call +49 (0) 841/89-37575

Rating: ☆☆☆☆

Tips: Start with the basic "Production - compact" tour. This covers the Press Shop, Body Shop, and Assembly area.

Tour: "Production - compact"
Schedule: English tour at 11:30 AM German tours at 10:30 AM, 12:30 PM, and 2:30 PM
Duration: 2 hours   **Cost:** € 7.- per adult

Tour Packages:
(Tours may be booked upon request in English or German. The tour packages listed below are just a sample of the 18 tours available at Audi - Ingolstadt)

"Steel and aluminium"
Detailed tour of the body shop
Group size: 20 people maximum
Duration: 2 hours   Cost € 150.- per group

"Journey to the future of body manufacturing"
Learn about metal technology
Group size: 30 people maximum
Duration: 2 hours   Cost € 80.- per group

"More than just paint"
Detail tour of body shop
Group size: 30 people maximum
Duration: 1½ hours Cost € 150.- per group

"The ecological side of production"
Learn about protecting the environment
Group size: 30 people maximum
Duration: 2 hours   Cost € 100.- per group

"How are cars made"
Tour for children age 6 to 10 years old
Group size: 20 people maximum
Duration: 2 hours   Cost € 40.- per group

"The making of an Audi A3"
Every step of the making an Audi A3
Group size: 10 people maximum
Duration: 6 hours   Cost € 350.- per group

Audi Forum Hours
▶ Monday to Saturday
8:00 AM to 6:00 PM

Contact Information

Audi Forum Ingolstadt
Ettingerstrasse
85057 Ingolstadt
Germany

Phone: +49 (0) 841/89-37575
Fax: +49 (0) 841/89-41860
E-mail: *welcome@audi.de*
www.audi.com/forums

Directions to Audi

From **Munich / Nürnberg by car:**
▶ Autobahn A9 (München-Nürnberg)
▶ Exit 60/Lenting direction Ingolstadt
▶ Follow signs to "Audi Forum Ingolstadt".
▶ When road reads "Ettinger Strasse" look for forum parking
▶ Enter Audi AG - parking lot is on the left side

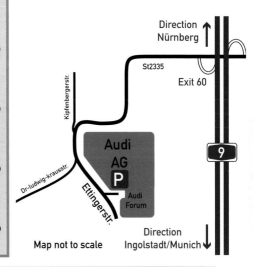

Map not to scale

Museum Mobile - Ingolstadt

A first time visitor to the Museum Mobile might be shocked to see that most of the vehicles on display aren't Audis. Or at least they don't say Audi. Welcome to the slightly complex and confusing history of Audi. Be rest assured that every vehicle in their permanent display is part of Audi's history, no matter what name is on the front. As visitors start their tour, they will witness the history behind the development of companies and brands such as Horch, DKW, Wanderer, NSU, and Auto Union - names that no longer grace the front grill of the modern Audi. Over time each one of these brands have merged into the company Audi AG, and today the Audi Museum Mobile is best way to explore this history first hand.

History of the Museum Mobile

Original museum was replaced by the new Audi Forum and Museum Mobile in 2000.

Museum Today

The museum today is 4 stories of steel and glass. Photographers may wish to consider visiting the museum on a cloudy day instead of a sunny one.

Quick Stats

- ▶ Plan on spending 2 to 4 hours at the museum and 1 to 2 more hours at the Audi Forum
- ▶ Over 130 exhibits
- ▶ Over 50 cars and 30 motorcycles
- ▶ 62,400 square feet

Architecture

The cylinder shaped building represents the annual rings of a tree trunk. The entire museum is wrapped in glass and feels very open. It should be no coincidence that there are 4 circular floors in the museum and 4 rings in the Audi emblem.

The Collection Theme

The most fascinating vehicles on display are part of the early history of Audi through the 1930s.

Must See

Auto Union 16 Cylinder Bergrennwagen Type C/D and the Audi Avus quattro Concept Car.

Opposite: *Overview of Museum Mobile.*
Right: *Audi quattro A2 of Michele Mouton.*

The Exhibitions

The permanent exhibit consists of the top two floors with each floor further divided into 7 sections with interactive displays. Start by taking an elevator in the basement level to the top level. The top floor will start with cars dating back to 1899 and a number of vehicles by Horch. The word "**Audi**" is the Latin word for the German word "**Horch**" (which means "*listen*" or "*hear*" in English).

Next level down starts at 1946 and covers the company's history up to the present day. The second floor is where the modern race cars are displayed including the Le Mans winning Audi R8 LMP.

The main floor is reserved for special exhibits. During our visit, the exhibit on display was "*Horch ein Audi*".

There is a 4 story rotating "*paternoster*" elevator of cars (world's largest). This constantly moving exhibit rotates cars (mostly prototypes and concept cars between the ground floor and the top floor). The Audi Avus quattro is on display here.

Horch
- 1903 Horch 10-12 PS Tonneau
- 1923 Horch 10/35 PS Phaeton
- 1927 Horch 8 Type 303 Phaeton
- 1932 Horch 670 V12 Sport-Cabriolet
- 1937 Horch 853 Sport-Cabriolet
- 1939 Horch 855 Special-Roadster

Audi
- 1913 Audi 14/35 PS Type C Limousine
- 1923 Audi 8/22 Type G Phaeton
- 1930 Audi 20/100 PS Type SS "Zwickau" Pullman Limousine
- 1934 Audi Front UW Limousine
- 1939 Audi 920 Limousine
- 1965 Audi 72 Limousine 2 door
- 1969 Audi 100 (C1) Limousine 4 door
- 1974 Audi 80 (B1) Limousine 2 door
- 1977 Audi 50 LS
- 1982 Audi quattro
- 1982 Audi 200 5 Turbo (C2)
- 1983 Audi 100 (C3)

Wanderer
- 1923 Wanderer 5/15 PS Type W8
- 1928 Wanderer W10/II Limousine
- 1936 Wanderer W40 Cabriolet 2 Fenster (*2 Window*)
- 1938 Wanderer W 25 k Roadster

DKW
- 1932 DKW Front (F1) Cabrio-Limousine
- 1936 DKW Schwebeklasse
- 1937 DKW F5 Front-Lexus Cabriolet
- 1958 DKW 3=6 Monza Coupe

Audi Race Cars /Rally Cars
- 1983 Audi Rallye quattro A2
- 1990 Audi V8 quattro DTM
- 2000 Audi R8 LMP

Audi Concept Cars
- 1993 Audi ASF Study IAA Frankfurt
- 1991 Audi Avus quattro

Auto Union

- 1937 Auto Union 16 Cylinder Streamliner Type C
- 1939 Auto Union 16 Cylinder Bergrennwagen (*Hill Climb Race Car*) Type C/D

Motorcycles

Don't miss the amazing collection of DKW motorcycles from 1921 to 1957.

Tours

"museum mobile - compact"
Overview tour of the museum
Duration: 1 hour
Cost € 4.- for adults, € 2.- for seniors
Held every hour Monday to Saturday.
Sunday - 11:00 AM, 1:00 PM, 3:00 PM

"More than just car stories"
Intensive tour of the museum
Duration: 1½ hours
Group size: 20 people maximum
Cost € 120.- per group

"A fascinating history of success"
Tour of the race cars in the museum
Duration: 1½ hours
Group size: 20 people maximum
Cost € 120.- per group

Group tours are by request. Please call Audi at +49 (0) 841/89-37575.

Contact Information

See "Contact Information" on page 41

Opposite: *DKW Schwebeklasse and the black Wanderer W40 Cabriolet behind it.*

Top: *Audi Union 16 cylinder Type C/D.*

Right: *Audi R8 LMP #8 - 2000 Le Mans winner - Biela, Kristensen, Pirro.*

Admission

Adults	€ 2.-
Under 18 & Seniors	€ 1.-
Groups (per person)	€ 1.-

Hours

- Monday to Sunday, Public Holidays - 9:00 AM to 6:00 PM

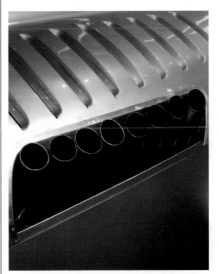

Neckarsulm

Neckarsulm History

The company NSU used Neckarsulm as a manufacturing center since 1880 but did not start building cars until 1906. On April 26, 1969, an agreement was reached by NSU shareholders to accepted a proposal of a merger between NSU AG and Auto Union GmbH. A little known footnote in history is that in 1976, Audi started building the **Porsche 924** under contract with Porsche. Audi continued to manufacturer Porsches through the **Porsche 944** and 944 Turbo models with production stopping in 1991.

Audi Forum Neckarsulm

The Audi Forum in Neckarsulm is a three story masterpiece of design. The Forum has more than 107,000 square feet of space and houses a restaurant, gift shop, a new car display, and a small museum on the top floor with a display of historic Audis.

The Forum is also the gateway to all the available Neckarsulm factory tours as well as the Delivery Center for new car customers. Since the Forum opened to the public in 2005, almost 1 million people have visited.

Factory Tour - Neckarsulm

Duration: 1 hour 40 minutes   **Cost:** € 6.-

Meeting Point: 2nd floor Audi Forum. The tour group will take a tour bus to the factory when the tour commences.

Where to book tour: Call Audi at +49 (0) 841/89-37575

Rating: ☆☆☆☆

Schedule: English tour at 1:45 PM German tours at 10:00 AM, 11:00 AM, and 1:00 PM (or upon request)

Tips: There are three possible tours. The best deal is the basic tour for € 6.- as both the Audi A8 Aluminum and R8 tour cost € 150.-. The Audi Forum in Neckarsulm has a lot of Audis on display on all three floors, so plan to arrive early.

Comments: Casual tour with a small group. Tour guide was able to change tour route per our wishes.

Tour:

1:45 - Meet guide

1:55 - Leave Audi Forum by bus

2:00 - Station 1 - "Press Shop"

2:10 - Station 2 - "Body Shop"

2:30 - Bus to final assembly area, detour to Audi R8 chassis assembly

2:50 - Detour by request to final assembly area of Audi R8

3:05 - Station 3 - "Final Assembly"

3:25 - Tour ends, return to Audi Forum on bus.

Worth Noting: Lamborghini bodies are manufactured in Heilbronn (sorry, no tour is available) and then painted at the Neckarsulm Audi factory.

Amenities
- Gift Store
- Restaurant Nuvolari

Opposite: Inside the Audi Forum in Neckarsulm.

Audi Forum/Restaurant Hours
- Monday through Saturday 8:00 AM to 6:00 PM

Contact Information

Audi Forum Neckarsulm
NSU-Strasse 1
74172 Neckarsulm
Germany
Phone: +49 (0) 841/89-37575
E-mail: *welcome@audi.de*
www.audi.com/forum

Directions to Neckarsulm

From **Nürnberg / Speyer by car:**
- Autobahn A6 (Nürnberg-Mannheim)
- Exit 37/Heilbronn/Neckarsulm
- South on B27
- First possible right on to Heilbronnerstrasse
- At roundabout, exit on to Rötelquerspange
- Turn right on Kanalstrasse
- Follow Kanalstrasse north under Autobahn.
- Left on Hafenstrasse to garage

Map not to scale

Interview with Hans-Joachim Stuck

Hans-Joachim Stuck was born January 1, 1951 in the small Bavarian town of Garmisch-Partenkirchen, a town at the foot of the Alps and in the shadow of the tallest mountain in Germany, the "Zugspitze". His father, Hans Stuck, was a racing legend with 411 wins and 7 Grand Prix victories. Hans-Joachim Stuck has followed in his fathers footsteps... With over 37 years of racing experience, he has won Le Mans twice in a Porsche 962, raced in 81 Grand Prix, and more recently raced an Audi R8 LMS. Currently he lives with his wife Sylvia in Ellmau, Austria near the famous ski resort of Kitzbühel. Via Corsa had the distinct pleasure of talking with Hans-Joachim Stuck for "*Via Corsa Car Lover's Guide to Southern Germany*".

VIA CORSA: We have heard you called many nicknames, please tell us about the nick name *"Strietzel"*.

HANS-JOACHIM STUCK: This is the one and only. This is the nickname my Auntie gave me when she was holding me in her arms during baptism and she said "Oh he looks like a Strietzel!" (A Strietzel is a sweet honey cake). So obviously I was looking funny in these days!

VC: We have heard about the "Mini Nürburgring" near Grainau (about 1 kilometer from Garmisch-Partenkirchen). What was that?

HJS: Yes this is the place I grew up. It was behind our house. It was a field where people cut logs out of the forest...My dad got permission and organized a bulldozer and on this field put in sort of a little Nürburgring with some corners and ups and downs and stuff like this you know and it's where I started to learn driving. He organized a BMW 600 which was the follow up car to the famous BMW Isetta and he took the body work off the frame...

put the seat on top with the steering wheel and speedometer and it is where I learned to drive a car. It was fantastic for me.

VC: On June 15, 1969 in a BMW 2002, you had your first race. It was on the Nürburgring. What were you thinking as your started your first race?

HJS: I couldn't wait for it...I took some BMW driving schools so I was really waiting for my first race and finally when it came up I was very happy and very proud to be at the same track that my dad was driving. To me up to now, the Nürburgring is the most famous race track of the whole world.

VC: In the 1970s when you raced a BMW 3.0 CSL "Batmobile", you had another nickname, the *"Jungewilden"*. What is *"Jungewilden"*?

HJS: Ah the *"Die Jungewilden"*! That's how they called us because we were the young guys. It was myself and some other drivers, and we were compared to those guys like Jacky Ickx. We were the *"Young and Wild"*.

VC: We heard it was a lot of fun back then!

HJS: Oh yes it was. Definitely. It was a great time of my career no doubt.

VC: Back then, racing was real racing. There were no driver aids, headlights were really bad, and the seats didn't fit...

HJS: Ja. Looking back, we didn't know of any of those things and we had to take it. Now a days I would say racing with the ASR, ESP, ABS doesn't make the racing easier, it makes it more controllable. In the days when we were racing, we were watching 5 or 6 instruments...oil pressure and water temperature. That's all past now. Since we can now concentrate on the driving, the competition became a lot tougher.

VC: Now looking back at your career, what was your absolute favorite race car to drive?

HJS: I don't have to think for a second, it was the 962 Porsche. Because it was the car with a lot of Aero(dynamics), and it had these ground effects, it had a 650-750 hp engine, huge wings, big tires, and great competition. This was by far the best car.

VC: You won Le Mans twice in the Porsche 962.

HJS: Won Le Mans twice and became the long distance world champion with my friend and fellow driver Derek Bell. I would say that this and the success with Audi winning the German Championship was the best time.

VC: If you to pick a car for the Nordschleife, not the fastest, but the most enjoyable, what would it be?

HJS: (Laughs) Good Question..It's always the last one. Right now it's the Audi R8 LMS..(laughs)..So the R8 LMS, it's the latest spec of car for the Nürburgring. It's fantastic because it's a mid engine car which makes it nice for all the bumps and humps and everything. With the V10 power of the Audi and the ABS and big tires we have. I also did my fastest lap last year (8:14.1) ever on the Nordschleife and for me it was the best car I've had there. There are 6-7 different possibilities on which kind of track to be set up for the Nordschleife. (For example) Without the Grand Prix circuit, with half Grand Prix circuit, with or without the Mercedes arena, and in combination, it was my fastest lap.

VC: What are your plans for the future?

HJS: I am coordinating the Motorsports of the Volkswagen Group, with all our 11 different brands, that means there is a lot to do as motorsports is in a moment of

change with emissions and going green. Second, I'm going to do a little bit more racing including the 24 Hours Nürburgring with the Audi R8 LMS and find some time to enjoy life...

VC: We understand that your eldest son Johannes races too. What are his plans?

HJS: Yes, he just finished 7th today in an Audi R8 LMS as well...He is in the complete VLN (*Veranstaltergemeinschaft Langstreckenpokal Nürburgring*) championship and also the FIA GT 3 championship. The smaller one Ferdinand just turned 18 and he is an official Porsche Factory Youngster and he is doing the Porsche Carrera Cup this year.

Thank you Hr. Stuck for your insights!

Please see his favorite Bavarian drive on page 282.

Below: *Hans-Joachim Stuck.*

BMW

During our factory tours and meetings with BMW (Bayerische Motoren Werke AG) during the creation of this book, there was one thing in particular everyone at BMW shared. It was pride. Pride in their company, their product, and their heritage and history. Everyone made sure we knew that this "little" company from Bavaria was a community of workers united in their efforts to create not only the best cars and motorcycles possible, but to build them to a standard that reflects the legacy created over the last 94 years.

History of BMW

Originally a manufacturer of airplane engines, the firm was founded in Munich on March 7, 1916. The name was Bayerische Flugzeugwerke.

1928 - First car is made, the BMW Dixi 3/15 PS.

1936 - BMW 328 Roadster debuts at the Nürburgring.

1951 - BMW 501 debut and the first car to be completed in Munich.

1955 - BMW Isetta, the best selling BMW of the 1950s debuts.

1956 - BMW 507 debuts - only 252 are ever made.

1959 - BMW is reorganized under the direction of Herbert Quandt.

1966 - BMW 1600 debuts. BMW celebrates its 50th anniversary.

1967 - BMW buys the automobile firm Hans Glas GmbH and its factories in Dingolfing and Landshut.

Opposite: BMW World Headquarters in Munich. To the left is the "Four Cylinder Building", right is the "Museum Bowl".

1973 - BMW builds a new corporate headquarters and museum (aptly named the "Four Cylinder Building" and "Museum Bowl" in Munich across from the Olympiapark (*Olympic Park*). The BMW 2002 Turbo debuts.

1975 - The BMW 3 Series is created.

1978 - The first modern BMW supercar and race car from the new M GmbH is born - the BMW M1.

1987 - The Regensburg plant opens.

1988 - BMW Z1 debuts.

2000 - BMW engines return to Formula 1 with Williams.

2004 - BMW Series 1 debuts as BMW's smallest car made.

BMW Logo - After BFW purchased Rapp Motoren Werke in 1916, the firm was renamed BMW GmbH. It was from this merger that the new logo was born. Company records show that in 1917, the new BMW logo was based on Rapp's circular logo which had the word "RAPP" written across the top and horse placed in the center.

BMW Welt - Munich

BMW Welt

Since late 2007, the new BMW Welt has been opened for visitors wishing to experience a new type of thrill. Of course the new forum has restaurants and stores, but also several interactive displays and exhibits. In its own way, this new forum is an extension of the newly renovated BMW museum. Except it's free. There are tours available (and recommended). Contact *infowelt@bmw-welt.com*

Architecture

Of all the different manufacturer's forums, this by far is the most fascinating from an architectural point of view. From the outside, BMW-Welt resembles a *"Double Cone"* while the inside is a mix of suspended walkways, stairways, and balconies.

"Jahreswagens"

When I moved to Munich, I decided my first car should be a BMW. So every Saturday, I would dutifully browse the Süddeutsche Zeitung looking for something to peak my interest. Why Saturday? It was when the newspaper ran their special car classified section. One Saturday, there was that ad. "6x BMW M3 Jahreswagen". Jahres-what? 6 of them? I had to call. Turns out, I had discovered what many Germans already knew. A "Jahreswagen" is a new vehicle owned by BMW and used by one of their employees for roughly one year. Of course Jahreswagens are professionally maintained by BMW and loaded with options. Yes, I bought the black one.

  ✋ *Ron Adams*

Factory Tour - Munich

Duration: 2 hours   **Cost:** € 8.-

Meeting Point: Info Desk, then BMW Welt at the doors to Production Forum 1

Distance: 3 kilometers walking

Where to book tour:
Call +49 (0) 1802/118822 or
E-mail: *infowelt@bmw-welt.com*

www.bmw-plant-munich.com

Rating: ☆☆

Schedule: English tour at 11:30 AM and 3:00 PM with German tours at 9:00 AM and 6:30 PM

Tips: Fridays are the busiest

Comments: Very crowded tour with a lot of back tracking and staircases. The tour route used catwalks over the factory floor rather than allowing the group to approach the machinery. There are better BMW tours than this one.

Tour:

3:00 - BMW video presentation about BMW and Munich plant.

3:10 - Introduction by guide & visitors receive headsets and safety goggles.

3:15 - Walk (if it is raining, you will get wet) to BMW Werk 1.1 Tor 1.

3:20 - Station 1 - "Press Shop".

3:35 - Robotic testing area.

3:40 - Station 2 - "Body Shop" - use safety goggles here to protect against sparks.

3:55 - Video on BMW paint process.

4:05 - Station 3 - "Paint Shop".

4:20 - Station 4 - "Final Assembly" - tour starts at the end of the line first.

4:30 - Tour walks past upholstery and seats but does not stop.

4:40 - Finishing area for new BMWs.

5:00 - Tour ends. Walk back to BMW Welt.

Opposite: BMW Welt (BMW World) in Munich by the Olympiapark.

Hours of BMW Welt
▶ Monday to Saturday 9:00 AM to 6:00 PM Sunday and holidays 10:00 AM to 6:00 PM

Contact Information

See "Contact Information" on page 59

Directions to BMW

From **Stuttgart by car:**
▶ Autobahn A8 (Stuttgart-München) to Autobahn end
▶ Follow Verdistr/Menzingerstrasse
▶ At "Y" intersection, left on Wintrich/ Georg-Brauchle-Ring (Not seen on map below)
▶ Follow George-Brauchle-Ring
▶ Just past BMW Welt, exit right, then left onto Lerchenauerstrasse
▶ Immediate left into garage

By train:
▶ Take a train to the Munich Hauptbahnhof
▶ Take escalators down to the subway system or "U-Bahn". Take U3 direction Olympiapark. Exit at last stop.

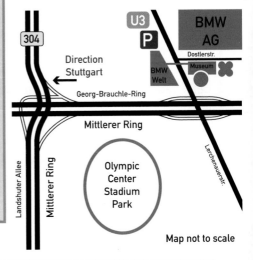

Map not to scale

BMW Museum - Munich

In 1973, the world had its first look at the new BMW "Museum Bowl" and the "Four-Cylinder Building" towering over it. For decades both have come to symbolise the cultural and business center of the world wide brand known as BMW. The buildings have appeared in postcards, travel shows, and promotional catalogs becoming icons as unique to Munich as, say, the Eifel tower is to Paris. As time has moved forward, so has BMW and its museum. Back in 1973, BMW was a smaller but respectable car manufacturer, and its museum a reflection of that brand and culture. Today BMW is a global phenomenon. Its vehicles are sold worldwide from manufacturing plants across the planet and today its museum reflects that global presence. One thing is for sure, the new BMW museum is still at the center of this automotive and cultural brand.

History of the Munich Museum

In 1973, the famed Viennese architect Professor Karl Schwanzer helped design a new complex of buildings for BMW across from the newly built Munich Olympiapark. The building that gained the most fame was the new BMW headquarters known as the "Four-Cylinder Building". The new museum named the "Museum Bowl" sat next to it. This new museum was the first of its kind and BMW one of the first car manufacturers to build a museum that incorporated its vehicles into a context of brand identity, culture, and technology.

For over 30 years, the BMW "Museum Bowl" had attracted an average of 200,000 visitors a year (ranking second behind the Deutsches Museum in popularity for all of Munich's museums). But as BMW grew over the years, so did the museum. In late 2005, the museum was closed, renovated, and expanded. The construction lasted 2 ½ years and the new museum opened June 2008.

Museum Today

The BMW Museum is only one part of a much larger interactive complex. The new BMW Welt across the street and connected by a pedestrian bridge is as much a part of the BMW experience as the BMW Museum. Both are a fascinating look at the brand and culture of BMW today.

Opposite: Temporary exhibit in the BMW Museum Bowl - "Art in Motion".
Right: Cockpit of the 1956 BMW 507.

Quick Stats

▶ Plan on spending 2 to 4 hours at the museum and 1 to 2 more hours at BMW Welt
▶ Over 125 exhibits
▶ 25 exhibition rooms
▶ 7 theme houses
▶ 53,800 square feet

The Architecture

From the outside, the museum has not really changed. The "Four Cylinder" building and the "Museum Bowl" are still there. Inside however, the museum's interior is a system of ramps and passageways creating an "urban transportation" structure.

The Collection Theme

Chronological walk through both BMW corporate, racing, and manufacturing history. There is a temporary exhibit in the original 1973 "Museum Bowl" of the museum.

Must See

BMW H2R World Speed Hydrogen Record Car and the BMW M3 DTM race cars.

The Exhibitions - Theme Houses

All the vehicles on permanent display are placed inside one of these seven houses. Each house is further divided into exhibition rooms. Some houses extend over two to three levels so different exhibition rooms within each house may be seen at different times.

Design House

Experience the process of creating a new BMW. Exhibition rooms are -

- ▶ Design, Inspiration, Ideas in Flow.
- ▶ Studio. Design in Dialogue.
- ▶ Treasury. Inheritance as Inspiration.

Company House

Learn about early years of BMW.

- ▶ First Steps. How it all Started.
- ▶ Aspects. Thinking and Acting.
- ▶ Chronology. Milestones of History.

Motorcycle House

BMW Motorcycle production.

- ▶ Passion. Quality and Innovation since 1923.
- ▶ Passion. Re-interpretation since 1969

Technology House

BMW's technological innovations.

- ▶ Lightweight Construction. Less is More.
- ▶ Aerodynamics. Shaped by the Wind.
- ▶ Engines. The Name Says it All.

Above: Touring cars. In the Fast Lane.

Motorsport House

Racing to win around the world.

- ▶ Champions. The Will to Win.
- ▶ Motorcycle Racing. Success on Two and Three Wheels.
- ▶ Touring Cars. In the Fast Lane.

Model Series House

Explore everything from 7 series to performance of the M series.

- ▶ BMW 7 Series. Luxury in its Most Dynamic Form.
- ▶ BMW M Models. M: the Most Powerful Letter in the World.

Brand House

BMW is more than just a car.

- ▶ Advertising. Over the Years.
- ▶ Encounters. Experience and Lessons Learned.
- ▶ Visions. Paths into the Future.

Museum Bowl

Temporary exhibit "Art in Motion". Art Car Collection of 16 BMWs created by artists **Roy Lichtenstein**, **Andy Warhol**, and others.

Vehicles

Just a sample of the cars, motorcycles, and engines on display!

Roadsters
▶ BMW 3/15 PS Wartburg
▶ BMW 315/1
▶ BMW 328
▶ BMW 507
▶ BMW Z1
▶ BMW Z3 1.8
▶ BMW Z8

Motorcycles
▶ BMW R 90 Butler & Smith Daytona
▶ BMW G/S Paris-Dakar 1981
▶ BMW F 650 RR Paris-Dakar
▶ BMW K 1200 R Power Cup

Formula 1
▶ Brabham BT 52
▶ 2006 Formula 1 Sauber

Engines
▶ M49 (BMW 3.0 CSL)
▶ P85 (F1 V19 Williams)
▶ P75 (BMW V12 LMR)
▶ P60/B40 (V8 BMW M3 GTR E46)
▶ P54 (R6 BMW 320i E46)

Lightweight Technology
▶ BMW 303 chassis and suspension
▶ BMW 328 Racing Saloon Spaceframe
▶ BMW M6 "Body-in-White"

Touring cars
▶ BMW 2000 TI
▶ BMW 3.0 CSL IMSA
▶ BMW 320 Group 5 (E 21)
▶ BMW M3 Group A (E 30)
▶ BMW M3 GTR (E 46)

BMW M Series
▶ BMW M1
▶ BMW M3 Sports Evolution
▶ BMW M5 E 28
▶ BMW M635CSi
▶ BMW M Roadster
▶ BMW M3 CSL

Concept Cars
▶ BMW 531 Prototype
▶ BMW Turbo
▶ BMW Z22
▶ BMW CS1
▶ BMW GINA
▶ BMW X Coupe
▶ BMW Mille Miglia Concept 2006

Below: Exhibit "Aspects. Thought and Action." - part of the "Company House".

Tours

Public tours

Individuals and small groups may participate in public tours. There is a maximum of 15 visitors per tour.

Individual guided tour including admission	€ 15.-

Individual guided tour with reduced price including admission*	€ 10.-

Exclusive tours

Exclusive tours are available for private groups of 5 to 15 visitors. If your group is larger than 15 people, it is not possible to book several tours at the same. However it might be possible to arrange tours for large groups on the same day.

Group tour   € 150.-
Group tour with   € 100.-
reduced price*
Tickets must be picked up 30 minutes before starting the tour at the Tickets and Information Counter of the BMW Museum. Payment may be made in cash or credit card. Prepayment isn't possible.

Guided tours last roughly 1 ½ hours. Shorter tours are also available and depend on the group's interest.

Guided tours hours -
Monday to Friday
9:00 AM to 4:00 PM
Saturdays, Sundays, and holidays
10:00 AM to 4:00 PM
Tours are available in German and English.

∗ Reduced rates apply to children, students up to 18 years of age, Disabled persons with an accompanying person, military, and BMW club members. Please see the BMW museum website for additional persons that may also qualify.

Booking Tours

To book a tour, contact BMW Welt Info Service at the below phone or e-mail.

Phone: +49 (0) 1802/118822 between 8:00 AM and 10:00 PM (0.06 Euro per call inside Germany)

E-mail: *infowelt@bmw-welt.com*

Amenities

▶ Museum Shop
▶ M1 Café Bar in BMW Museum

Parking

First and second hour	€ 1.50
Each additional hour	€ 1.-
Maximum daily rate	€ 10.-

Admission

▶ Adults	€ 12.-
▶ Under 18 & Seniors	€ 6.-
▶ Group of 5+ (per person)	€ 9.-

Opposite: *BMW 328.*
Above Left: *Production BMWs.*
Above Right: *2006 BMW Sauber F1.06.*

Events

The BMW Museum is available for evening events. For further information contact BMW at -

Phone: +49 (0) 1802/118822 between 8:00 AM and 10:00 PM (0.06 Euro per call inside Germany)

E-mail: *events.museum@bmw.de*

Hours

▶ Tuesday to Sunday, Public Holidays - 10:00 AM to 6:00 PM
▶ Closed on Mondays
▶ Closed December 24-26, 31, January 1

Contact Information

BMW Museum / BMW Welt
Am Olympiapark 1 & 2
80809 München
Germany

Phone: +49 (0) 180/211-8822
www.bmw-museum.com or
www.bmw-welt.com

Dingolfing

Dingolfing History

In 1883, **Hans Glas GmbH** started manufacturing agricultural machinery in Dingolfing. In 1951, Glas started building scooters and 4 years later in 1955, the first Glas automobile, the new **Glas Goggomobil**, made its debut. But the Hans Glas company wasn't without its problems. Despite selling over 280,000 Goggomobils and 87,585 **Glas Isars**, the company still struggled. After only 11 years in the automobile business, the Hans Glas Company and their two factories were sold to BMW.

On November 10, 1966 the purchase of Glas by BMW was complete and by 1969, the last Glas automobile was built.

1973 - BMW begins manufacturing in Dingolfing with the BMW 5 Series and by 1975 had built 100,000 cars.

1977 - The first BMW 6 series and 7 series roll down the production line.

1982 - 1,000,000 BMWs made.

1989 - The short lived BMW 8 series is made in Dingolfing.

1992 - 25th anniversary in Dingolfing.

Factory Tour - Dingolfing

Duration: 2 hours, 30 minutes **Cost:** Free

Meeting Point: Reception room at the BMW 2.40 Tor 3 (*Gate 3*)

Where to book tour:
www.bmw-plant-dingolfing.com
Click on "Guided Plant Tours". Expect an e-mail confirmation with questionnaire.

Rating: No rating - we had a press tour.

Tips: There is a small gift store on the right hand side of the road as you approach Tor 3 (*Gate 3*) just past the visitor center.

Comments: There are three large BMW factories in Bavaria. Munich, Regensburg, and Dingolfing. First impressions are that each tour would be the same. That is not the case and the tours at Regensburg and Dingolfing are the far better tours.

Tour:
We chose to photograph the final assembly area of the BMW 5 Series including the "Marriage" of the chassis to the body. There is a factory tour open to the public. It covers all aspects of the manufacturing process.

See page 62 for tour photos.

Dingolfing Today

Out of all the BMW manufacturing facilities in the world, the factory in Dingolfing is BMW's largest manufacturing plant and in 2008, BMW reached a milestone by hitting the five million BMW 5 series made. In 2010 the sixth generation of the 5 series entered production in addition to manufacturing the second generation BMW 6 series and fifth generation 7 series.

Amenities
▶ Gift Store
▶ Hours of gift store are Monday to Friday 10:00 AM to 4:00 PM

Contact Information

BMW AG
Werk Dingolfing
Landshuterstrasse 56
84122 Dingolfing
Germany

www.bmw-werk-dingolfing.de

Directions to BMW - Dingolfing

From **Munich by car:**
▶ Autobahn A92 (München-Deggendorf)
▶ Exit 17A/Dingolfing-West
▶ Follow signs to BMW & "BMW Werk 2.4 - Tor 3"
▶ Once at roundabout, take the first right and follow "Besucher" signs to the gate. Enter gated parking lot by pressing button.

Opposite: Gate 3 and main entrance of the BMW plant in Dingolfing.

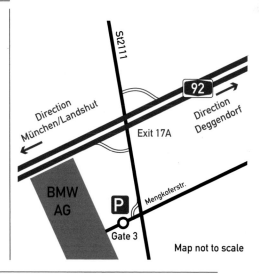

Map not to scale

Exclusive Factory Tour of BMW Dingolfing

Without exception, there is one rule for all factory tours. No photos. Period. So of course with every rule, there is an exception. In conjunction with the BMW Press Department in Dingolfing, here is a look into the final assembly of a BMW 5 Series. There are three different types of BMW 5 Series currently manufactured at the Dingolfing plant. The 5 Series Sedan, 5 Series Touring, and 5 Series Grand Tourismo. The M versions of the Sedan are also made here.

1 & 2: 6 speed gearboxes.

3 & 4: Suspension and brake systems are moved to the line via automatic trollies.

Via Corsa Car Lover's Guide to Southern Germany

5: Engines from Munich waiting in storage racks.

6: Gearbox mounting plates.

7: Gearbox and engines are assembled.

The BMW Final Assembly -

By the time the BMW 5 Series reaches this point, it has passed through four main production stations. Here the final assembly will require an additional 10 hours before the car reaches the last stop, the "Finish Area".
Station 1 - Metal Stamping "Presswerk"
Station 2 - Assembly "Karosseriebau"
Station 3 - Paint "Body in White"
Station 4 - Buffer (To help arrange "Just in sequence" production)
Station 5 - Final Assembly Area (pictured below)

8: A BMW 5 Series body about to get "Married" to the chassis.

9: BMW 5 Series Grand Tourismo shock waiting installation.

10: Chassis Assembly.

12 & 13: Installation of front nose.

11: The "Marriage" of the chassis & body.
15 & 16: BMWs enter final assembly.

14: Lets go to the "Market" for parts.

Regensburg

Regensburg History

The history is still in the making in Regensburg. The factory opened for production only 24 years ago and was built to keep up with the demand of the BMW 3 Series.

1997 - 50,000 BMW M3s

2000 - The one millionth 3 Series

2001 - The factory builds its 2 millionth car & undergoes an expansion

2004 - The new BMW 1 Series begins production

2009 - Production of the second generation BMW Z4 begins

Regensburg Today

The factory today sports some impressive statistics.

- ▶ 9,300 employees
- ▶ 1,200 cars made per day
- ▶ 1 Series, 3 Series, Z4, and M3 are all made here
- ▶ The factory has 550 suppliers
- ▶ 600 trucks a day visit the factory
- ▶ BMW M3 Carbon Fibre roof is made in Landshut and shipped to Regensburg
- ▶ 970 Kuka robotic arms
  See *www.kuka-robotics.com*

Above: BMW Regensburg plant - Gate 2.

Factory Tour - Regensburg (Best Tour!)

Duration: 2 hours, 30 minutes **Cost:** Free

Meeting Point: Reception room at the BMW 6.1 Tor 2 (*Gate 2*).

Distance: 5 kilometers walking

Where to book tour:
www.bmw-werk-regensburg.com
Click on "Guided Plant Tours". Expect an e-mail confirmation with questionnaire.

Rating: ☆☆☆☆☆

Schedule: English tour at 1:00 PM German tours at 8:30 AM and 1:00 PM

Tips: If you arrive early, visit the BMW gift store at Tor 1 (*Gate 1*).

Comments: Great tour with multiple video presentations. Casual tour despite the large group with a lot of walking. A large portion of the walking is outside, so be prepared if it looks like rain. No one under the age of 14 years allowed.

Tour:

1:00 - BMW video presentation with information about BMW and the Regensburg plant.

1:30 - Introduction by tour guide & visitors receive headsets.

1:45 - Walk to Station 1 - "Press Shop".

2:00 - Walk to Station 2 - "Body Shop". Safety goggles handed out to the tour and the group was shown another video presentation.

2:30 - Walk to Station 3 - "Paint Shop".

2:45 - Watching the two paint production lines.

3:00 - Walk to Station 4 - "Final Assembly" tour group shown a multi media presentation on 8 flat panel TVs.

3:30 - Tour ends at a customer lounge inside the BMW factory. Tour guide offered free soda and water and stays around to answer questions.

Amenities

▶ Gift store at Tor 1 (*Gate 1*) Open Monday to Friday 8:00 AM to 4:00 PM

Contact Information

BMW AG Werk Regensburg
Herbert-Quandt-Allee
93055 Regensburg
Germany

www.bmw-werk-regensburg.com

Directions to BMW - Regensburg

From **Munich by car:**

▶ Autobahn A9 to Autobahn A93
▶ Autobahn A93 direction Passau/Deggendorf
▶ Exit 101/Regensburg-Ost
▶ West/right on Leibnizstrasse
▶ Left on Max-Planck-Strasse
▶ Left on Herbert-Quandt-Allee
▶ Follow signs "BMW Werk", enter plant through Tor 2 (*Gate 2*)
▶ Park in gated "Besucher" lot to your left. Press button to enter lot.

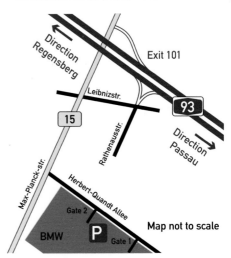

Mercedes-Benz

The automobile was born in 1886 with the issuance of a patent. Who was the father of the automobile? Karl Benz. A year earlier, Gottlieb Daimler built the high speed "Grandfather Clock" engine and precursor to the modern 4 stroke engine. Never meeting, the two of them worked independently of each other during these formative years to help create a dynasty that over the next 120 years would touch all facets of transportation. Today Daimler AG, the parent company of Mercedes-Benz, has 14 brands on 5 continents selling over 2 million vehicles a year.

Daimler-Benz History

The history of Mercedes-Benz is as much a history of the automobile as it is about the company its self.

1883 - Karl Benz forms "Benz & Co. Rheinische Gasmotorenfabrik" in Mannheim. Independently Gottlieb Daimler files for patents on the first gas engine.

1886 - On January 29, the motor car is born with the filing of patent number DRP 37435. The motor car makes its public debut on July 3rd.

1889 - Gottlieb Daimler and Wilhelm Maybach develop a new 2 cylinder engine.

1890 - The "Daimler-Motoren-Gesellschaft" (DMG) is founded by Gottlieb Daimler.

1893 - DMG presents the first fully functional car to the USA. Maybach invents the spray jet carburetor.

Opposite: Statue of Juan Manuel Fangio and the Mercedes-Benz W 196 by artist Joaquim Ros Sabaté.

1900 - Gottlieb Daimler dies at age 65. Daimler and Benz never meet. Businessman Emil Jellinek markets and sells Daimler automobiles under the name "Mercedes" (named after his daughter Mercédès Jellinek).

1910 - Barney Oldfield sets a world record of 211 km/h with his 200 hp Blitzen Benz at Daytona Beach.

1926 - DMG and Benz Cie. merge to form the new company Daimler-Benz AG.

1935 - Rudolf Caracciola wins the first of his three European championships driving a Mercedes-Benz W25.

1954 - The SL Series is born with the debut of the 190 SL and 300 SL

1998 - Daimler-Benz AG becomes DaimlerChrysler AG. Chrysler was sold in 2007 and the new firm was renamed Daimler AG.

Mercedes-Benz Emblem - Each point of the three point star inside the Mercedes-Benz emblem represent the three main methods of transportation - air, sea, and land.

Stuttgart-Untertürkheim

Untertürkheim History

In 1900, the Daimler-Motoren-Gesell-schaft signs a contract to buy 185,000 square meters of land to build their new plant.

1903 - Production starts in December

1947 - Body shop and final assembly moves to Sindelfingen.

1967 - New test track with 90° banked curves is unveiled.

1970 - Three millionth passenger car engine since 1946 is built.

1984 - The "Research and Development" building is opened.

Untertürkheim Today

Today this Stuttgart factory is the corporate headquarters of Daimler AG. Even though there are no vehicles made here, this factory builds engines, axles, transmissions, and other components. Over 16,000 employees produce over 710,500 motors and 920,000 transmissions per year. Also unique to the plant is a research and development facility as well as a 15,460 meter long banked test track.

Above: *Chassis-Montage at the Daimler-Motoren-Gesellschaft in Untertürkheim, in 1921.*

Factory Tour - Untertürkheim

See engines, transmissions, and axles being manufactured. There are no cars being assembled here. See <u>page 79</u> for information about tours at the Sindelfingen plant. We did rate the factory tour at Untertürkheim.

Tours are available Tuesday through Friday. There are a total of two tours each day with one in German and one in English. Tours may be booked at the museum ticket counter on the day of your visit. Advanced bookings are not possible. Groups interested in a factory tour should contact Mercedes-Benz by e-mailing: *werkbesichtigung.ut@daimler.com*

Admission

▶ Tickets available on day of tour

Restrictions

▶ Only over 16 years of age (due to insurance)

Hours

▶ 11:50 AM Tuesday - Friday in German

▶ 11:50 AM on Friday in English. The cost is € 4.- and lasts roughly 90 minutes

Contact Information

Mercedes-Benz Untertürkheim Plant
Mercedesstrasse 137
70327 Stuttgart
Germany

Phone: +49 (0) 711 /17-0
www.daimler.com

Directions to Mercedes-Benz

From **Ulm/Munich by car:**
▶ Autobahn A8 (Stuttgart-München)
▶ Exit 55/Wendlingen to B313
▶ North on B313 to B10/ Stuttgart-Zentrum
▶ West on B10 to signs "Neckerpark Traffic"/Mercedes-Benz Museum
▶ Follow signs

From **Karlsruhe by car:**
▶ Autobahn A8 (Karlsruhe-Stuttgart)
▶ Exit 51/Stuttgart to A831
▶ North on A831 to B14/ Stuttgart-Zentrum
▶ Follow B14 as it merges with B10 and follow the signs for Neckerpark Traffic and Mercedes-Benz Museum
▶ Exit on Benzstrasse and follow signs

From **By Train:**
▶ Take a train to the Stuttgart Hauptbahnhof
▶ S-Bahn Line S1 heading Kirchheim (Teck) to Neckerpark (Mercedes-Benz)

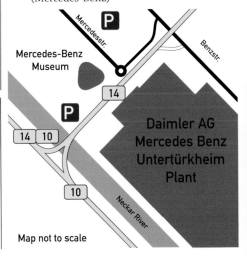

Mercedes-Benz Museum

We all know the feeling of elation when spotting a single exotic car in a random parking lot. Some of us may also know what its like to be overwhelmed when looking at hundreds of exotics at a car show. However at some point in time, even the most ardent car enthusiast may admit to being overwhelmed by this kind of sensory overload. But don't fret, it happens to the best of us. If you have never felt that sensation, the new Mercedes-Benz Museum is just the place you need to visit. Here is a museum that houses 160 vehicles. But not just any vehicles. World famous chapters in history worthy of their own history book vehicles. It is a overwhelming experience to see a car of legend, however it is an entirely new experience to see dozens of the rarest cars on the planet lined up in pristine displays. Visiting this museum is a mandatory stop for anyone visiting Germany.

History of the Mercedes-Benz Museum

The Mercedes-Benz Museum seen today is only a few years old, however some of the cars inside have been on display for over 100 years. In 1899, The Historic Department of the Daimler-Motoren-Gesellschaft (DMG) was at the first international motor show in Berlin with a display of "classic" decade old vehicles. But it took until 1936 for a proper museum to take shape at Untertürkheim. By then the automobile was 50 years old.

By the 1950s, efforts were underway to complete a collection that spanned roughly 70 years and plans were made in 1958 for a separate 35,000 square foot museum to house it. By the 100th anniversary in 1986, this museum underwent an extensive renovation to increase the size of the museum to 62,000 square feet with a front glass facade. This museum would remain open until the museum we see today was built.

In 1999, plans were made for a brand new museum and an architectural competition was held in 2001. In January 2002 the winner was announced: UNStudio van Berkel & Bos of Amsterdam. Construction began in September 2003 and lasted until 2006 when the last of the exhibits were placed. The new museum opened in May 2006. By June 2007 the museum welcomed its one millionth visitor.

Opposite: *Entrance to Museum.*
Right: *1886 Benz Patent Motorwagen and first car in the world.*

Museum Today

The Mercedes-Benz Museum is actually part of a larger complex called "Mercedes-Benz World" that includes the Mercedes-Benz Center Stuttgart.

Quick Stats

- Plan on spending a full day
- Over 160 vehicles
- Over 1,500 exhibits
- 177,540 square feet
- 9 levels in building

The Architecture

The Mercedes-Benz Museum is a modern interpretation of a "double helix". There are also no enclosed rooms, no straight walls, and 1,800 windows, none of which are the same. Visitors start their tour by walking through the chronological history of Mercedes-Benz (Legend Tour) on a single continuous ramp, while detouring to a second helical route of stairs to tour the various side collections.

The Collection Theme

The museum is a comprehensive collection highlighting the history of Mercedes-Benz over the last 125 years.

Must See

1955 Mercedes-Benz 300 SLR Uhlenhaut Coupé and the Mercedes-Benz ML 320 from the 1997 movie "The Lost World: Jurassic Park".

The Exhibitions

The museum is divided into two types of exhibits. One theme is the "Legend Tour" and the other is the "Collection Tour".

The Legend Tour

This is a chronological look at the history of Mercedes-Benz. Follow the main ramp to see all 7 Legend exhibits.

- Legend 1: Pioneers - The Invention of the Automobile, 1886 - 1900
- Legend 2: Mercedes - Birth of the Brand, 1900 - 1914
- Legend 3: Times of Change - Diesel and Supercharger, 1914 - 1945
- Legend 4: Post-War Miracle - Form and Diversity, 1945 - 1960
- Legend 5: Visionaries - Safety and the Environment, 1960 - 1982
- Legend 6: New Start - The Road to Emission Free Mobility
- Legend 7: Silver Arrows - Races and Records

The Collection Tour

The five collections are not in chronological order and are detours off the main Legends walk way.

- Collection 1: Gallery of Voyagers
- Collection 2: Gallery of Carriers
- Collection 3: Gallery of Helpers
- Collection 4: Gallery of Celebrities
- Collection 5: Gallery of Heroes

The Cars

There are many historically significant cars in the museum. Here are the highlights, including some celebrity owned cars -

▶ 1886 Benz Patent Motorwagen
▶ 1928 Mercedes-Benz SSK
▶ 1936 Mercedes-Benz 500 K Special Roadster
▶ 1937 Mercedes-Benz 770 Grand Open Touring Car
▶ 1955 Mercedes-Benz 300 SLR Uhlenhaut Coupé
▶ 1973 Mercedes-Benz Experimental Safety Vehicle ESF 22
▶ 1980 Mercedes-Benz 230 G Popemobile
▶ 1984 Mercedes-Benz 190 E 2.3 AMG owned by Ringo Starr
▶ 1991 Mercedes-Benz 500 SL owned by Princess Diana Spencer

Opposite: 1962 Mercedes-Benz 300 SL Roadster in the foreground with the legendary silver 1955 Mercedes-Benz 300 SLR Uhlenhaut Coupé to the left.

Above: Mercedes-Benz race cars from the 1950s and part of the "Legend 7: Silver Arrows" exhibit.

The Race Cars - Silver Arrows

These race cars are on display in the Legend 7: Silver Arrows -

▶ 1937 Mercedes-Benz W 25 Streamlined AVUS
▶ 1937 Mercedes-Benz W 125
▶ 1938 Mercedes-Benz W 154 3-liter
▶ 1939 Mercedes-Benz W 165 Tripoli 1.5-liter
▶ 1955 Mercedes-Benz W 196 R 2.5-liter
▶ 1989 Sauber-Mercedes C 9 Group C
▶ 1990 Sauber-Mercedes C 11 Group C
▶ 1994 Penske-Mercedes PC 23 Indy
▶ 1997 Mercedes-Benz CLK-GTR GT
▶ 1997 McLaren-Mercedes MP4-12 Formula One
▶ 1998 McLaren-Mercedes MP4-13 Formula One
▶ 2005 AMG-Mercedes C-Class DTM

Tours

There are several tours including a factory tour of the nearby Mercedes-Benz factory. Tickets for museum tours may be purchased at the main ticket counter on the main floor.

Fascination of Technology

Explore the research, design, and development at Mercedes-Benz. Group tours start on the hour every hour with a maximum of 20 people. Tours start at 11:00 AM to 4:00 PM. Guided tours in German start at 2:00 PM and English at 4:00 PM. Tour lasts roughly 60 minutes. Cost: Free

Art and Architecture Tours

Take a tour with an architect and learn the secrets behind this fascinating building and the cars it displays. Tours available roughly twice a month on Fridays at 4:00 PM. Please ask about the availability upon arrival. Cost: € 4.- in addition to entry fee.

Open Guided Vehicle Tours

This chronological tour of the 160 vehicles on display is the best way to gain an overview of Mercedes-Benz history. Open Guided Vehicle Tours in English start at 10:45 AM and 2:30 PM in Germany. These tours are generally available from Tuesday to Sunday. Cost: € 4.- in addition to entry fee.

Electronic Audio Guide

This is a self-guided tour and at your own pace. Cost: Free

Groups

Travel groups are asked to contact the museum's Customer Care Center prior to arrival. Each group is limited to 20 visitors per guide and it is possible to book guides for larger groups. Group tours lasts roughly 75 minutes.

Factory Tour of Untertürkheim

Tours are available. Please ask at the museum reception. Please see page 71.

Events

There is an open air stage for concerts on level 0 to an open terrace with views of the Neckar Valley on the roof. Contact the Customer Care Center for more information.

Amenities

▶ Museum Shop
▶ Lounge, Restaurant, and Café

Admission

▶ Adults   € 8.-
▶ Ages 15 to 17   € 4.-
▶ Under the age of 15   Free
▶ Group of 10+ (per person)   € 7.-
▶ Annual ticket   € 32.-

Opposite: *1955 Mercedes-Benz 300 SL Coupe Gullwing.*

Above: *"75 Years Silver Arrow" - Mercedes-Benz on display.*

Hours

▶ Tuesday to Sunday, Public Holidays - 9:00 AM to 6:00 PM
▶ Ticket Office closes at 5:00 PM
▶ Closed on Mondays
▶ Closed December 24-25, 31, January 1

Contact Information

Mercedes-Benz Museum GmbH
Mercedesstrasse 100
70372 Stuttgart
Germany

Mercedes-Benz Customer Center
Phone: +49 (0) 711/17-30000
Fax: +49 (0) 711/17-30400
E-mail:
classic@daimler.com
www.mercedes-benz.com/museum

Sindelfingen

History of Sindelfingen

Originally opened in 1915 as an aircraft plant, today the factory builds Mercedes-Benz C-Class, S, E, CL, CLS, SLS AMG, and Maybach.

1919 - Vehicle production begins.

1955 - The 1,000th Mercedes-Benz 300 SL is built at Sindelfingen.

1959 - Crash testing starts.

1971 - The one millionth diesel rolls off the factory assembly line.

1981 - New customer center opens.

2002 - Maybach manufacturing facility opens for production.

Sindelfingen Today

Here are some statistics we learned during our factory tour -

▶ 1,500 delivery trucks each day
▶ Cars are finished in four days
▶ Every 30 seconds, a new Mercedes-Benz is finished
▶ Roughly 2,100 cars built per day
▶ 1,000 E-Class and 50 CLS per day
▶ Each E-Class has 20 kg of paint
▶ Each E-Class body has 450 parts
▶ 50 tons of paint are used daily
▶ 70 days to build a Maybach
▶ 350 Maybach are built per year

Above: *Sindelfing Customer Center.*

Tour - Sindelfingen

Duration: 1 hour, 45 minutes **Cost:** Free

Meeting Point: Inside the Mercedes-Benz Customer Center by the Kino/Cinema

Where to book tour: Call +49 (0) 7031/9070-403

E-mail: *werkbesichtigungen.w050@daimler.com*

Rating: ☆☆

Schedule: English tour at 11:20 AM 6 German tours per workday starting at 9:15 AM and lasting until 2:30 PM

Tips: Arrive early. There is a lot to see at the Customer Center.

Comments: Tour started late by a tour guide more occupied with his cell phone than the group and the tour completely skips the Press and Paint departments. The minimum age is 6 years and factory tours are run Monday through Thursday only.

Tour:

11:25 - Watch power point presentation

11:50 - Into bus with safety goggles and headsets to the factory

11:55 - "Body Shop"

12:10 - Information Center for E-Class body inside the factory

12:25 - Back in bus to "Final Assembly"

12:30 - "Final Assembly" for all Mercedes-Benz including S-Class and SLS AMGs

12:55 - "Finish Area" including several SLS AMGs

1:00 - Back in bus to return to the Customer Center

1:10 - Tour over

Worth Noting: Mercedes-AMGs such as the SLS AMG are finished here in Sindelfingen and not in Affalterbach. During our visit, there were several dozen SLS AMGs in the "Finish Area".

Hours

▶ Monday to Friday 8:00 AM to 4:00 PM

Directions to Mercedes-Benz - Sindelfingen

From **Stuttgart by car:**

▶ Autobahn A81 (Stuttgart-Sindelfingen)

▶ Exit 23/Böblingen-Sindelfingen

▶ North on Rudolf-Diesel-Strasse

▶ West/left on Käsbrünnlestrasse

▶ Follow Käsbrünnlestr. around bend

▶ Enter Gate 8 / Kundencenter

Contact Information

Mercedes-Benz Sindelfingen Plant Bela - Barenyi - Straße 71063 Sindelfingen Germany

Phone: +49 (0) 7031/90-0 *www.daimler.com* or *www.mercedes-benz.de/ kundencenter-sindelfingen*

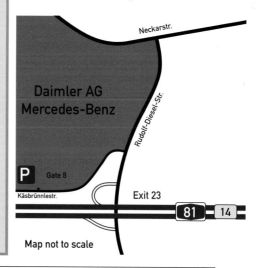

Map not to scale

Mercedes-AMG

History of AMG

In 1967, AMG's founders Hans Werner Aufrecht and Erhard Melcher started a business tuning Mercedes-Benz. But they did more than just "tune". They also raced, specifically the 1971 24 hour endurance race at Spa-Francochamps. They placed second. In the late 1980s, AMG gained fame racing its legendary 190 E 2.5-16 Evolution against the BMW M3s in DTM. In 1991 Daimler-Benz acquired controlling interest in AMG and in 1999 the new firm Mercedes-AMG was formed.

AMG Today

All of the Mercedes-Benz vehicles built today with an AMG engine have one thing in common - the very best engine in terms of performance, quality, and reliability. In a process unique to AMG, each engine is hand assembled by the same technician from start to finish on one of two large floors in the Mercedes-AMG factory. In 2010, the AMG 6.3 liter V8 engine won the "International Engine of the year" award.

Above: Mercedes-AMG showroom.
Opposite: Follow this sign!

Factory Tour - Affalterbach

Duration: 2 hours   **Cost:** Free

Meeting Point: Mercedes-AMG reception desk

Where to book tour:
Contact your Mercedes-Benz dealer or contact AMG directly at +49 (0) 7144/3020. The AMG contact form is *www.mercedes-amg.com/contact*

Rating: ☆☆☆☆☆

Schedule: Flexible and there is no set time. Our tour began at 1:00 PM

Tips: Finding Affalterbach isn't that hard, but finding lunch in Affalterbach is. Arrive at least 15 minutes early and well fed. If you own a Mercedes-AMG, write down the name of your engine builder (look at the plaque on top of your engine) as you might meet him or her.

Comments: The Mercedes-AMG tour may be individually tailored for an AMG owner and could detour, or stop, at the owner's request. One request cannot be granted - No pictures.

Tour:

Performance Studio - All the special cars are made here. This includes the FIA Formula 1 Safety & Medical Cars.

Dyno Testing - Engine testing room.

Engine Manufacturing - Watch one technician build each Mercedes-AMG engine from start to finish on one of the two spotless factory floors.

Worth Noting:
AMG is primarily an engine manufacturer. There is however an apply supply of new Mercedes-AMG vehicles all over the factory grounds.

Showroom Hours (open to public)

- ►   Monday to Friday
  9:00 AM to 5:00 PM

Contact Information

Mercedes-AMG GmbH
Daimlerstrasse 1
71563 Affalterbach
Germany

Phone: +49 (0) 7144/3020
www.mercedes-amg.com

Directions to Mercedes-AMG

From **Stuttgart by car:**

- ►   East on B14 direction Leutenbach for roughly 16 kilometers
- ►   Exit Winnenden on to Winnenderstrasse / L1127
- ►   North/ left on L1127 direction Affalterbach for roughly 7 kilometers
- ►   Once entering Affalterbach town limits, left at Robert-Bosch-Strasse

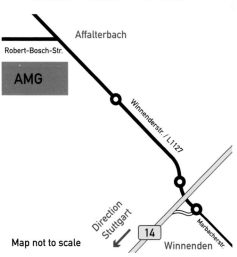

Map not to scale

Interview with Susie Stoddart

Susie Stoddart was born in Oban, Scotland in 1982. As most young race drivers these days, she had her start in karting. Before her debut in the German DTM series, she also raced in Formula Renault and Formula 3 with three podium finishes in 2004 alone. In 2006, she made her debut in DTM (Deutsche Tourenwagen Masters) racing a Mercedes-Benz C-Class. Now starting her fifth year, Susie is a rising star for Mercedes-Benz, DTM, and the world racing scene. Recently Susie teamed up with Mercedes-Benz USA to launch the new Mercedes-AMG SLS by driving demonstration laps at Mazda Laguna Seca to highlight the capabilities of this amazing car. Susie was also kind enough to talk to Via Corsa and talk a little bit about her time spent with Mercedes-Benz.

VIA CORSA: Susie, thank you for talking with us! Please tell us how and when did you start racing?

SUSIE STODDART: I started karting when I was 8. My parents have a motorcycle dealership in Scotland so I always had small bikes to play on since the age of 3. For my 8th birthday I got a kart and it all started from there.

VIA CORSA: When was your big break? The one that would eventually lead you to the DTM series?

SUSIE STODDART: In 2003 I was nominated as one of the 6 finalists in the prestigious McLaren Autosport Young Driver of the Year Award. It was the first time a female had ever made the finals and this brought me to the attention of a lot of people, including Mercedes-Benz Motorsport boss Norbert Haug.

VIA CORSA: In 2006, you made your debut in DTM in a Mercedes-Benz C-Class. What was that first race like?

SUSIE STODDART: It was amazing. Norbert Haug told me to look at the Mercedes grand stand on the formation lap, I had no idea why but when I got there the whole grand stand were holding up cards that formed together to read "Welcome Susie". It was really amazing. I finished 10th in this race so it was a good start.

VIA CORSA: We hear DTM is pretty rough (U.S. does not currently have a chance to watch DTM). Some people call it the European version of NASCAR. Is there really that much contact?

SUSIE STODDART: Yes, we race hard but fair.

VIA CORSA: What challenges did you encounter as a woman in a very aggressive and high contact race series such as DTM?

SUSIE STODDART: It is tough not just for me as a woman but for all the drivers. It is a very competitive championship so you really have to push for every last tenth of a second.

VIA CORSA: Currently you drive for TV Spielfilm/ Persson Motorsport. Is this considered a privateer team or a factory Mercedes-Benz team?

SUSIE STODDART: This is not the factory team but also not a privateer team. Team Persson receive all the cars, parts, data, and support from the factory team.

VIA CORSA: What are your plans for 2010? You will be once again driving a Mercedes-Benz? Persson Motorsport?

SUSIE STODDART: Yes.

VIA CORSA: What advice would you give to any young woman wanting to race?

SUSIE STODDART: If you have a passion for racing, go to your nearest kart track and give it a go!

VIA CORSA: Which Southern German racetrack do you most enjoy and why?

SUSIE STODDART: I have a special liking for Hockenheim as I did my first ever DTM race there. The season opener and finale are always at Hockenheim so somehow there is always a very special atmosphere.

VIA CORSA: If you were to be handed the keys to any Mercedes-Benz past or present to drive the Autobahn, what would it be?

SUSIE STODDART: The new SLS is really fun to drive and would be my car of choice although the C63 AMG is also a favourite of mine.

VIA CORSA: What are you plans for the future?

SUSIE STODDART: To stay with Mercedes-Benz and continue racing.

VIA CORSA: Do your plans include any racing here in the U.S.? How about Formula 1? Or Endurance racing?

SUSIE STODDART: As I am a Mercedes-Benz driver, I am only permitted to drive Mercedes-Benz cars. This limits which championships and where I can race. Of course Formula 1 is the dream of every driver but first I need to concentrate on having more success in the DTM.

VIA CORSA: During your time in Southern Germany, did you ever have a favorite drive? Perhaps, somewhere that you either drove for your team to test, or somewhere just to relax?

SUSIE STODDART: As I live in Switzerland and often have to drive to Stuttgart (where Mercedes-Benz is based), I enjoy the drive passing through Austria, Bregenz to Stuttgart. When the roads are quiet it is great as there is an open speed limit!

Opposite: *Susie Stoddart.*
Above: *Susie at the Nürburgring in 2009.*

Porsche

Porsche is number one. Yes, there is a Porsche 356 "Number 1" on display at the new Porsche Museum, but Porsche is number one in a lot more ways. According to J.D. Power, Porsche is ranked number one in quality (2006 & 2007 IQS - Initial Quality Study) and durability (2010). Ask just about anyone involved in motor sports, and they will say Porsche is number one as well. Number one in winning, number one in reliability, and their number one choice as a car to campaign. It's no coincidence that Porsche is the sports car of choice by enthusiasts everywhere.

History of Porsche

1875 - Ferdinand Porsche is born.

1900 - Ferdinand Porsche develops an all wheel drive race car.

1909 - Ferdinand "Ferry" Anton Ernst Porsche, son of Ferdinand Porsche, is born.

1923 - Ferdinand Porsche designs the Mercedes Compressor sports car for DMG.

1934 - Porsche receives the order to build the Volkswagen Beetle prototype. Three are built in the garage of Porsche's Stuttgart villa.

1935 - Ferdinand "Butzi" Alexander Porsche, son of "Ferry" Porsche, is born.

1948 - Porsche 356 "Number 1" is built.

1950 - Porsche 356 production begins.

1953 - The Porsche 550 debuts at the Paris Auto Show.

Opposite: Porsche Platz and Plant II in Zuffenhausen/Stuttgart.

1963 - Porsche 901 is introduced at the Frankfurt Auto Show.

1968 - Porsche 907s win top three spots at 24 Hours of Daytona race.

1970 - Porsche wins Le Mans with a 917K driven by Herrmann /Attwood.

1973 - Mark Donohue walks away with the Can-Am championship with his twin turbo 5.4 liter Porsche 917-30.

1974 - Porsche 911 Turbo debuts at the Paris Automobile Salon.

1976 - Porsche 924 enters production and is built in Neckarsulm.

1985 - Porsche 959 street car debuts.

1986 - Derek Bell, Hans-Joachim Stuck, and Al Holbert win Le Mans 24 Hours in a Porsche 956C.

1996 - Porsche Boxster debuts. One millionth Porsche built.

2003 - Porsche Carrera GT supercar debuts at Geneva Motor Show.

2005 - Porsche Cayman debuts.

2009 - Four door Porsche Panamera sedan debuts in Shanghai, China.

Zuffenhausen

Zuffenhausen History

The origins of the Porsche factory in Stuttgart can be traced back to 1931 when Porsche opened an office for "Engineering and Consultation on Engine and Vehicle Design".

1944 - Porsche KG relocates to Gmünd in Austria.

1950 - Porsche KG returns to Stuttgart-Zuffenhausen.

1969 - The factory expands and a new assembly operation added.

1988 - New Body Shop building is added.

Zuffenhausen Today

Zuffenhausen is still the world headquarters and cultural center for Porsche AG. However the factory does not build all the different Porsche models. The factory in Leipzig builds the Cayennes and, for now, Boxsters and Caymans are built in Finland. They will soon be built in Austria. All Porsche engines are still made in Zuffenhausen. One unusual feature of the Porsche factory today is the enclosed bridge 15 meters above Schwieberdingerstrasse that moves the finished bodies to the paint shop.

Factory Tour - Porsche

Duration: 1 hour, 45 minutes   **Cost:** Free

Meeting Point: Inside the Porsche Museum on ground floor by reception.

Where to book tour: Book through an authorised Porsche dealer or by e-mail. (See *www.porsche.com*)

E-mail: *factorytours@porsche.de*

Rating: ☆☆☆☆

Schedule: English tour at 10:00 AM

Tips: All 10:00 AM tours meet in the same place. We almost left with the German speaking group by accident. If you book a factory tour on Monday, the museum will be closed.

Comments: This is the only tour to cover the upholstery department. In fact our tour guide let us help ourselves to leather samples.

Tour:

Receive a "Porsche Besucher-Tour" sticker with date stamp to wear and walk across Schwieberdinger Strasse to the factory.

Porsche Body - Steel bodies are assembled by hand and robot.

Paint Shop - Five step process is used to paint all Porsches.

Porsche Engines - All Porsche engines are built in Zuffenhausen.

Porsche Seats - Leather skins are cut with a jet of water.

Porsche Wedding - Chassis and engine meets the painted body.

Porsche Final Assembly - Last step in car's assembly and the Porsche tour.

Worth Noting: Factory tours are suspended during August and are only available Monday though Thursday the rest of the year. Check with Porsche for age restrictions.

Opposite: Porsche Museum with the Porsche Zentrum Stuttgart to the right.

Porsche Crest

In 1952, **Max Hoffman**, a U.S. Porsche importer, was having dinner with Dr. Ferry Porsche in a New York restaurant. After Mr. Hoffman mentioned all cars of some standing have a badge, Dr. Porsche grabbed a napkin and started drawing. He started with the Baden-Württemberg crest, the name Porsche, and the black prancing horse from Stuttgart, and replied "How about something like that?"

Contact Information

Porsche AG
Porscheplatz 1
70435 Stuttgart, Germany

Phone: +49 (0) 711/911-20911
www.porsche.com

Directions to Porsche

From **Munich/Karlsruhe by car:**

▶ Autobahn A8 to Autobahn A81
▶ North on A81 direction Heilbronn
▶ Exit 17/Stuttgart-Zuffenhausen
▶ South on B10 to Zuffenhausen
▶ Merge onto Schwieberdingstrasse
▶ Parking is under Museum

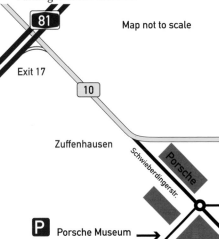

Map not to scale

Exit 17

Zuffenhausen

Porsche Museum →

Porsche Museum

Only a few short years ago, the Porsche Museum was just a single door to a tiny rectangular exhibition hall next to the Porsche Delivery Center. It was small and dark with the world's best race cars lined up in two narrow rows. Today the Porsche Museum is a world class art gallery of motor sports that makes all other car museums seem a bit lacking. Notice there are no ropes holding back the visitors from interacting with these priceless automobiles. Each and every pristine Porsche may be examined from every side and angle. A visitor may also lean inside some of the cockpits of these famous cars. This is a brave move by Porsche and unique to this museum. In fact, the lack of any boundary between the car and its enthusiast create a three dimensional interaction and relationship of which no photo or text can do justice.

Via Corsa Car Lover's Guide to Southern Germany

History of the Porsche Museum

The new Porsche Museum started in 2004 with the announcement by the Porsche management to build a new museum at Porscheplatz in Zuffenhausen. A competition was announced to design the new museum and out of 170 entries by architects across Europe, the firm Delugan Meissel of Vienna, Austria was announced as the winner.

In 2006, the new museum began to take shape. Over the next two years, over 21,000 cubic meters of concrete and 4,000 tons of reinforced steel were used to create this architectural wonder. Construction lasted until the end of 2008.

Museum Today

Quick Stats
- Plan on spending 2 - 4 hours
- Over 80 cars
- 60,250 square feet
- Opened January 2009

The Architecture
From the outside, the new Porsche Museum seems to hover in space with three concrete "cores" holding up an angular three story glass and concrete structure. When the visitor steps through the doors and enters the ground floor reception, it is a world of white. Even before entering the museum above, it's pretty obvious that something special awaits.

Opposite: Porsche 956 #17 Rothmans.
Right: 1948 Porsche 356 "Number 1".

The interior space of the museum is a contemporary mix of angles, slopes, ramps, and steps. Almost all the cars are placed on or against a monochromatic mix of shiny white floors, black backgrounds, and shades of gray. Photography buffs need not worry about the weather or sun outside as almost all the cars are very well lit and under artificial lights.

The Collection Theme
The inside is as open as the architecture that surrounds it. Visitors may tour the museum in chronological order or simply wander about in any number of possible directions. There is no single path and no arrows on the floor pointing the way.

Must See
- The 1948 Porsche 356 "Number 1" prototype is the very first car Ferry Porsche made (in the town of Gmünd, Austria) bearing his name and was the start of the Porsche dynasty.

The Exhibitions

The museum exhibits are on two of the three floors above the ground floor. There are several paths to take when entering the museum, but the most common path follows the exhibits in their chronological order. There are no proper exhibition halls, but rather cars grouped together in displays on platforms, balconies, ramps, and rises. Additional exhibits ranging from engines to trophies are spread through out the museum next to the cars.

The Cars

There are roughly 80 vehicles in the museum. Many of the Porsches leave the museum to travel ("Museum on Wheels") and may be spotted at prominent events around the world. For example, the Porsche 718 W-RS Spyder in the photograph on page 93 displays a 2008 "Goodwood Festival of Speed" entry sticker. Here is a list of the most significant exhibits -

▶ 1939 Type 64 "Berlin-Rome Car"- Four cylinder boxer engine and 33 hp. The car has been referred to as the "Original Porsche" and the "Great-Grandfather".

▶ Volkswagen Beetle - Ferdinand Porsche presented the concept of the VW Beetle in 1934 with a study titled "Construction of a German People's Car". The Beetle on display is the eighth car built under him.

▶ 1948 Porsche 356 "Number 1" - This is the first car built carrying the "Porsche" name and brand. It was a single prototype with a 35 hp Volkswagen engine.

▶ 1950 Porsche 356 Coupe "Ferdinand" - This particular car was a birthday gift to Ferdinand Porsche in 1950 when he turned 75 years old.

The Road & Concept Cars

The prototype and concept cars at the museum are an amazing display of cars that have evolved into the Porsches seen on the street today. Here is a sample -

- ▶ 1953 Porsche 356 America Roadster
- ▶ 1956 Porsche 550 A Spyder
- ▶ 1956 Porsche Type 597 Jagdwagen concept car
- ▶ 1959 Porsche Type 754 "T7"
- ▶ 1960 Porsche 356 B 2000 GS Carrera GT

- ▶ 1964 Porsche 911 2.0 Coupe
- ▶ 1969 Porsche 914/8
- ▶ 1970 Porsche 915 Prototype
- ▶ 1970 Porsche 911 S 2.2 Targa
- ▶ 1976 Porsche 911 Turbo 3.0
- ▶ 1981 Porsche 924 Carrera GTS
- ▶ 1983 Porsche 928 S
- ▶ 1989 Porsche Panamericana Concept Car
- ▶ 1996 Porsche Boxster
- ▶ 1997 Porsche 911 GT1 "Street Version"

- ▶ 1999 Porsche 911 Carrera "Biggibilla"
- ▶ 2003 Porsche Carrera GT
- ▶ 2008 Porsche 911 Carrera S Cabriolet

Opposite: Porsche 917 KH Coupe #23.

Above Top: Porsche 959 with an upside down Porsche 956 of Jacky Ickx and Derek Bell.

Above: Porsche Type 64.

Right: Porsche RS Spyder #7.

Right Bottom: Porsche 550 Spyder Carrera Panamericana #55.

The Porsche Race Cars

Porsche and racing go back to the dawn of the firm. This is just a sample of what is on display.

- ▶ 1947 Porsche Type 360 Cisitalia
- ▶ 1954 Porsche 550 Spyder Carrera Panamericana #55
- ▶ 1960 Porsche 718 RS Spyder
- ▶ 1962 Porsche 718 W-RS Spyder
- ▶ 1964 Porsche 904 Carrera GTS
- ▶ 1970 Porsche 908/03 Spyder #40 Gulf Racing
- ▶ Porsche 908 LH Coupe #64
- ▶ 1973 Porsche 911 Carrera RS 2.7 Coupe
- ▶ Porsche 911 Carrera RSR
- ▶ 1976 Porsche 935 Jacky Ickx and Jochen Mass/ Martini #41
- ▶ Porsche 962 C Le Mans - Derek Bell and Hans-Joachim Stuck #17
- ▶ 1988 Porsche 959 #203
- ▶ 1986 McLaren TAG MP 4/2 C Formula 1

The Porsche 917s

The Porsche 917s on display is part of the museum's "Powerful" display and a tribute to these famous race cars.

- ▶ Porsche 917 KH Coupe #23
- ▶ 1973 Porsche 917/30 Mark Donohue #6
- ▶ Porsche 917 KH Coupe Martini Racing Team #22
- ▶ Porsche 917/20 "Pink Pig" #23
- ▶ Porsche 917 LH Coupe Martini Racing #21
- ▶ Porsche 917 KH Coupe Gulf #2
- ▶ Porsche 917 PA Spyder

"Porsche before 1948"

This theme features milestones that were instrumental in the life of Ferdinand Porsche. Porsche 356 "Number 1" is inside this theme display.

"Lightweight"

The lightweight exhibit focuses on power to weight ratios of the Porsche 356 and Porsches that raced in the Targa Florio in Italy.

"Clever"

Porsche has been a leader in technological advancements since its founding. Several of the Porsches on display highlight those "Clever" innovations. The 1960 Porsche 356 B 2000 GS Carrera GT is a good example of "Clever".

"Fast"

Raw horsepower without control meant little to Porsche. Hence Porsche has been at the forefront in the evolution of aerodynamics. Take a look at the upside down Porsche 956. In theory its aerodynamics allow it to drive on a ceiling at 200 mph.

There are several more themes inside the Porsche museum. Each is relevant to the history of both Porsche and their respective cars. For example there is a display on the "Consistent Idea" and the "Intense Idea". Visitors may also see how a Porsche is created with a look inside Weissach Research Facility and cutaway models. The final display is centered on "My Porsche" and the current year models.

Opposite: 1962 Porsche 718 W-RS Spyder. This is Porsche's first two liter eight cylinder vehicle and was nicknamed the "Grandmother" by its mechanics.

Porsche Archives

The archive has 2.5 million pictures, 3,000 car books, and over 1,500 hours of video. Visitors are allowed access to the archives with advance registration.

Workshop

Inside the museum building is a very special workshop. It is the workshop where all the museum's cars are serviced and it is open to the public. If you are an owner of a classic Porsche, you may inquire about their services.

Events

Third level of the museum and its open terrace is reserved for corporate events. The area hosts seminars, lectures, and new car presentations.

Amenities

- ▶ Museum Shop
- ▶ Christophorus Restaurant
- ▶ Coffee Bar
- ▶ Museum Restaurant "Boxenstop" (We recommend the "Boxster-Burger")

Admission

- ▶ Adults   € 8.-
- ▶ Under 14   Free
- ▶ Annual Pass   € 32.-
- ▶ Parking garage   € 2.-

Hours

- ▶ Tuesday to Sunday, Public Holidays - 9:00 AM to 6:00 PM
- ▶ Last admission is 5:00 PM
- ▶ Closed on Mondays, Closed December 24-26, 31, January 1
- ▶ Christophorus Restaurant - Tuesday to Saturday 11:30 AM to 12:00 PM, Sundays to 2:30 PM

Contact Information

Porsche Museum
Porscheplatz 1
70435 Stuttgart
Germany

Groups & special tours:
Phone: +49 (0) 711/911-20911

Public relations:
Phone: +49 (0) 711/911-24026

General visitor enquiries:
Phone: +49 (0) 1805/356-911
E-mail: *info.museum@ porsche.de*

Event information:
Phone: +49 (0) 711/911-21911
Fax: 49 (0) 711/911-21356
E-mail: *events.museum@ porsche.de*

www.porsche.com/international/aboutporsche/ porschemuseum

Interview with Derek Bell

Derek Bell has won Le Mans four times for Porsche. His record is a testament to both Porsche as a dominate manufacturer in the world of motorsports as well as Derek Bell as one of the best drivers they have ever had. Derek Bell was kind enough to talk to Via Corsa about his racing career with Porsche.

Derek has a career spanning almost 40 years with at least 52 first place finishes. He has raced just about every Porsche that has existed between 1971 and 1991 including the following Porsches: 908/3, 917, 934, 935, 936, 956, 962

Career wins at the 24 Hours of Le Mans -

1981 - Porsche 936 - 1st overall
Co-driver: Jacky Ickx
1982 - Porsche 956 - 1st overall
Co-driver: Jacky Ickx
1986 - Porsche 962C - 1st overall
Co-driver: Hans-Joachim Stuck
1987 - Porsche 962C - 1st overall
Co-drivers: Hans-Joachim Stuck, Al Holbert

Career wins at the 24 Hours of Daytona -

1986 - Porsche 962 - 1st overall
Co-drivers: Al Holbert, Al Unser Jr.
1987 - Porsche 962 - 1st overall
Co-drivers: Al Holbert, Al Unser Jr., Chip Robinson
1989 - Porsche 962 - 1st overall
Co-drivers: John Andretti, Bob Wollek

VIA CORSA: When is the first time you raced a Porsche competitively?

DEREK BELL: I won with a Porsche 917 at the 1,000 Km Buenos Aires...I won the first race of the year in 1971.

VC: Was this a factory team or a privateer team?

DB: Not all the cars were factory cars. They put me in cars because they wanted me to drive for private teams that represented them.

VC: How did you get your initial ride with Porsche as a factory driver?

DB: It started really through John Wyer of the Gulf Team. I was invited by him to drive the (Ford) GT-40 in '68. I had only been racing three years then...I had been invited to drive the GT-40 Gulf car with Pedro Rodriguez at Le Mans in September 1968. They said we want you, but Ferrari wouldn't release me...and so I didn't drive it. Subsequently when I drove for Ferrari in 1970 at Spa (in Belgium) which was my first sports car race in the 512, I then went on to drive at Le Mans for the factory..and from that, because we ran well, John Wyer then phones me up and asks if I could go for a test drive at Goodwood. So I went in the Porsche 917 which was the Gulf Porsche 917 which was the factory team. So I went to Goodwood and drove against Ronnie Peterson. I got the Porsche 917 drive. Then my first Porsche race was in 1971 which was in Buenos Aires, which I won. Then at the end of the year I won the last race, the Paris 1,000 Km race.

VC: Between all of the different Porsches you have driven, which one was your favorite?

DB: My favorite is the 962. It has to be, because at the end it was such an amazing car. I can't say whether it was the "C" or the "IMSA" car. Although the "IMSA" car I preferred because it had more power. 800+ horsepower. Either one, the 962C or 962 on its own which were wonderful as I won so much, I won 35 races or something. That was very special for me. The 917 was probably the most memorable because it was the 917.

VC: When did your time as a factory Porsche driver end?

DB: I drove on and off, they brought me back here and there. I started in 1971 and then I did the odd race during the '70s.... I was always a factory driver..after my first year I wondered why I hadn't received a second contract. Peter Falk (the Porsche team manager) said *"Well we will see you for testing in January at Paul Ricard"* I said *"I haven't been asked to drive for you next year"*. *"Once you're a Porsche driver, you are always a Porsche driver."*...Once you were in the family, you were always in the family and even to this day the people who are there from that era, of course there aren't too many, are treated like we are all part of the same team. I still drive. They bring cars from the museum for me to drive... So I am still very much part of Porsche in that respect. But my last real race for them was in 1993. The last time I drove for them, I drove for Joest. Joest was the Porsche Team. He ran the Porsche works team.

"Once you were in the family, you were always in the family..."

VC: Between the Nürburgring and Hockenheimring, which racetrack do you most enjoy?

DB: Oh Nürburgring. It has to be.

VC: Would that be the Grand Prix Circuit?

DB: No, the big track. The Nordschleife. If you are lucky enough to have driven on the greatest track in the world as many times as I have, without winning it..never had won the bloody thing..it's just the most demanding and most exciting place to go around in the world. You can't treat it lightly. It brings out the best in many drivers. You cannot afford to give up on anything...It's the most unforgiving track

Right: Derek Bell today.

in the world, it's the hardest track in the world to learn a track with 170 corners...I go there every year. I was driving a Bentley there last July. I did an eight minute lap.

VC: If you were to be given the keys to any car to drive the Autobahn, what would it be?

DB: A Porsche Carrera GT. The hot one. It's one I've never driven, funny enough.

VC: What are you plans for the future?

DB: I just love racing. I work with Bentley world wide and I work with Porsche all over the place. I just love driving race cars. I drive the Bentley Le Mans twice a year at different events. I would race every week if I could, but obviously no one is going to ask me at my tender age. I just enjoy driving the best cars. I'm not that keen on historic cars having said that. I go back just as far as the 917, which is historic in most people's books.

VC: Did you ever have a favorite drive around Stuttgart?

DB: Yea, I think one of the most enjoyable drives I ever had driving was a long time ago in a Porsche 914/6. Me and three or four other guys from Gulf Porsche flew into Stuttgart and picked up three or four 914/6s. And then drove down into Italy to Monza where we then raced Porsche 917s. I just remember that drive. It was just so fabulous over the Alps..To be honest I don't get much chance to go out and have a great drive...

Southern German Museums

What is the difference between a car collection and a museum? Well, not much. In fact a large number of the museums listed here are just that - a car collection. A car collection owned by a passionate and dedicated owner(s) willing to share their enthusiasm with the rest of the world. Do be aware that most smaller museums either close or have reduced hours during the fall and winter months

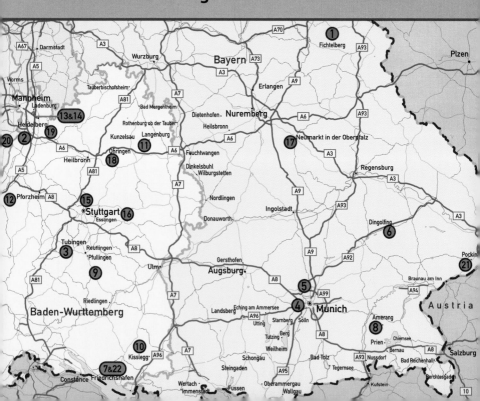

Car Related Museums

Museum	City	Time to see Museum
1 - AMF	Fichtelberg	1 - 2 hours
2 - Autovision	Altlussheim	2 - 4 hours
3 - Boxenstop	Tübingen	2 - 4 hours
4 - Deutsches Transport	Munich	3 - 6 hours
5 - Deutsches Aircraft	Munich	3 - 6 hours
6 - Dingolfing Industrial	Dingolfing	2 - 4 hours
7 - Dornier	Friedrichshafen	3 - 6 hours
8 - EFA	Amerang	3 - 6 hours
9 - Engstingen	Engstingen	1 - 2 hours
10 - Fritz B. Busch	Wolfegg	2 - 4 hours
11 - Langenburg Automuseum	Langenburg	2 - 4 hours
12 - Marxzell Fahrzeugmuseum	Marxzell	1 - 2 hours
13 - Automuseum Dr. Carl Benz	Ladenburg	2 - 4 hours
14 - Karl Benz Mansion	Ladenburg	1 hour
15 - Daimler Memorial	Stuttgart	1 hour
16 - Daimler Birth House	Schorndorf	1 hour
17 - Maybach	Neumarkt	2 - 4 hours
18 - Motormuseum	Öhringen	1 - 2 hours
19 - Sinsheim Technical	Sinsheim	1 day +
20 - Speyer Technical	Speyer	1 day +
21 - Toyota Museum	Pocking	1 - 2 hours
22 - Zeppelin	Friedrichshafen	2 - 4 hours

AMF Museum

A MF stands for Automobile, Motorcycle, and Flugzeug (or airplane in English). Anyone interested in the history and technological developments of each of these respective modes of transportation should definitely visit the AMF Museum.

History of AMF Museum

The AMF Museum was founded by Perry and Timo Eckert as a dedication to their passion for things that move. The museum is a big draw to the town of Fichtelberg, which is otherwise well known for its spa, and not for car museums.

Above: *Display of sports cars inside the AMF-Museum.*

AMF Museum Today

This private museum has one main hall for cars and motorcycles and a second hall with a historic workshop and assorted tractors. There are 8 airplanes and helicopters outside including a Russian **MiG-21** and Russian **Mil Mi 9** helicopter. Their motorcycle collection includes a **1910 NSU** racing bike and a **MV Augusta 750 S Sport**.

Quick Stats

- Plan on spending 1-2 hours
- Over 200 exhibits
- Over 140 cars
- 30 motorcycles
- 4 airplanes

The Collection Theme

The 100 plus year history of the car from the 1886 Daimler Motor Carriage to a 1991 Lamborghini Diablo.

The Exhibitions

There are 2 exhibition halls covering 3 floors of cars, motorcycles, and planes.

The Cars

Here are the highlights -

- 1897 Panhard & Levassor - 4 cylinder, 8 hp
- 1936 Lagonda BJ 36
- 1936 Jaguar SS 100 Roadster
- 1950 BMW 507 Sport Touring
- 1954 Talbot Lago 2.5 Liter Sport Coupe
- 1968 Iso Rivolta S4 Fichia - 1 of 192 built
- 1968 Lamborghini 400GT Espada
- 1973 Bitter Diplomat CD Coupe
- 1984 Bayer TC 3 Prototype

Directions to AMF

From **Nürnberg by car:**

- Autobahn A9 (Nürnberg/Berlin)
- Exit 39/Bad Berneck to B303
- East on B303 direction Frankenhammer for more than 20 kilometers
- Right on Jahnstrasse direction Fichtelberg
- Left on Naglerweg to museum

Amenities

- Restaurant "Museo" scheduled to open in spring 2011

Admission

- Adults   € 8.50
- Students   € 6.-
- Group of 20+ (per person)   € 6.-

Hours

- April to October - 10:00 AM to 5:00 PM (closed on Mondays)
- November to March - 3:00 PM to 5:00 PM (closed on Mondays)
- Open holidays all year long from 10:00 AM to 5:00 PM

Contact Information

AMF-Museum Fichtelberg
Naglerweg
95686 Fichtelberg
Germany

Phone: +49 (0) 9272/6066
Fax: +49 (0) 9272/6066
E-mail: *info@amf-museum.de*
www.amf-museum.de

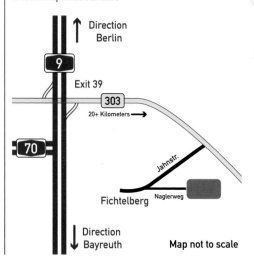

Autovision Museum

A utovision is a car museum and science center. There are several exhibitions that combination their automobiles and engines into interactive displays that appeal to all ages. In addition to the museum, there is a biergarten, theater, coffee lounge, gift store and a solar service station. There is a lot to explore here for adults and is a great place for youngsters too.

History of the Autovision Museum

Autovision is the private museum of Horst Schultz and opened to the public in 2002 in Altlussheim. His goal was to show the public the history of the automobile as well as current technologies and the future of the automobile. In addition to the permanent exhibits, the museum rotates special exhibitions that are shown on a temporary basis. The museum is just a few minutes away from the famous race track - the Hockenheimring.

Autovision Today

This modern and open museum features several educational and interactive displays that go beyond the typical car museum. This is a child friendly museum that promotes a hands on approach and is a must see for all car enthusiast families.

Quick Stats
▶ Plan on spending 2-4 hours
▶ Opened in 2002
▶ 3 stories high
▶ Over 60 cars & 80 motorcycles

The Collection Theme
There are 5 exhibitions under one roof. Each explores a different facet of the automobile's history and future.
▶ 125 years of Mobility
▶ Mobility after the World Wars
▶ Wankel engine
▶ AUTOVISION
▶ Science Arena

Directions to Autovision

From **Mannheim by car:**
▶ Autobahn A6 (Mannheim-Nürnberg) to Autobahn A61 (Speyer-Koblenz)
▶ Autobahn A61 west direction Koblenz
▶ Exit 63/Speyer to B9
▶ South on B9 direction Schwegenheim
▶ East on B39 direction Altlussheim/ Walldorf
▶ Merge right onto Hauptstrasse
▶ Drive through Altlussheim
▶ Museum Autovision on right

Opposite: *Museum Autovision.*
Top: *Evolution of children's pedal cars.*

The Exhibitions

125 years of Mobility
Before the dawn of the automobile, there was first the invention of the bicycle. Follow the evolution of the world of mobility as the 19th century manufacturers start building two wheeled bicycles.

Mobility after the World Wars
Explore the rebirth of Germany as a center for manufacturing after World War II. After the war ended, bicycles were the first to enter production, then motorcycles, and finally the automobile.

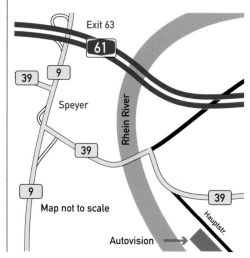

What is a Wankel Engine?

In the 1950s a German engineer by the name of **Felix Wankel** worked for the now defunct company NSU Motorwerke AG (NSU is now part of Audi AG). It was during this time at NSU that Wankel developed a new type of internal combustion engine using a rotary design rather than reciprocating pistons. This engine is now known around the world as the **Wankel rotary engine**. These engines have been used for years by Mazda in everything from the Mazda RX-8 to the Formula Mazda race cars.

What is the advantage of a rotary engine? They are lighter, cheaper, and have fewer moving parts than the traditional piston engine. They last longer, have lower maintenance costs, rev higher, and run without valves, connecting rods, or a crankshaft. An additional benefit is that a rotary engine rarely, if ever, fails or blows up.

Wankel Engine

Autovision has the only permanent Wankel rotary engine display. This German (not Japanese) invention is explored fully through the use of educational displays and stories. The museum claims that this is also the largest display of Wankel rotary engines and cars with 20 cars and 80 engines on display.

▶ Cut display of the RO80 (Original IAA Show car)
▶ Mercedes-Benz C111
▶ 4 Wankel motorcycles
▶ There are over 80 Wankel rotary engines on display

AUTOVISION

Glimpse the future today with a peek at alternative fuel vehicles and technologies.

▶ Electric vehicles -
Follow the 200 year evolution of the battery. Autovision starts with the 19th century battery to electric concept cars.
▶ Hybrid vehicles -
Explore the hybrid engine and its ability to recover kinetic energy with interactive displays and hybrid concept cars.
▶ Fuel cell vehicles -
160 years of fuel cell research and development are explored with both displays of fuel cells and the 1997 methanol fueled Mercedes-Benz Necar3 Concept Car.
▶ Hydrogen vehicles -
This 2001 BMW 730 hL is the first hydrogen operated car.

Science Arena

Parents rejoice! Here is an area for children to explore. There are no ropes or areas off limits. The Autovision science Arena explores the following -

- Physics -
  50 different models exploring magnetism, electricity, and mechanics.
- Automobile Power -
  Explore gears, crankshafts, and all sorts of other moving parts.
- Engines -
  Look inside engines and their related parts.
- Computer Simulators -
  Test drive a car with one of Autovision's 6 computer terminals.

Events

The forum, garden, and biergarten are available for rental for events. The forum holds up to 120 people, the garden holds up to 200 people, and the biergarten up to 60 people. Each location may host lectures, meetings, or casual dinners and events.

Opposite: *A red 3rd generation Mazda RX-7 next to a white 2nd generation Mazda RX-7 and a Mazda rotary engine.*
Above: *1925 NSU Type 5. This is an example of Motorsports of the 1920s.*
Right: *BMW 730 hL Hydrogen.*

Amenities

- Gift Store
- Movie Theater
- Biergarten
- Coffee Lounge
- Museum tours

Admission

- Adults   € 5.-
- Students   € 3.-
- Group of 20+ (per person)   € 4.-

Hours

- Tuesday to Sunday,
  Public Holidays -
  10:00 AM to 5:00 PM
- Closed on Mondays
- Closed December 24-26, 31,
  January 1

Contact Information

Museum Autovision
Hauptstrasse 154
68804 Altlussheim
Germany

Phone: +49 (0) 6205/307661
Fax: +49 (0) 6205/307662
E-mail: *post@autovision-tradition.de*
www.museum-autovision.de

Boxenstop Museum

Boxenstop, or as it is translated to English, "*Pitstop*", is a quaint little museum in the very pretty university town of Tübingen. Beyond its entrance is more than just another car and toy museum, but more a way of life.

History of the Boxenstop Museum

Opened in 1985, Boxenstop is the private museum of founders Rainer and Ute Klink. Initially the museum was only 2,100 square feet. But over the years it has expanded in three phases over the years to almost 9,700 square feet today.

In 1987, as the museum was expanding its car and toy collections, Rainer Klink took the museum into a new direction. He began to host trips and events to many of Germany's classic car rallies and hill climbs. If that wasn't enough, in 1993, Klink began hosting trips around all of Europe, including trips to Le Mans, Goodwood, and the Mille Miglia.

Boxenstop Today

Today Boxenstop is one of Germany's oldest private car museums. The unusual thing about the cars at Boxenstop is that every single car is road worthy. The museum is more than just static cars, but rather a place dedicated to a passion that should never stop moving. Boxenstop continues to host trips around Europe, and has a dining room on the top floor.

Quick Stats

- ▶ Plan on spending 2-4 hours
- ▶ Over 70 cars, bikes, and motorcycles
- ▶ Interesting cars include a Bugatti 37 and a Maserati 4 CL
- ▶ Over 1,000 vintage toys in their original condition

Directions to Boxenstop

From **Stuttgart by car:**

- ▶ Autobahn A8 (Stuttgart-München)
- ▶ Exit 53a/Stuttgart-Degerloch
- ▶ South on B27 direction Tübingen
- ▶ Right on Stuttgarterstr./L1208
- ▶ Left on Willhelmstrasse
- ▶ If a left is allowed, left on Schlachthausstr./Nordingstr.
- ▶ Otherwise continue on Wilhelmstrasse
- ▶ Street renames Hölderlinstrasse
- ▶ Left on any cross road - Keplerstrasse or Gmelinstrasse
- ▶ Left back onto Willhelmstrasse
- ▶ Right on Schlachthausstrasse
- ▶ Follow as road renames to Brunnenstrasse
- ▶ Museum on left side

Opposite: Ground floor entrance.

The Collection Theme

The three themes here are cars, motorcycles, and toys. Of course, to most of us, cars are toys, so it only goes to say that here is the best of both worlds. The museum displays motorcycles, toys, and cars together on all three floors.

The Exhibitions

The Cars

Here are some highlights -

- ▶ Aermacchi ala d`Oro
- ▶ BMW Sportwagen 319/1
- ▶ Bugatti Type 37
- ▶ Chevron B16
- ▶ EuroBrun ER188/ Ford Cosworth F1
- ▶ Ferrari 250 GT Pininfarina Coupe
- ▶ Jaguar XK 120
- ▶ Jaguar SS 100
- ▶ Maserati 4 CL
- ▶ March Formula 1
- ▶ March Formula 3
- ▶ Mercedes-Benz 300 SL Gullwing
- ▶ Porsche 906 Carrera 6
- ▶ Marsh-Porsche 90P Indy

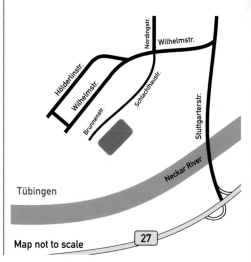

Map not to scale

Above: 1970/71 March Type 701/Ford Cosworth Formula 1 in Boxenstop's "Rastelli" Restaurant.

Opposite Top Right: 1966 Porsche 906/ Carrera 6.

Opposite Bottom Right: Bugatti Type 37.

Below: The very unusual March-Porsche 90A #4 Indy car. This car was raced by John Andretti at the 1990 Indianapolis 500. Porsche sadly announced in September 1990 that they would conclude its Indy Car program leaving this as one of the last examples of oval racing by Porsche in the U.S.

The Toys

Toys everywhere! There are pedal cars, dolls, airplanes, and scale cars. There are vintage toys and recently released toys. Two traditional German toy companies are featured prominently here - Märklin Trains and Steiff bears The **Märklin Train Company** was founded in 1858 and is still the benchmark for HO scale trains world wide. The **Margarete Steiff Company** was founded in 1880 and is best known for the company that invented the Teddy Bear. There are no ropes or barriers holding the little ones back from (carefully) exploring the toys on display.

Events

Through out the year, Boxenstop is host to a number of events and meets. The annual highlights are the "Steam Meeting" (to highlight steam powered cars and toys), the annual model train show, and classic car meet with live music and parade.

Hours

- April to October
  Wednesday to Friday 10:00 AM
  to 12:00 PM, 2:00 PM to 5:00 PM
- Saturday, Sunday, Holidays
  10:00 AM to 5:00 PM
- November to March
  Sunday and Holidays
  10:00 AM to 5:00 PM

Travel

The 2010 travel itinerary at Boxenstop lists around 2 dozen different trips around Europe. Just about every major event is listed ranging from Le Mans to Goodwood to the Millie Miglia. Check with Boxenstop directly if you are interested in accompanying them on one of their trips.

Heidi

Not "Heidi of the Alps", but rather "Heidi the vintage 1964 Swiss bus". Take 37 of your closest friends for a trip around the Alps in this bus for hire.

Restaurant "Rastelli"

On the top floor Boxenstop is a dining room called "Rastelli". Boxenstop has a full crew with chef and staff available to serve the best regional dishes. There are not many places where you can dine next to a Formula 1 car.

Amenities

- Restaurant on top floor
- Gift Store

Admission

- Adults   € 6.-
- Children ages 10 - 14   € 5.-
- Children under 7   Free

Contact Information

Boxenstop Auto-und-Spielzeugmuseum Tübingen
Brunnenstrasse 18
72074 Tübingen
Germany

Phone: +49 (0) 7071/929090
Fax: +49 (0) 7071/929099
E-mail: *info@boxenstop-tuebingen.de*
www.boxenstop-tuebingen.de

Deutsches Transport Museum

The Deutsches Museum, or German Museum, is the collectively the world's largest science and technology museum. Until recently, the transportation section of this massive collection was housed at the main museum on an island in the Isar River.

History of the Deutsches Transport Museum

The main museum **Museum Insel** (*Island*) was founded in Munich in 1903 by Oskar von Miller on a small island in the middle of Munich on the Isar River. It was heavily damaged during the second world war and again during a 1980s arson attempt.

In 2003, the cars and trains were moved to the new the Deutsches Museum Verkehrszentrum (*German Transport Museum*). It opened in what was once the Munich convention center. It is also worth mentioning that the exhibition halls are beautiful historic buildings that date back to 1908 and were part of the original **Messe München** (*Convention Center*).

Deutsches Transport Museum Today

The Transport Museum consists of 3 halls (all historic buildings) with each hall highlighting a different theme. In addition to the Transport Museum featured here and the Museum Insel in downtown Munich, there is the Deutsches Aircraft Museum in Schleißheim (see page 114) just outside of Munich and a branch in Bonn.

Quick Stats

- ▶ Plan on spending 3-6 hours
- ▶ In you plan on visiting the main Island Museum, plan on spending 1 to 2 full days to see it all
- ▶ Parking is amazingly difficult, try using the subway for this one
- ▶ 4,500 exhibits

Directions to Deutsches Museum

From **Munich by car:**

- ▶ From city center, west on Bayerstrasse
- ▶ Left on Martin-Greif-Strasse
- ▶ Stay right as you approach the Theresienwiese
- ▶ Park anywhere you see!
- ▶ While it is possible to drive to this museum, we recommend you use public transportation. Parking is difficult at best.

By Train:

- ▶ Take the U-Bahn U4 or U5 direction Laimerplatz, exit at Schwanthalerhöhe
- ▶ Museum is a few minute walk away

Opposite: *Inside Hall 1 "Urban Transport".*
Above: *Entrance at Hall 3.*

The Collection Theme

Trains, no planes, and automobiles! The museum features cars and trucks through out all 3 exhibition halls of the museum and are placed according to the theme of each respective hall.

There is a very impressive train collection in Hall 2 and assorted motorcycles, helicopters, and (of all things) skis spread about all 3 halls. This museum is rich with child friendly displays and activities with Hall 3 being the best place for children to explore. The halls are named "Urban Transport", "Travel", and "Mobility and Technology".

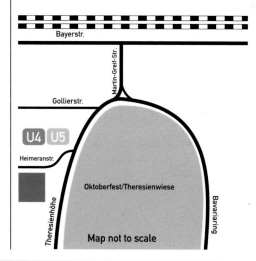

Hall 1

"Urban Transport"

This is a single floor display at the far end of the museum (The main entrance is at Hall 3). The focus is on both public and private transportation. Here there are electric street trams, subway cars, and personal cars. The entire hall is laid out as if it were 4 city blocks. There are streets, a crosswalk, and even a stop light.

There are 140 different displays here with most centered around 6 color coded areas. Additional displays are spread through out the hall.

Must See

▶ The BMW 118i crash test. This safety display not only shows the car, but also the crash test parameters and the barriers used.

Inside Hall 1

▶ Safety and rescue vehicles
▶ Learning center for children
▶ Driving school information and simulator
▶ Historical bicycle shop
▶ Traffic and the environment
▶ ADAC helicopter
▶ BMW "Clean Energy / Powered by Hydrogen" Car
▶ City and traffic planning display

Several of the displays are interactive and are geared for younger enthusiasts.

Above: Hall 2 - "Travel" Hall with various trains and automobiles.
Left: Hall 1 - Crash Testing a BMW 116i.
Opposite: Hall 2 - From Left to Right - 1958 Kassbohrer-Setra S Bus, 1985 ICE-V, 1912 Bavarian S 3/6.

Hall 2

"Travel"

This hall has two levels and the top level is a gangway that is great for photos of the trains below.

The focus of this hall is the evolution of mass transportation during the 19th and 20th centuries. This includes a stellar railroad display.

Must See

▶ The ICE-V Train Engine (Inter City Experimental). This particular engine is the experimental engine first run in 1985 as a test bed for the entire ICE (Inter City Express) program. Technical innovations include the use of composites and an on-board diagnostic system. In 1988 it broke the world speed record reaching 406.9 km/h. It was retired in 2000. Today the ICE trains still run regularly all over Germany.

Inside Hall 2

▶ The origins of the vacation - an interactive display going back to the dawn of automobile. This display is great for children to explore.
▶ Route 66 tribute display - cars and the culture surrounding Route 66 and the open road.
▶ Travel by motor coach.
▶ The culture and evolution of train travel.
▶ The art of travel.
▶ Movement of freight traffic.
▶ Horse and carriage simulator (to experience how the composer Mozart may have travelled).

Displays include vintage train engines and passenger cars, motor coaches and buses, horseless carriages, classic cars, military vehicles, and one pink 1959 Cadillac. The children's area in Hall 2 includes books and story boards and seating for reading.

Hall 3

"Mobility & Technology"

This is the first hall a visitor will see and here is where the rare cars are located. Most of the other displays here are dwarfed by the awesome cars in the evolution of motorsports display.

Hall 3 is split into 2 different levels. The bulk of the displays and cars are located on the main floor. The auditorium and lockers are located to the right of the entrance, while the café and gift store are located to the left.

Must See

▶ The Formula 1 car upstairs and under glass. It is disassembled and near the 1978 Renault Formula 1. It is easy to miss if you are in a hurry.

Inside Hall 3

▶ Evolution of motorsports and pursuit of speed.
▶ Bicycle racing.
▶ Model railway.
▶ Temporary / special exhibits.

The Cars (and some Motorcycles)

▶ Benz Patent Motor Car. This one cylinder engine car is universally heralded as the first car made. In 1886, Karl Benz patented the concept of a "vehicle with gas engine operation".
▶ 1907 Prontos New York-Paris Race Car. This car took place in the 1908 race covering over 21,000 kilometers.
▶ 1914 Audi Type C "Alpinesieger"
▶ 1922 Mercedes 1.5 Liter Compressor 1955 Messerschmitt 200
▶ 1931 Alfa Romeo 6C Grand Sport
▶ 1936/37 Auto Union Type C
▶ 1955 Mercedes-Benz 300 SLR
▶ 1959 BMW 507
▶ 1956 NSU "Delphin III" World Record Holder.
▶ 1967 Porsche 911 S in stainless steel. This is a one off car that served as a test model by Porsche for studying corrosion.
▶ 1978 Renault RS01 #15 Jean-Pierre Jabouille Formula 1.
▶ BMW-Williams Ralf Schumacher Formula 1.
▶ While not a car, there is a fun HO scale train layout on the second floor.

Events

Events at the museum range from bicycle workshops to lectures to film screenings in the theater (in German of course). There is also the chance to book a birthday party for your child here. See contact information on the opposite page.

Left: 1978 Renault Formula 1.
Opposite: *Hall 3 - Evolution of Motorsports.*

Tours

Daily guided tours in German start at the times listed below. There is no cost for the daily tours, but group tours need to be booked in advance. Please e-mail the museum for group rates.

h.klotzbier@deutsches-museum.de

▶ 10:00 AM, 11:00 AM, 1:30 PM, 2:00 PM, 2:30 PM, and 3:00 PM

Amenities

▶ Café-Station
▶ Gift Store
▶ Lecture/forum area
▶ Children's play area
▶ Story boards and information in English

Admission

▶ Adults 16 and older   € 6.-
▶ Children ages 6 - 15   € 3.-
▶ Children under 7   Free
▶ Groups 20+ (per person)   € 4.-

Hours

▶ 9:00 AM to 5:00 PM daily
▶ Closed January 1, Easter, Christmas
▶ Please see website for additional closings

Contact Information

Deutsches Museum Verkehrszentrum
Theresienhöhe 14a
80339 München
Germany

Phone: +49 (0) 89/500-806-762
Fax: +49 (0) 89/500-806-501
E-mail:
verkehrszentrum@deutsches-museum.de

www.deutsches-museum.de/ verkehrszentrum

Contact for events:
Birgit Breitkopf, M.A.
E-mail:
b.breitkopf@deutsches-museum.de

Deutsches Aircraft Museum

Nestled in the far corner of a quiet airport is one of the best airplane museums in Germany. This is the Deutsches Museum's airplane museum in Schleißheim and part of the museum system that recently opened the Transport Museum.

History of the Deutsches Museum Flugwerft

The airport in Schleißheim was founded in 1918 by the Royal Bavarian Flying Corps and is one of Germany's oldest air fields. Over the decades it has been used by the U.S. Army Air Corps and the German Luftwaffe (*Air Force*) as a training center for pilots.

In 1992, the Deutsches Museum moved its ever growing collection of aircraft and aircraft engines here. The museum extensively renovated a number of buildings that used to house the original control tower and hangers. One of the original hangers is a maintenance hanger dating back to 1918. Today it is the main hanger of the museum.

Deutsches Museum Flugwerft Today

Several new buildings and additions have been made to the original hangers and control tower. These new glass structures don't distract from these historic structures, but add a modern "air" (excuse the pun) to the complex.

Quick Stats

- ▶ Plan on spending 3-6 hours
- ▶ Home to a world class restoration shop.
- ▶ Children can test simulators at the "Flying Circus".
- ▶ Located in a historic hanger and control tower.

The Collection Theme

The first question might be why are we covering an airplane museum in a car book? The major car manufacturers here in Germany are also builders of airplane engines as well. In fact BMW began as an airplane engine manufacturer, not as a car manufacturer.

Directions to Deutsches Museum

From **Munich by car:**

- ▶ Autobahn A99 (northern section of the Munich Autobahn loop)
- ▶ Exit 12a/München-Neuherberg (one exit west of the A9/A99)
- ▶ Turn on/straight to Jägerstrasse
- ▶ Follow Jägerstrasse to the museum

Opposite: Eurofighter EF 2000 DA 1. This prototype took flight in 1994 and is first of seven prototypes. It last flew in 2006.
Above: *Entry Foyer and Hanger.*

The main focus of the museum is, of course, the airplane. Engines are few and far between, but the connection to the automotive world is here.

Must See

- ▶ The restoration shop is a world class facility that actively restores planes and helicopters. This "live" action shop is set between two hangers with visitors able to watch from a catwalk above.

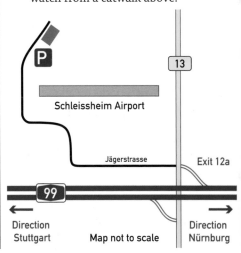

The Exhibitions

The museum has two main exhibition areas. The historic hanger and the main exhibition hall. The restoration shop is located in between the two.

The Historic Hanger
The main entrance is located just off the historic hanger. The noteworthy aircraft -

▶ Fokker D VII
▶ Fieseler Fi 156C
▶ MBB 223 Flamingo "Porsche"

The Exhibition Hall
Larger than the historic hanger, this houses the bulk of the museum's collection. The noteworthy aircraft -

▶ Heinkel He 111 H-16 (appeared in the movie "The Battle of Britain")
▶ Dornier Do 31 E-3 (One of two surviving prototypes. The other is at the Dornier Museum. See page 122.)
▶ Douglas DC-3 (C-47D)
▶ Dornier Do 24 T-3 Flying Boat
▶ EADS/ Boeing X-31
▶ Eurofighter EF 2000 DA 1
▶ North American F-86 Sabre
▶ MiG-21 MF
▶ MiG-23 BN
▶ Saab J 35 Draken A

Top Left: 1944 BMW 801 TJ turbo charged 14 cylinder engine.

Bottom Left: 1986 MBB 223 Flamingo PFM with a Porsche PFM 3200 Aviation engine. From a total of 97 Flamingos, this is the last and only Flamingo with a Porsche air-cooled flat six engine.

Opposite: 1955 Sikorsky HH-19 B from the US Airforce Museum, Dayton, Ohio under restoration.

The Engines

In addition to the Porsche powered MBB 223 Flamingo, the museum has a number of fascinating engines. The noteworthy engines -

- BMW 132A
- BMW M2B 15
- BMW 801 TJ
- BMW 803
- Daimler D IV
- Daimler-Benz DB 610

The Restoration Shop

In between the two halls is a world class restoration shop. Visitors are allowed to watch the work in progress from a second story catwalk. The current project is a 1955 Sikorsky HH-19 Helicopter from Dayton, Ohio.

Tours

Guided tours in German start at the times listed below. There is no cost for the daily tours and it lasts about 20 minutes. These tours only take place Monday to Friday and cover just a portion of the museum. Group tours are available for a fee. Please contact the museum at least 6 weeks in advance at this e-mail - *fuehrungen-fws@deutsches-museum.de*

- 10:30 AM - Historic Hanger
- 11:30 AM - New Exhibition Hall
- 2:30 PM - Historic Hanger
- 3:30 PM - New Exhibition Hall

Admission

- Adults 16 and older   € 6.-
- Students   € 3.-
- Children under 6   Free
- Family Ticket   € 12.-

Hours

- 9:00 AM to 5:00 PM daily
- Closed January 1, Good Friday, Easter, May 1, November 2, and December 24, 25, 31
- Please see website for additional closings

Amenities

- Restoration shop
- Gift store
- Children activities at the museum range from building model airplanes and rockets to learning how to pilot a plane. Seminars and classes are in German. Please see the website for current information.

Contact Information

Deutsches Museum Flugwerft
Schleißheim
Effnerstrasse 18
85764 Oberschleissheim
Germany

Phone: +49 (0) 89/315714-0
Fax: +49 (0) 89/315714-50
E-mail: *fws@deutsches-museum.de*
www.deutsches-museum.de/flugwerft

Dingolfing Industrial Museum

Tucked away in the quiet town of Dingolfing is a hidden gem of a museum. Its meek appearance from the street gives the visitor little idea of the treasures within. This little industrial museum pays tribute to the defunct company Glas Auto and the world renown car company that acquired it, BMW AG.

History of the Museum Dingolfing

The museum itself just opened in 2008. But the three buildings it occupies can trace its origins to 1410. The most interesting is the Ducal Castle (part of the museum) next to the main entrance to the museum.

This historic castle dates back to the 15th century and has been a museum for the town of Dingolfing since 1959.

The other main building is the grain storage building that dates back to 1477. It was destroyed in 1743, rebuilt in 1750, and served as a school house from 1892 to 2003.

Museum Dingolfing Today

The museum opened in 2008 and is owned by the town of Dingolfing. It is a collection of three medieval buildings that focus on three distinct themes. Local city history, industrial history, and archaeology. There is also a restaurant, café, and a gift store. The cars are located in the industrial section.

Directions to Museum Dingolfing

From **Munich by car:**

- ▶ Autobahn A92 (München-Deggendorf)
- ▶ Exit 17A/Dingolfing-West
- ▶ South on St2111
- ▶ Follow St2111/Brumatherstrasse
- ▶ Right on Bahnhofstrasse and cross Isar River
- ▶ Left onto Bruckstrasse and into Dingolfing Old City
- ▶ Right at Speisemarkt
- ▶ Follow Steinweg
- ▶ Follow Obere Stadt and the one way streets to museum.
- ▶ Museum is on left side. There is no dedicated museum parking lot.

Opposite: *Main entrance next to the right of the castle entrance.*

Above: *Glas Auto Sign.*

Quick Stats

- ▶ Plan on spending 2-4 hours
- ▶ Bavarian Museum Award winner 2009
- ▶ Several automobiles by Glas Auto on display
- ▶ Color coded interactive displays

The Collection Theme

The car related exhibits are in the industrial section of this museum. The industrial museum displays focus on the defunct Glas Automobile Company and BMW AG. The museum is color coded with themes running vertically through several different floors.

Must See

- ▶ The Kuka Industrial Robot located on the bottom floor. This brand and type of robot is used extensively by BMW at the nearby manufacturing plant of Dingolfing. It's job here is to retrieve 1/18 scale diecast BMWs from a nearby storage case. See *www.kuka-robotics.com*

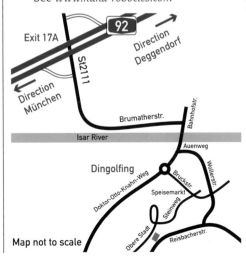

Map not to scale

The Exhibitions

There are three main vertical themes. Each are represented by a color coded display on each floor. Each floor's display ties into that same theme even though each floor focuses on a different topic.

The Upper Floor

The top floor explores the dawn of the 18th century industrial revolution and how it affected Dingolfing. Various technologies that were developed and used are displayed.

- ▶ Blue display - Technological inventions and science
- ▶ Green display - Industry of the day
- ▶ Yellow display - Everyday tools and devices

The Ground Floor

The Hans Glas Automobile Company was founded in 1895, but didn't start manufacturing cars until 1955. The company was sold to BMW in 1966.

The town of Dingolfing that the Glas Automobile Company once called home is now home to the largest BMW factory in the world.

- ▶ Blue display - Automobile inventions
- ▶ Green display - Dingolfing becomes an important industrial hub
- ▶ Yellow display - The post war boom of industry creates a wealth and prosperity

The Basement

BMW has become an integral part of Dingolfing and the largest BMW factory in the world.

- ▶ Blue display - Technology drives the auto industry and creates lighter weight cars
- ▶ Green display - Dingolfing's radius of influence both in the region and worldwide
- ▶ Yellow display - The automobile becomes a technological marvel.

The Cars

The range of cars manufactured in Dingolfing are displayed starting with Glas Auto. The noteworthy cars -

- ▶ Glas 1204
- ▶ Glas 1304 GL
- ▶ Glas Goggo Coupe 250
- ▶ Glas Goggomobile
- ▶ BMW 520
- ▶ BMW 850i

Top Left: *Kuka robot retrieving a 1/18 scale BMW model.*

Opposite Left: *Glas Auto technology of the 1950s.*

Opposite Right: *BMW Automobile technology of today.*

Tours

Prices start at € 35.- for one hour and increase in price with each additional half hour.

Amenities

▶ Tingula Restaurant & Café
▶ Gift store

Admission

▶ Adults 16 and older   € 4.-
▶ Students   € 2.-
▶ Seniors   € 2.-
▶ Family Card   € 10.-

Hours

▶ Tuesday and Wednesday
1:00 PM to 5:00 PM
▶ Friday to Sunday
10:00 AM to 5:00 PM
▶ Closed December 24, 25, January 1, and Good Friday

▶ Please see website for additional closings.

Contact Information

Museum Dingolfing Industriegeschichte Stadtgeschichte Veranstaltungen
Obere Stadt 19
84130 Dingolfing
Germany

Phone: +49 (0) 8731/312228
E-mail: *info@museum-dingolfing.com*
www.museum-dingolfing.de

Tingula Restaurant
Obere Stadt 21
84130 Dingolfing

Phone: +49 (0) 8731/3269911
www.tingula.de

Dornier Museum

Dornier and the town of Friedrichshafen are both central to the history of aviation in Germany. After the age of the Zeppelins, Dornier was founded in Friedrichshafen as a high tech aviation firm developing cutting edge aircraft and rockets.

Dornier Museum Friedrichshafen History

After 18 months of construction, The Dornier Museum opened on July 24, 2009 to celebrate both aviation history and the history of Dornier Aircraft Manufacturing Company. The inspiration behind this new museum was **Silvius Dornier**, the oldest living son of Claude Dornier, the founder of Dornier. The town of Friedrichshafen is where the firm was founded and now the location of this private museum. In October 2009, the museum debuted a special temporary exhibit known as James Turrell's Light Installation. This artist from Flagstaff, Arizona is known for exploring light and space.

Dornier Museum Friedrichshafen Today

The Dornier Company was founded in 1914 and became famous for its flying boats and the Do 31 vertical take off prototypes. Dornier was acquired by Daimler AG in 1985. It was sold once again to Fairchild in 1996. Today there is little left of this historic and significant part of aviation history.

The Architecture

The museum building is a multi story glass and concrete wonder of modern architecture. It is designed to give museum visitors a feeling of open space on the inside and a feeling of integration with the landscape and nearby airport on the outside.

Directions to Dornier

From **Munich by car:**
- Autobahn A96 (München-Lindau)
- Exit 3/Sigmarszell
- West/right on B31/B308 direction Friedrichshafen
- Exit to B30 by using exit ramp. Left on Länderöschstrasse
- Right on B30/Ravensburgerstrasse
- Left at Roundabout to Am Flughafen
- Look for museum to the right of airport tower

By Train:
- Take a train to the Friedrichshafen Trainstation
- Transfer to the bus service and take bus line 7486. For more info, see *www.stadtverkehr-fn.de*

Opposite: *Dornier Do 28 D2 outside.*
Above: *Interactive miniature wind and drag tunnel in the gallery of the museum.*

Quick Stats
- Plan on spending 3-6 hours
- Over 54,000 square feet of exhibition space
- Opened in 2009
- Cost over $30 million to build

The Collection Theme

The focus is on the history of Dornier from the dawn of aviation to the space age.

Must See
- Dornier Do 31 E1 - one of two prototypes made for vertical take offs and landings. The other is at the Deutsches Aircraft Museum (see page 114).

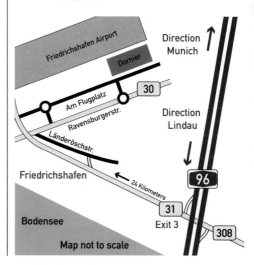

The Exhibitions

The museum is divided into three different areas - The Museum Box, The Gallery, and The Hanger.

The Museum Box
This permanent exhibit is the core to learning the history and the development of Dornier over the last 100 years. The interactive displays and scale models on the top floor of the museum are an in depth look at the company's progression over time.

The Gallery
The remaining portion of the second floor is a 100 meter long gallery dedicated to interactive technological developments used by aviation, space, and automobiles.

The Hanger
The majority of the planes on display are inside the main indoor hanger. This includes the Do 31. In addition to the main hanger, there is a cinema playing a short movie about Dornier. There are also a number of space and rocket related displays and aircraft engines.

Once visitors are done looking at the aircraft inside the hanger, there are additional aircraft outside near the entrance. Once visitors pass through the gift store, there is a restaurant, cafeteria, and access to a children's play area and a Dornier Do 27 with a built in slide. This airplane "Jungle Gym" is an excellent place for the children to play while the adults dine.

The Airplanes

All the aircraft here are important historic examples and some are even flight worthy. Here is a list of most of the aircraft -

- Brequet 1150 Atlantic
- Dornier Do Alpha Jet
- Dornier Do 27
- Dornier Do 28
- Dornier Do 29
- Dornier Do 31
- Dornier Do 228
- Dornier Merkur
- Fiat G.91 Fighter

Events

Over 32,000 square feet is available for events and is ideal for corporations looking to hold functions. Contact the museum at - *event@donniermuseum.de*

Amenities

- Restaurant and cafeteria
- Gift store
- Theater
- Children's Dornier Do 27 aircraft display/jungle gym outside
- Story boards and information in English

Admission

- Adults   € 9.-
- Children 11 and under   € 4.50
- Group up to 15 people   € 8.-
- Family tickets   € 20.-

Combo with Zeppelin Museum

- Adults   € 14.-
- Group up to 15 people   € 13.-
- Family tickets   € 33.-

Hours

- May to October - Daily from 9:00 AM to 5:00 PM
- November to April - 10:00 AM to 5:00 PM (closed on Mondays)

Contact Information

Dornier Museum Friedrichshafen
Am Flughafen
Claude-Dornier-Platz 1
88046 Friedrichshafen
Germany

Phone: +49 (0) 7541/4873600
Fax: +49 (0) 7541/4873651
E-mail: *info@donniermuseum.de*
www.donniermuseum.de

Opposite: *Dornier Do 31 E1 Experimental.*
Above: *Daimler Benz DB 603 12 cylinder engine with supercharger.*

EFA Museum

The EFA - Museum für Deutsche Automobilgeschichte (*Museum for German Automobile History*) is tucked away in the Bavaria countryside just north of the popular holiday destination spot Chiemsee. This little known museum is a large modern day exploration into the history and culture of Germany and the automobile. The museum should be enough of a temptation to go, but it is also a very pretty drive.

EFA Museum History

Founded in 1989 by entrepreneur Ernst Freiberger after a two year effort to find and purchase auto-mobiles that depict the history and changes over the years of automobiles and Germany.

In the 20 years since the museum opened, several other museums such as the Deutsches Museum in Munich and the Technical Museum in Berlin have lent the EFA Museum cars to display in addition to the collection created by Mr. Freiberger.

EFA Museum Today

Set in a modern building and full of light, there are 100 years of German automobiles on display at the EFA Museum. There is a gift store with scale die cast models and wide variety of car books and a model railway in the basement. The museum continues to receive cars on loan from other museums around Germany and hopes its visitors leave the museum with an emotional connection to the cars and Germany.

Quick Stats
▶ Plan on spending 3-6 hours
▶ 220 automobiles
▶ 64,000 square feet
▶ Model railway display is over 5,000 square feet in size and has almost 7,000 linear feet of track

Directions to EFA Museum

From **Munich by car:**
▶ Autobahn A8 (München-Salzburg)
▶ Exit 106/Bernau
▶ North on Prienerstrasse direction Prien
▶ At Prien, left on St2092/Seestrasse, then an immediate right on Rimstingerstrasse direction Bad Endorf/Halfing
▶ Once at Halfing, right on Bahnhofstr/St2360 direction Ammerang
▶ Follow road through town, signs will direct you to the museum at the north end of the town

Opposite: *Rows of classic cars.*
Above: *Front entrance.*

The Collection Theme
The museum follows the development of the German manufactured automobile for 100 years. There are displays focusing on the 1930s, 1950s, and 1960s. There is also an impressive Porsche display called "Abteilung Porsche" (*Porsche Division*).

Must See
▶ The cross section of a 1987 Porsche 959 Coupe. The Porsche 959 is a 2.8 liter 450 hp supercar with twin turbos and four wheel drive. When the car debuted, it was a technological marvel.

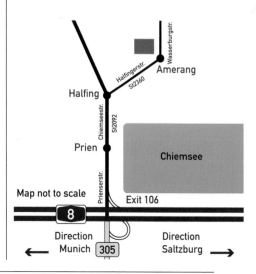

The Exhibitions

The museum directs foot traffic in a one way circle of the main building. Each row of cars highlights a different theme.

Because this museum is housed in a building with so many windows and skylights, photographers will find this museum a completely different experience on a sunny day versus an overcast day.

The Collections

The museum curator has divided the museum into 20 different collections. Here is our brief overview of some of the collections. We combined some prewar and postwar collections to save a little space.

Auto Union
12 cars ranging from a Horch 8 cylinder Type 400 to a DKW P15 Cabrio.

BMW
11 BMW's from 1928 to 1943. The collection includes a BMW 328 Sportswagen. 11 more post war BMW's including a BMW 507, BMW 3.0 CSL Coupe, BMW M365Csi Coupe, and a BMW M1.

Borgward
4 Borgwards spanning 1949 to 1961.

Ford
7 Pre-war Fords ranging from a Model T to a 1941 Ford V8 Cabriolet and 5 post war Fords.

Above: 1987 Porsche 959.
Opposite Top: Map of the museum.
Opposite: "Abteilung Porsche" display.

Maybach
2 Maybachs - A Maybach SW 38 Cabriolet and a SW 42 Cabriolet.

Mercedes-Benz
14 Mercedes-Benz prior to 1942 including a 540 K Cabriolet and 19 post war Mercedes-Benz including a Mercedes-Benz 300 SL and a 300 Gullwing.

Porsche
8 Porsche street cars and an amazing collection of Porsche race cars. EFA has a Porsche 917, Porsche 935, Porsche 956, Porsche 961, and Porsche "Dauer" 962 Le Mans.

Volkswagen
9 VW's ranging from 1946 to 1982.

Small cars of the 1950s
This mix of odd little cars include a Messerschmitt, Goggomobil, BMW Isetta, and NSU Wankel Spider. 18 cars in total.

Cars from East Germany
Here the little Trabant "Trabby" has found a home. 6 of these outcasts from the old DDR are on display.

Amenities
- ▶ Gift Store
- ▶ Café-Bistro Boxenstop
- ▶ Story boards and information in English

Admission
- ▶ Adults   € 8.-
- ▶ Children 6 to 14 years old   € 4.-
- ▶ Group up to 20 people   € 7.-

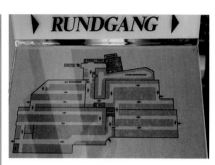

Hours
- ▶ April to October - Tuesday to Sunday 10:00 AM to 6:00 PM
- ▶ Closed Mondays
- ▶ Museum closes for the winter in November. Contact museum for exact closing date.

Contact Information
EFA - Museum für Deutsche Automobilgeschichte
Wasserburgstrasse 38
83123 Amerang
Germany

Phone: +49 (0) 8075/8141
Fax: +49 (0) 8075/1549
E-mail: *info@efa-automuseum.de*
www.efa-automuseum.de

Engstingen Museum

The entry prices are written by hand on a note pad at the entrance and the cars inside are just alright. In fact this museum isn't really the best. The whole museum lacks the overall shine that grace the museums in Stuttgart an hour or so to the north. But it is still worth a visit. Situated on two floors next to a restaurant, there are roughly 120 cars, motorcycles, and scooters. One nice bonus to this museum is the great drive through the countryside of the Swabian Alb to reach it!

Engstingen Museum Today

The museum is a good distance from any Autobahn or large town, in the heart of the rolling hills of the Swabian Alb (*Plateau*). In 2010, the museum opened a new display with cars from the 1960s, 1970s, and 1980s.

Quick Stats
- Plan on spending 1-2 hours
- 120 cars & motorcycles
- 13,000 square feet
- Minutes away from Schloss Lichtenstein (If you like Schloss Neuschwanstein, you will love this other fairy tale castle). See their website at - *www.schloss-lichtenstein.de*

Admission
- Adults   € 4.-
- Children 12 to 18   € 2.-
- Children 11 and under   € 1.-
- Group up to 15 people   € 3.-

Amenities
- Restaurant Engstinger Hof is next door. It is open daily.

Hours
- Good Friday to end of October - Saturday & Sunday Noon to 5:00 PM
- School vacation hours - Tuesday through Sunday Noon to 5:00 PM
- Museum closes November 1

Contact Information

Automuseum Engstingen
Kleinengstingerstrasse 2
72829 Engstingen
Germany

Phone: +49 (0) 7129/9399-0
Fax: +49 (0) 7129/9399-99
E-mail: *info@engstingen.de*
www.automuseum-engstingen.de

Directions to Engstingen

From **Stuttgart by car:**
- Autobahn A8 (Stuttgart-München)
- Exit 53A (Stuttgart-Degerloch)
- B27 direction Reutlingen
- Merge onto B28 direction Reutlingen
- Drive through Reutlingen city center
- Merge onto B312/B313 south direction Pfullingen/Riedlingen
- Follow either B312 or B313 into Engstingen
- Turn onto Kleinengstingerstrasse

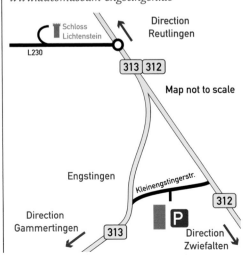

Opposite: *From left - 1942 Fiat Sport, 1966 Fiat 850, 1940 NSU-Fiat Weinsberg Sport Roadster, NSU Prinz 4.*

Above: *Museum entrance.*

Fritz B. Busch Museum

The Automobilemuseum von Fritz B. Busch tells the story of Germans and their automobiles. This is a little different than the usual car museum in that it places rather ordinary cars into the context of the German culture behind them. Foreigners may not understand or appreciate this museum at first glance, so we recommend a guided tour for the die hard enthusiasts.

History of the Museum Fritz B. Busch

The history of the museum is also the history of one man, its founder and creator - Fritz B. Busch. Mr. Busch was born in 1922 and has become a very well respected German automotive journalist. He founded his museum in 1973 with 32 cars in part of a historic castle. In 1998 the museum was expanded to a second building - a 400 year old barn about 100 feet from the main museum.

Busch Museum Today

This private museum is still housed in the 500 year old stables of the royal castle of Waldburg-Wolfegg. The second building, a quick walk down the street, is in a slightly more modern 400 year old building.

Quick Stats

- ▶ Plan on spending 2-4 hours
- ▶ 32,000 square feet on display
- ▶ 200 vehicles
- ▶ Founded by famous German automotive journalist Fritz B. Busch

The Collection Theme

Of all the museums covered in this guidebook, this museum has the most complex theme. The collection of cars reflect and display the human condition at various points of time in Germany. Please ask the staff more to fully appreciate the cars and displays.

Directions to Fritz Busch

From **Munich by car:**
- ▶ Autobahn A96 (München-Lindau)
- ▶ Exit 7/ Waltershofen
- ▶ North on L265 direction Kisslegg
- ▶ Once at Kisslegg, north/right on L265/Schlossstrasse
- ▶ Left/east on L330/Krumbachstrasse direction Rötenbach
- ▶ Once in Rötenbach, right on L315/ Wolfeggerstrasse direction Wolfegg
- ▶ Follow signs for museum. Use public parking as the museum does not have its own parking lot

Opposite: *Museum entrance at the 500 year old stables of the Waldburg-Wolfegg Castle.*
Above: *1923 Fiat 501 S, 1921 AGA.*

Must See

The Legendary Jaguar E Type made famous by Mr. Busch by aptly calling the his car "Pure Whisky on wheels" or just "Whisky Pur". There is an article on the museum's website explaining more. See - *www.automuseum-busch.de/whiskypur.htm*

The Exhibitions

There are two buildings to the museum. Each are two story and are roughly 100 feet apart. Both buildings are relatively dark and can be a challenge to photograph. The museum staff will direct you to building 2 of the museum.

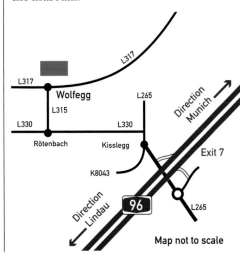

Map not to scale

Who was Fritz B. Busch?

Most readers of either U.S. or English car magazines may have never heard of this famous automotive journalist. But those who read either *Auto Motor und Sport*, *Der Stern*, or *Motor Klassik* know exactly who Fritz B. Busch is. For those who enjoy the challenges of reading German, Mr. Busch has written articles for those respective magazines plus authored several books, many of which are on *www.amazon.com*.

Mr. Busch has written reviews of cars that focus more on the human condition rather than the actual technical specifications of the car. When asked in a 2007 interview about the future of man and automobile design, he replied "Es wird ganz schlimm werden"..or *It looks pretty bad*". Sadly Fritz B. Busch passed away in 2010.

The Cars

The museum says that it doesn't take pride in having the rarest cars, but ones that reflect the personality of its founder. There are more than 200 cars in the museum, here are the highlights -

- ▶ 1918 Benz 8/20 Sport Phaeton
- ▶ 1923 Fiat 501 S
- ▶ 1930 BMW Dixi
- ▶ 1930 BMW Ihle Sport
- ▶ 1933 Framo LTH 200
- ▶ 1934 Fiat 500 (Topolino)
- ▶ 1952 Cadillac von Hans Albers
- ▶ 1954 BMW 501 A
- ▶ 1957 Zündapp Janus
- ▶ 1958 Porsche Junior Tractor
- ▶ 1959 Auto Union AU 1000 SP
- ▶ 1962 Messerschmitt Kabinenroller
- ▶ 1962 Jaguar E Type Series 1 "Whisky Pur"
- ▶ 1966 Porsche 906 Long Tail

Here are two of the car collections themes in the museum.

War Shortages Collection -

It is hard for a lot of us to imagine life after World War II, but people in Germany during the 1950s lived with a short supply of even basic materials. While the world was focused on rebuilding Europe, luxury goods and the money to buy them were scarce. The little cars of this time period are on display and reflect the feelings of a nation during those years.

The Italian Vacation Collection -

Every August, all of Europe (still) shuts down for the month. Families packed up their station wagons and hooked up their Wohnwagen (*camper trailer*) for their annual migration to Italy. The Autobahnen were clogged with epic Stau's (*traffic jams*) and all traffic ground to a stop. Fathers put their cars in park, turned off the engine, and patiently wait in the heat. Today air conditioning, GPS, and satellite radio are the norm, but back in the 1950s, it was a different story. Cars were a fraction of the size and amenities all but nonexistent. Travel was slow, crowded, and hot. But as the museum shows, people were also happy. Explore the cars that moved families around Europe during this mad August vacation rush.

Amenities
▶ Gift Store in building 2

Opposite: Building 1, main hall.
Above: The "Barn Find" - A 1952 Lloyd 250.
Right: Jaguar E Type Series 1 "Whisky Pur".

Admission
▶ Adults   € 7.-
▶ Children ages 5 to 14   € 3.-
▶ Group 20+ people   € 6.-

Hours
▶ April to October Tuesday to Sunday 10:00 AM to 5:00 PM
▶ November to March the museum is open only on Sundays from 10:00 AM to 5:00 PM

Contact Information

Automuseum von Fritz B. Busch
Fritz B. Busch Weg 1
88641 Wolfegg
Germany

Phone: +49 (0) 7527-6294
E-mail: *info@automuseum-busch.de*
www.automuseum-busch.de

Langenburg Museum

Looking for a scenic drive and great views? Pay a visit to the picturesque town of Langenburg and the Deutsches Automuseum Langenburg! This museum is located in the town of Langenburg and sits on a hill over looking the Jagst River below. Next door to the museum is the residence of the Hohenlohe family, the historic castle "Schloss Langenburg".

History of Langenburg

Founded in 1969 by Fürst Kraft von Hohenlohe and Richard von Frankenberg, the original name of this museum was "Deutsches Auto-Museum Heidelberg". In 1970 the museum moved from Waibstadt to Langenburg. In 1972 a gallery was added and in 1977 the museum expanded again to include the third building, a coach house. From the initial 25 cars in 1970, the museum today has expanded to over 70 cars in three different exhibition halls.

Langenburg Today

In March 2010, this private museum celebrated its 40th birthday. With the cooperation of the Porsche Museum in Zuffenhausen, the museum presented 9 extraordinary Porsches as part of a temporary exhibit including a Porsche 716 Le Mans winner and a Porsche 804 Formula 1. The museum continues to host both permanent and temporary exhibits with the cooperation of both the Porsche Museum and the Mercedes-Benz Museum.

Quick Stats
▶ Plan on spending 2-4 hours
▶ Over 21,500 square feet
▶ Over 70 cars
▶ Hosts Langenburg Historic Car Rally every April.
  See *www.langenburg-historic.de*
▶ Next door to Schloss Langenburg
  See *www.schlosslangenburg.de*

Directions to Langenburg

From **Heilbronn by car:**
▶ Autobahn A6 (Heilbronn-Nürnberg)
▶ Exit 44/ Ilshofen-Wolpertshausen
▶ North on L1042/Hörlebacherstrasse direction Obersteinach
▶ Continue north direction Nesselbach on L1042/Steinacherstrasse
▶ Keep right in Nesselbach and follow L1036 over Jagst river
▶ Right on Bächlingerstrasse direction Langenburg/Schloss Langenburg
▶ Public parking available by castle. Pay for parking as you leave.

Opposite: Museum entrance next to Schloss Langenburg.

Above: *1982 Porsche 956C.*

The Collection Theme

The central theme here is the German automobile. There are however brands from around the world such as Buick, Jaguar, and Maserati. There are some NSU motorcycles on display as well, but they aren't central to the museum.

Must See
▶ The Porsche race cars - 956C raced by Hans-Joachim Stuck (see **page 48**) and Derek Bell (see **page 94**), 911 GT1, Porsche-March CART, and 953 "Paris-Dakar" rally car.

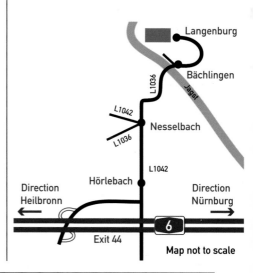

The Exhibitions

The entrance is a single large wooden door that gives the visitor the impression the museum is quite small. That impression couldn't be more wrong. There are three halls here and the museum is deceptively big.

The Cars

There are more than 70 cars in the museum. Here are the highlights -

▶ 1938 Alvis 4.3 Liter Vanden Plas
▶ 1957 BMW 600 "Isetta"
▶ 1916 Buick Roadster D-6-55
▶ 1937 Horch Type 853
▶ 1946 Jaguar Mark IV
▶ 1939 "K-Wagen" (Mercedes-Benz 170V - 1 of 5 pieces)
▶ Lancia Astura IV Pininfarina Cabriolet (1 of 25 pieces)
▶ 1962 Maserati Sebring GT
▶ 1951 Mercedes-Benz 300 Cabrio
▶ 1956 Mercedes-Benz 300 SL
▶ 1940 NSU/Fiat "Topolino"
▶ 1949 Talbot Lago Record Cabrio
▶ 1910 Sizaire-Naudin 4 Touring

The Porsche Race Cars

▶ 1982 Porsche 956C - Hans-Joachim Stuck, Derek Bell, Frank Jelinski
▶ 1984 Porsche 953 Paris-Dakar Jacky Ickx/Claude Brasseur (The pair finished in sixth place)
▶ 1998 Porsche 911 GT1 - Hans-Joachim Stuck, Terry Boutsen, Bob Wollek
▶ 1990 Porsche-March CART - Theo Fabi

The Porsche Street Cars

▶ 1960 Porsche Junior Tractor
▶ 1961 Porsche 356 B 1600 S
▶ 1970 Porsche 914/6 Prototype
▶ 1979 Porsche 928 S 4 door
▶ 2002 Porsche Boxster - "Cross Section Model"

Events

The museum hosts events such as rallies and rents its exhibition halls for any number of functions.

Amenities

▶ Small gift store
▶ Schloss Langenburg is next to Museum and combo-tickets are available to see both.

Admission

▶ Adults   € 4.90
▶ Students   € 4.-
▶ Children under 14 years   € 3.-
▶ Group of 20+ people   € 4.-

Hours - Low Season

▶ Low season is April to the beginning of May & late September and October.
▶ Saturday, Sunday, and Holidays 10:30 AM to 5:00 PM

Opposite: *1990 Porsche-March CART and 1998 Porsche 911 GT1.*

Above: *A white 1957 BMW 600, a 1957 Zündapp Janus, and a red 1968 Goggomobil T 250 Limousine.*

Hours - High Season

▶ High season is May to September
▶ Tuesday to Friday 11:00 AM to 4:00 PM
▶ Saturday, Sunday, and holidays 10:30 AM to 5:00 PM
▶ Closed every Monday.

Winter

▶ Museum closes for the winter in November and reopens in April.

Contact Information

Deutsches Automuseum
c/o Fürstliche Verwaltung
Schloss Langenburg
Schloss 1
74595 Langenburg
Germany

Phone: +49 (0) 7905/94190-0
Fax: +49 (0) 7905/9419066
E-mail:
museum@schlosslangenburg.de
www.deutsches-automuseum.de

Marxzell Museum

If the manufacturer's museums by Audi, BMW, Mercedes-Benz, and Porsche represent a pinnacle of achievement for all that a car museum can possibly be, the Marxzell Museum is the anti-museum. It is everything that these factory museums are not. The best single word to describe this museum is "eccentric". Actually words cannot describe a museum that is so different from everything else we have ever seen. Yes, it is worth a visit.

History of the Marxzell Museum

Bernhard Reichert started collecting in 1958 and 10 years later he opened his museum. The museum was supposed to be housed in Karlsruhe but when the town backed out of the deal, a suitable property was found in Marxzell. The family bought an old sawmill and founded the museum in 1968. Today, the Reichert family still owns and operates this one of a kind museum.

Marxzell Today

Expect to walk into this museum, shake your head, and then laugh to yourself wondering out loud "Now what is that?!". We actually like this museum. It is so far removed from everything considered normal or "German". The owners are very proud of their museum and are friendly fellows.

Quick Stats

▶ Plan on spending 1-2 hours. Actually 1 of 2 things will happen. Either you will walk in and the walk right out...or want to spend all day here.

▶ At least 30 cars in various condition. Most are whole cars.

▶ Museum was founded 42 years ago and is located in a historic saw mill.

▶ Has an impressive little collection of fire trucks.

Directions to Marxzell

From **Karlsruhe by car:**

▶ Autobahn A5 (Karlsruhe-Freiburg)

▶ Exit 47/Ettingen

▶ South on Karlsruhestrasse

▶ Left on B3/L562

▶ Follow L562 south

▶ Merge onto Pforzheimerstrasse

▶ Merge right onto L564/ Herranalberstrasse

▶ Road renames from Herranalberstrasse to Albtalstrasse

▶ Look for museum on left side before you enter the town of Marxzell

Opposite: The side of the museum.
Above Right: Dis-membered Mercedes-Benz. We have no idea why...

The Collection Theme

We aren't really sure what the theme is here. There are cars, trucks, and fire engines. There is also mannequins, dead animals, miniature versions of Laurel and Hardy, antlers, and wicker baskets.

Must See

▶ The Citroën Kegresse in the basement is also worth a look as are the 1922 American La France and 1915 Benz Feuerwehr fire trucks. Also look for the embalmed animals. It reminds us of the 1987 movie - "Lost Boys".

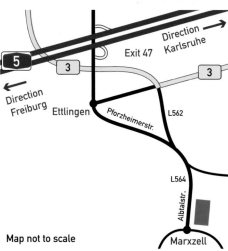

Map not to scale

The Exhibitions

The building has a large main floor that is divided into at least three different rooms. One room houses the fire trucks and another holds a few cars and the Mercedes-Benz front grills. The main room (where the entrance is located) houses most of the cars. There is also a basement with yet more.

The Cars

There are some interesting cars here, however it is dark and they may be hard to find. Here are the highlights -

- ▶ 1938 BMW 328 Roadster Sportwagen
- ▶ 1952 BMW 502 3.2 V8
- ▶ 1950 Cadillac Fleetwood
- ▶ 1957 Chevrolet Bel Air
- ▶ 1960 Chevrolet Corvette
- ▶ 1963 Chevrolet Corvette
- ▶ 1969 Chevrolet Corvette
- ▶ 1924 Citroën Torpedo
- ▶ 1958 Ford Thunderbird
- ▶ 1957 Fuldamobil
- ▶ 1953 Mercedes-Benz 300 "Adenauer"
- ▶ 1951 Messerschmitt KR 175
- ▶ 1953 Pontiac Chieftain
- ▶ Rolls Royce Phantom III 12 cylinder. First owner - Queen Mary
- ▶ 1949 Vanden-Plas Princess

The Rest of the Museum

This place is packed to the ceiling with more than just cars. We will skip listing each embalmed animal and try to stick to the stuff with wheels. More highlights -

- 1927 Böhmerland - 3 passenger motorcycle
- 1915 Benz Feuerwehr fire truck
- 1922 American La France fire truck
- Citroën Kegresse - 1 of 3 used to cross the Himalayas in 1931

Amenities
- Theater (of sorts)

Admission
- Adults   € 5.-
- Students   € 3.-
- Children 5 and under   Free
- Group of 10 people   € 4.-

Hours
- Tuesday to Sunday
  2:00 PM to 5:00 PM
- Museum is open all year long

Contact Information

Fahrzeugmuseum Marxzell
Neuenbürgerstrasse 1
76359 Marxzell
Germany

Phone: +49 (0) 7248/6262
Cell: +49 (0) 172/7232817
Fax: +49 (0) 7248/9249901
E-mail: *Reichert-Marxzell@t-online.de*
www.fahrzeugmuseum-marxzell.de

Opposite Top: *1957 Chevrolet Bel Air with helicopter behind.*

Opposite Below: *Main exhibition hall.*

Top: *Citroën Kegresse - 1 of 3 used to cross the Himalayas in 1931.*

Above: *Classic fire trucks.*

Mercedes-Benz Partner Museums

This is a special museum sub-section for the Mercedes-Benz partner museums and sites. Under the direction of Mercedes-Benz, there are a number of private museums that have been incorporated into an official network of Mercedes-Benz related partner sites. This network allows the sites to coordinate with the Mercedes-Benz / Daimler Archives in an effort to preserve the history behind and culture of Mercedes-Benz. Some of these sites are historical landmarks commemorating the lives of the founders of Daimler AG while others are car museums in the traditional sense. All of these sites are worth visiting for any car enthusiast and not just the diehard Mercedes-Benz fan. Some of the sites are not photographed in this guide, but their contact information is provided.

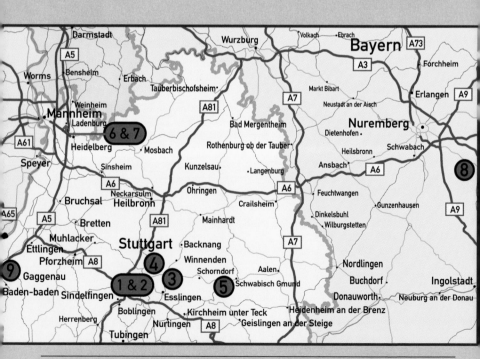

Mercedes-Benz Partner Museums & Sites

Site	City	Notes
1 - Mercedes-Benz Museum	Stuttgart/ Untertürkheim	Covered here, see page 72
2 - Mercedes-Benz Archives and Collections	Stuttgart/ Untertürkheim	Not covered in this book.
3 - Mercedes-Benz Classic Center	Fellbach/ Stuttgart	Not covered in this book.
4 - Gottlieb Daimler Memorial	Bad Cannstatt/ Stuttgart	Covered here, see page 151
5 - Gottlieb Daimler Birth House	Schorndorf	Covered here, see page 150
6 - Karl Benz Mansion	Ladenburg	Covered here, see page 146
7 - Automuseum Dr. Carl Benz	Ladenburg	Covered here, see page 147
8 - Maybach Museum	Neumarkt in der Oberpfalz	Covered here, see page 152
9 - Unimog Museum	Gaggenau	Not covered in this book.

Contact Information for sites not covered -

Mercedes-Benz Archives
Phone: +49 (0) 711/1730-000
Fax: +49 (0) 711/1730-400
E-mail: *classic@daimler.com*
www.mercedes-benz-classic.com

Mercedes-Benz Classic Center
Stuttgarterstrasse 90
70736 Fellbach
Germany
Monday to Friday
9:00 AM to 5:00 PM
www.mercedes-benz-classic.com

Unimog Museum
An der B 462
Ausfahrt Schloss Rotenfels
76571 Gaggenau
Germany

Phone: +49 (0) 7225/98131-0
Fax: +49 (0) 7225/98131-19
E-mail: *info@unimog-museum.de*
www.unimog-museum.de

Hours - Tuesday to Sunday
10:00 AM to 5:00 PM

Karl Benz Mansion

The town of Ladenburg near Mannheim is home to two different Mercedes-Benz sites. The Benz family started living in the mansion in 1905 and it remained occupied until 1969. The Automuseum was founded in 1996 & displays 70 cars.

The Karl Benz Mansion is a nice extra stop if you find yourself visiting Ladenburg for the Automuseum Dr. Carl Benz. The only portion of the mansion open to the public is a rather small basement, but there is a Benz Patent Motorwagen on display. This is the smallest exhibit of all the Mercedes-Benz related sites and is worth visiting in conjunction with the Automuseum Dr. Carl Benz.

Admission
▶ Everyone   Free

Hours
▶ Sundays only
    2:30 PM to 5:30 PM

Contact Information

Karl Benz Mansion
Dr. Carl-Benz-Platz 2
68526 Ladenburg
Germany

Phone: +49 (0) 6203/15924
*195.138.33.22/downloads/
history_places_en.pdf*

Left: *Benz Patent Motorwagen inside the Karl Benz Mansion.*

Opposite: *Museum entrance to the Automuseum Dr. Carl Benz.*

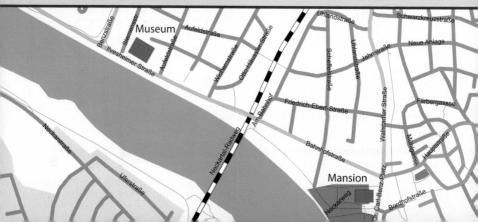

Automuseum Dr. Carl Benz

Directions to Museum

From **Mannheim by car:**

- ▶ Autobahn A5 (Karlsruhe/Darmstadt)
- ▶ Exit 35 / Landenburg
- ▶ West on L597
- ▶ Left/south on Benzstrasse
  (2nd possible left)
- ▶ Left on Ilvesheimer Strasse

Directions to Mansion

From **Automuseum Dr. Carl Benz:**

- ▶ East/left on Ilvesheimer Strasse
- ▶ Right on Wallstatter Strasse
- ▶ The mansion is to your right just
  before Dr. Carl-Benz-Platz

Map not to scale

Direction
Darmstadt

L597   Exit 35

Weinheimerstr.

5

Benzstr.

Ladenburg

Ilvesheimerstr.

Direction
Karlsruhe

Automuseum Dr. Carl Benz

Founded in 1996, the museum is housed in a period building that gives the visitor an idea of 19th century architecture. This Mercedes-Benz partner museum has 70 high quality and rare cars.

Quick Stats

▸ Plan on spending 2-4 hours
▸ More than 70 vehicles

The Collection Theme

Follow automotive history from the invention of the car to present day. The name implies that all the cars are Mercedes-Benz, but there are several other brands on display. Additional displays follow the life and accomplishments of Dr. Carl Benz.

Must See

▸ The race car collection in the rear of the museum

The Exhibitions

The museum is a single building with two different exhibition halls. The main hall houses the "Dr. Carl Benz Plaza" and "Mercedes Alley". The Plaza displays cars manufactured by Benz prior to 1926. The Alley displays cars manufactured 1926 and later. The other exhibition hall is the race cars. Maybe half are actually Mercedes-Benz, but all are interesting.

The Cars

The 70 cars are all in good condition and some are very rare. Here are the noteworthy cars -

▸ 1957 Mercedes-Benz 190 SLR W 121
▸ 1925 Benz & Cie. 10/35 PS Touring
▸ 1921 Benz & Cie. Avus 10/30 Race Car
▸ 1921 Amilcar CC race car
▸ 1886 Benz Patent Motorwagen

Events

The museum both holds various annual events and rents out its restaurant and bar. The annual events include a car auction, festivals, and dinners. See the website for more information.

Amenities

▶ Restaurant, café, and gift store

Admission

▶ Adults   € 4.-
▶ Children 11 and under   € 2.50
▶ Family ticket   € 8.-
▶ Group up to 15 people   € 3.-

Hours

▶ Wednesday, Saturday, & Sunday
  2:00 PM to 6:00 PM

Contact Information

Automuseum Dr. Carl Benz
Ilvesheimer Strasse 26
68526 Ladenburg
Germany

Phone: +49 (0) 6203/181786
Fax: +49 (0) 6203/2503
E-mail:
info@automuseum-ladenburg.de
www.automuseum-ladenburg.de

Opposite: *View into the back exhibition room.*
Top Right: *(From closest) - 1976 Brixner Group C Spyder, 1971 Brixner Group 7 Spyder, and 1983 Van Diemen 1600.*
Bottom Right: *2001 McLaren-Mercedes MP 4/16A - Mika Häkkinen, 1991 Sauber-Mercedes C 192 - Michael Schumacher & Karl Wendlinger.*

Gottlieb Daimler Birth House

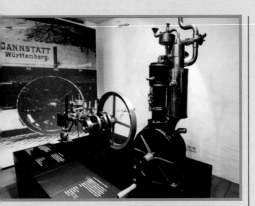

This single story exhibition in the pedestrian zone of Schorndorf is a collection of 19th century technology and inventions by Gottlieb Daimler.

Quick Stats
▶ Plan on spending 1 hour
▶ 1885 1 cylinder engine

Amenities
▶ Story boards in English

Directions to Birth House

From **Stuttgart by car:**
▶ B14 to B29 (no exit number)
▶ East on B29 direction Schorndorf
▶ Exit Schorndorf-Zentrum
▶ Waiblingerstr direction Zentrum
▶ At roundabout, head south on Benzstrasse
▶ West on Karlstrasse
▶ Park along Karlstrasse
▶ Walk to Museum (The entrance is inside a pedestrian zone)

Admission
▶ Everyone   Free

Hours
▶ Open Tuesday to Thursday 10:00 AM to 6:00 PM
▶ Open Friday 2:00 PM to 5:00 PM
▶ Closed Monday, Saturday, Sunday
▶ August by appointment only
▶ Closed between Christmas & New Years

Contact Information

Gottlieb Daimler Birth House
Höllgasse 7
73614 Schorndorf
Germany

Phone: +49 (0) 7181/66510
195.138.33.22/downloads/
history_places_en.pdf

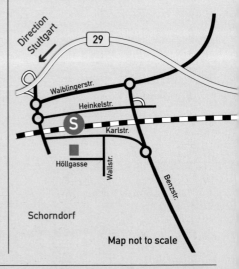

Gottlieb Daimler Memorial

This little villa in the Stuttgart suburb of Bad Cannstatt was converted into a workshop by Gottlieb Daimler in 1882. This serene working environment was where he and Wilhelm Maybach worked in secrecy to build the world's first high speed gas engine.

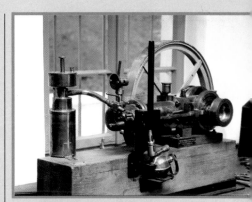

Quick Stats
▶ Plan on spending 1 hour
▶ The engines located at the Gottlieb Daimler Birth House were built here.

Admission
▶ Everyone   Free

Hours
▶ Monday to Friday 10:00 AM to 4:00 PM
▶ Closed Mondays & Public Holidays

Directions to Memorial

From **Stuttgart by car:**
▶ B14 East out of the Stuttgart city center
▶ Straight across the Neckar River
▶ Cannstatterstrasse turns into Waiblingstrasse
▶ Left on Wilhelmstrasse
▶ Right onto König-Karl-Strasse
▶ Follow road around corner to Memorial

By Train:
▶ Take S-Bahn to Bad Cannstatt

Opposite: The first high speed engine from 1883 to the left of the 1885 "Grandfather Clock" one cylinder engine.
Above: Gottlieb Daimler Memorial.

Contact Information

Gottlieb Daimler Memorial
Taubenheimstrasse 13
70372 Stuttgart
Germany

Phone: +49 (0) 711/569399
195.138.33.22/downloads/ history_places_en.pdf

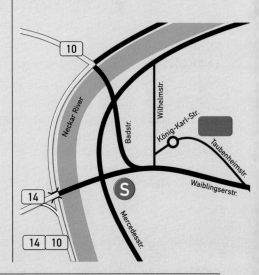

Maybach Museum

Wilhelm Maybach was born in Germany in 1846 and together with Gottlieb Daimler invented the 4 stroke high speed internal combustion engine. But the partnership with Daimler-Mercedes wasn't to last, and he left the firm in 1907 to build engines under contract for the Zeppelin Airship Company. In 1921, in part due to the Versailles Treaty, he started building automobiles. This museum highlights the very best from that era.

History of the Museum

The full name of the museum is the "Museum für Historische Maybach-Fahrzeuge" and is housed in the renovated complex of historic buildings that once housed the motorcycle and bike company Express Werke AG.

The museum's founders, Anna and Dr. Helmut Hofmann, purchased their first Maybach, a SW38 Pullman Cabriolet, in 1988. 21 years, and almost 18 cars later, the Hofmanns opened their museum on June 13, 2009.

Above: *Entrance to the Museum.*

Maybach Museum Today

The museum complex today consists of two exhibition halls, a foyer, offices, lounge, and rentable space. The total square footage under roof is over 28,000. It is the largest private Maybach collection in the world and partners with the Mercedes-Benz Museum, Zeppelin Museum, and Technik Museum Sinsheim.

Quick Stats
- Plan on spending 3-6 hours
- 18 to 20 cars on display
- Two exhibition halls consisting of over 27,000 square feet
- Roughly 1,800 Maybach were manufactured between 1921 and 1941. Only 160 remain today.

The Collection Theme
The biography of Wilhelm Maybach, his son Karl Maybach, and the

Directions to Maybach

From **Nürnberg by car:**
- Autobahn A3
  (Nürnberg - Regensburg)
- Exit 92/Neumarkt
- South on B299a direction Neumarkt
- Merge/south onto B299
- Left/straight on Ambergerstrasse direction Neumarkt
- Road changes to Dammstrasse
- Follow road south over the canal
- Left on Freystädterstrasse
- Right on Regensburgerstrasse
- Right on Ingolstadtädterstrasse
- Museum is on right side
- Use public parking

Above: Maybach SW 38 Sport Cabriolet - 1938 Geneva Auto Show Car.

Maybach automobiles are the focus of this museum. Additional information covers the partnership with Gottlieb Daimler and the Maybach automobiles of today. Maybach history in aviation is only briefly discussed, but it is worth noting there is a 1917 Type Mb. IVa aircraft motor on display.

Must See
- The cross section Maybach and the SW 38 Maybach show car at the front of the museum

The Exhibitions

The entry to the museum is on Holzgartenstrasse with the parking lot on Ingolstädterstrasse. The museum has two exhibition halls. The smaller hall is to the left of the forum entry and the larger exhibition hall is to the right. The museum has dimmed lighting and few windows, so photography could be a challenge for some.

The Bodies

Even though the cars are named "Maybach" and are adorned with the Maybach emblem, the bodies are not made by Maybach. The coachbuilder **Carosseriebau Hermann Spohn** of Ravensburg, Germany was responsible for most of the Maybach automobile bodies from this era.

The Cars

There are roughly 20 vehicles in the museum. There is some rotation of vehicles during the year.

- ▶ 1889 Stahlradwagen
- ▶ 1906 Mercedes Rennwagen
- ▶ 1920 "Weissen Mars" motorcycle
- ▶ 1921 – 1928 Maybach W 3
- ▶ 1926 Maybach W 5 SG
- ▶ 1930 Maybach DS 8 "Zeppelin" Roadster
- ▶ 1935 Maybach SW 38
- ▶ 1936 Maybach SW 38 Cabriolet
- ▶ 1937 Maybach Zeppelin

- 1937 Maybach SW 38 Pullman Cabriolet
- 1937 Maybach SW 38 Sport Cabriolet
- 1938 Maybach SW 38 4 door Pullman Limousine
- 1938 Maybach SW 38 Cabriolet
- 1938 Maybach SW 38 Standard Pullman Limousine
- 1939 Maybach SW 38
- 1939 Maybach SW 38/42 Sport Cabriolet
- 1939 Maybach SW 38 Pullmann Limousine
- 1939 Maybach DS 8 "Zeppelin" Pullmann Limousine
- 1938/1950 Maybach SW 38/42 Ponton Cabriolet
- 2009 Maybach 57 S

Events

- The museum has a large area available for corporate rentals.

Amenities

- Café - open Sunday and bank holidays from 1:00 PM

Admission

- Adults   € 9.-
- Students   € 5.-
- Children 5 and under   Free
- Group of 15 people   € 8.-
- Photo permission   € 3.-

Hours

- Tuesday to Sunday 10:00 AM to 5:00 PM
- Last admission at 4:00 PM

- Please look at website for museum closings

Corporate Events
Ms. Gradl or Ms. Engelbrecht

Phone: +49 (0) 9181/4877100
Fax: +49 (0) 9181/4877000
E-mail:
event@automuseum-maybach.de

Contact Information

Museum für Historische
Maybach-Fahrzeuge
Holzgartenstrasse 8
92318 Neumarkt
Germany

Phone: +49 (0) 9181/4877100
Fax: +49 (0) 9181/4877000
E-mail:
info@automuseum-maybach.de
www.automuseum-maybach.de

Opposite: *Maybach SW 38/42 & 2009 57S.*
Above: *1938 Maybach SW 38.*

Öhringen Museum

Just off an innocuous Autobahn exit, there is this secret little museum tucked away in a industrial section of a small town. In fact, once you arrive and stand at the front door, there is little to indicate there is a pretty neat car collection hidden inside.

History of the Öhringen Museum

One man's passion for cars has been the driving force behind the "Motor Museum Öhringen". Paul Heyd not only displays his car collection but also his motorcycle, fashion, glass, and camera collections here as well. The museum was founded in 1980 as a private museum next to the company Alfred Heyd GmbH & Co. KG.

As a side note, the Alfred Heyd firm next door to the museum manufacturers ball joints, tie rods, and steering components for both cars and trucks. His parts fit Alfa Romeo, Audi, BMW, Mercedes-Benz, and Volkswagen.

Öhringen Museum Today

The meek appearance of the museum shouldn't dissuade car lovers from visiting this museum. Its cars are interesting, it's just off the Autobahn, and it's near a number of other significant car museums and sites. Check the hours before visiting as this museum is not always open.

Quick Stats
▶ Plan on spending 1-2 hours
▶ Located at Alfred Heyd GmbH & Co. KG, a manufacturer of components used on a number of European built cars.
▶ Museum is also home to a "Fascination with Art and Glass" exhibit.
▶ Roughly 26 cars in the museum

The Collection Theme

This is an "Oldtimer" museum with sport and touring cars from the 1940s to the 1960s with just about every major automotive manufacturer represented. This theme runs well with both the camera and fashion

collections also on display. The collection of glass represents a step away from the cars, but the museum has made some interesting pairings by placing certain works of glass art next to accompanying automobiles. This probably isn't like matching wine with cheese, but it's kinda fun none the less.

Must See
▶ The Packard and Nash at the far end of the smaller exhibition hall.

Directions to Öhringen

From **Heilbronn by car:**
▶ Autobahn A6 (Heilbronn-Nürnberg)
▶ Exit 40/ Öhringen
▶ North on Neuenstadterstrasse
▶ Left on Westallee
▶ Follow Westallee under Autobahn
▶ Left on Verrenbergerweg
▶ Left on Stettinerstrasse

Opposite: *Main exhibition hall.*
Top Right: *Entrance to museum.*

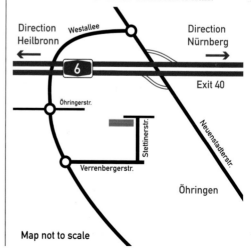

Map not to scale

The Exhibitions

The two major exhibits are the cars and the glass. In fact, when one glass collector website listed this museum, they joking told their glass enthusiast members - "Don't be put off by all the automobiles!".

The Cars

There are roughly 26 cars in the museum and more than 100 motorcycles.

- ▶ 1947 Alfa Romeo 6C 2500 SS
- ▶ 1958 Aston Martin DB 2/4 Mk III
- ▶ 1953 Bentley R-type
- ▶ 1957 BMW 503
- ▶ 1956 Borgward Hansa 2400 Pullman
- ▶ 1947 Buick Super 8
- ▶ 1963 Buick Rivera
- ▶ 1949 Cadillac Type 62 Cab
- ▶ 1949 Cadillac Type 61 Coupe
- ▶ 1951 Chevrolet Styleline

- ▶ 1949 Chrysler New Yorker
- ▶ 1951 Citroën 15/6
- ▶ 1948 Delahaye 135 MS
- ▶ 1961 Ferrari 250 GT Cabriolet
- ▶ 1951 Hotchkiss 2050
- ▶ 1959 Jaguar XK 150 Roadster
- ▶ 1955 Lancia B 24 S Aurelia Spider
- ▶ 1960 Maserati 3500 GT
- ▶ 1951 Mercedes-Benz 170 S
- ▶ 1952 Mercedes-Benz 220
- ▶ 1956 Mercedes-Benz 300 SC
- ▶ 1950 Nash Airflyte Statesman Super
- ▶ 1950 Opel Kapitän
- ▶ 1946 Packard Super Clipper Custom 8
- ▶ 1952 Rolls Royce Silver Wraith
- ▶ 1949 Talbot Lago T 26 Record
- ▶ 1951 Triumph Renown
- ▶ 1950 Volvo PV 444

Below & Opposite: *Main halls inside the Öhringen Museum.*

The Motorcycles

There are over 100 motorcycles built from the 1945 to 1975 on display. There are bikes from Adler, AJS, Ardie, BMW, BSA, DKW, Harley-Davidson, Hoffmann, Honda, Horex, Matchless, Moto-Guzzi, Norton, NSU, Puch, Scott, Triumph, Velocette, and Zündapp.

Modern Glass

The works of art in glass are everything from bowls and vases to modern interpretations of light and form.

Additional displays

There are over 350 vintage enamel signs on the walls, vintage cameras such as Leica and Pentacon (a little known German camera manufacturer once based in Dresden, Germany) in display cases, and 1950s fashions on mannequins by Christian Dior and Chanel.

Admission

▶   Adults   € 3.-
▶   Children & Seniors   € 2.-
▶   Children under 14 years   Free

Hours

▶   April to October -
     Tuesday to Thursday
     1:00 PM to 4:00 PM
     Sunday and Holidays
     1:00 PM to 5:00 PM
▶   Museum closes for the winter
     November 1

Contact Information

Motormuseum Öhringen
Stettinerstrasse 22
74613 Öhringen
Germany

Phone: +49 (0) 7941/8027
Fax: +49 (0) 7941/841 89-41860
E-mail: *museum@heyd.de*
Museum Director: Paul Heyd
www.motormuseum-oehringen.de

Sinsheim Technical Museum

Several adjectives come time mind when describing this museum. But rather than list a plethora of words that all mean really incredible, lets just say this place is over the top insane. This is Disneyland for technology enthusiasts and the only place in the world with both an Air France Concorde and Russian Tupolev supersonic jets on the roof. Plan on spending a lot of time here.

History of the Sinsheim Museum

Sinsheim opened on May 6, 1981 as a 50,000 square foot technology museum and its sister museum in Speyer opened in 1991. They have become the largest private museum in Europe. Both museums are sponsored by the Auto & Technik Museum e.V. and have roughly 2,000 members. The funding for the museum is based exclusively on membership subscriptions, donations, and admission.

Sinsheim Today

The full museum name "Auto & Technik Museum Sinsheim" hardly conveys the shear size and scope of this museum. It is a super car museum, a Formula 1 museum, an airplane museum, a military museum...and so on. There is so much here, that even a full day may not be enough to explore this place. If you have one day to chose one museum and only one museum, come to this museum.

Quick Stats
▶ Plan on spending 1 day (or more)
▶ Known for its "Blue Flame" and the 2 supersonic jets on the roof
▶ 1.5 million visitors a year
▶ Over 320,000 square feet of exhibition space
▶ More than 200 vintage cars and 100 race and sports cars

Directions to Sinsheim

From **Heilbronn by car:**
▶ Autobahn A6 (Heilbronn-Mannheim)
▶ Exit 33b/Sinsheim-Süd
▶ North on Dietmar-Hopp-Strasse to Neulandstrasse
▶ Right/east on Neulandstrasse
▶ Street renames to In Der Au
▶ Right on Unter Au
▶ Or just look for Concorde on roof. It is visible from the Autobahn. There are several parking lots available.

Opposite: Air France Concorde F-BVFB. *This last flew in 2003 before being retired to the Auto & Technik Museum Sinsheim.*

Above: clockwise from left - Ferrari F40, Ferrari 342 America, Ferrari 365GTB/4 Daytona, Lamborghini Muira P 400 S.

The Collection Theme
This museum focus is more on the automobile than its sister museum in Speyer. The theme is a mix of modern technological achievements and the history behind them. There isn't a specific car theme here. There are exotics next to classics.

Must See
▶ See the Formula 1 collection (largest permanent Formula 1 exhibit in Europe).

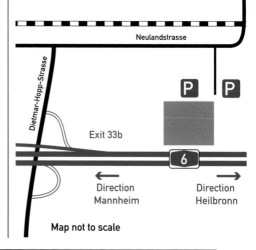

Neulandstrasse

Dietmar-Hopp-Strasse

Exit 33b

6

← Direction Mannheim

→ Direction Heilbronn

Map not to scale

The Exhibitions

This massive museum has two main buildings. Each of these buildings are further divided into different exhibition halls and areas. Start with the main building where the cashier is located.

The Cars

Trying to see and photograph all the cars here is futile. Even with a full day, the most adamant car lover will find himself passing up cars that on a normal sunny day would draw gasps and crowds.

There is one really nice photo spot located by the Ferraris in the main hall. It is a ladder leading up to a small platform and is open to the public to use. The photo on the opposite page was taken from that platform.

Lastly, some of the cars on display are owned by private individuals (who have lent the museum their cars) and are rotated in and out of the museum on a regular basis. So some cars from the list below might not be present during your visit. Here are some highlights -

The Vintage Cars

▶ Alfa Romeo 8C Monza
▶ Audi Alpensieger Type C
▶ American La France Funkenblitz
▶ Bentley 4.5 Liter "Le Mans"
▶ Bugatti Type 37
▶ Bugatti Type 57
▶ Cord 812
▶ Jaguar D Type
▶ Jaguar SS
▶ Mercedes-Benz SSK
▶ Mercedes-Benz 540 K
▶ Mercedes-Benz 770 K Cabrio
▶ Rolls-Royce Phantom III
▶ Rolls-Royce Silver Ghost

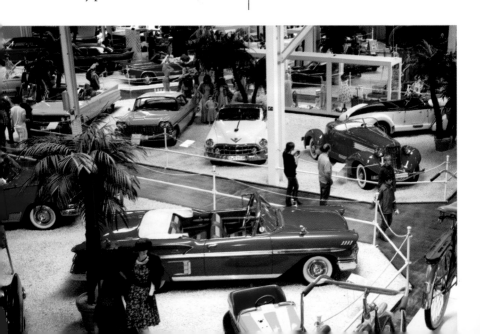

The Sports Cars

- De Tomaso Pantera GTS
- Ferrari Enzo
- Ferrari F50
- Lamborghini Countach LP 500 S
- Vector W 8 Twin Turbo

The Formula 1 Race Cars

- 1974 BRM P160 E #21
- 1975 March 751 #9
- 1976 Tyrrell P34 #3
- 1986 Lotus JPS 98 T - Senna
- 1991 McLaren MP4 - Senna
- 1991 Jordan 191 - Schumacher
- 1995 Benetton-Renault B195 - Schumacher
- 1996 Ferrari F310 - Schumacher
- 1997 Mercedes-McLaren MP4/9 - Häkkinen

Opposite Below: *The American Collection.*
Below: *Ferraris and Lamborghinis.*

The American Cars

- 1935 Auburn 851 Boattail Speedster Convertible
- 1958 Cadillac Eldorado Brougham Limousine
- 1958 Cadillac De Ville Convertible
- 1954 Chevrolet Corvette
- 1958 Ford Thunderbird Convertible
- 1956 Lincoln Continental MK II
- 1952 Oldsmobile Ninety Eight Convertible

The Blue Flame

The "Blue Flame" set a world record on October 23, 1970 when its driver/pilot Gary Gabelich hit 622.407 mph (or 1,000.671 km/h) at the Bonneville Salt Flats in Utah. A record that was to stand for the next 13 years. His car, the "Blue Flame" is now a center piece here in Sinsheim.

Exhibitions Continued -

Once past the cars, there is more. Much more...

The Locomotives

There are 20 locomotives total.

▶ 1919 Baden State Locomotive Series 18 built by Maffei

▶ 1942 "Kriegs" Locomotive Series 52

The Military Vehicles

Most tanks are World War II era

▶ German Panzer IV

▶ German Panther V

▶ Russian T34

▶ U.S. Sherman M4 A3

▶ U.S. Pershing M26

The Airplanes

It is all but impossible to miss the overwhelming presence of the airplanes at Sinsheim and if you enjoyed the airplanes here, be sure to visit the museum in Speyer (See page 166).

▶ Air France Concorde F-BVFP

▶ Canadair CL-215 Sea Plane

▶ De Havilland Venom jet fighter

▶ Douglas DC-3

▶ Iljuschin IL 18

▶ Heinkel He-111

▶ Junkers JU-52 (two examples)

▶ Junkers JU-87

▶ Junkers JU-88

▶ Messerschmitt Me-109

▶ Tupolev Tu-134

▶ Tupolev Tu-144

Six aircraft may be toured - Canadair CL-215, Concorde, Douglas DC-3, Junkers JU-52, Tupolev Tu-134, and Tupolev Tu-144.

Top: The "Blue Flame".
Left: Mercedes-McLaren MP4/9.
Opposite Top: 46 Liter 12 cylinder "Brutus" Experimental Prototype.
Opposite Bottom: One of many Bugattis.

Events

Through out the year, the museum hosts a number of annual club events. The schedule may be found on the museum web page (see below).

Amenities

- 2 Restaurants - "Concorde" (German cuisine) & "Airport" (mostly Italian cuisine) - Open from 9:00 AM to 6:00 PM
- IMAX 3-D - Screen is 72 feet by 88 feet. There is a showing every hour on the hour and lasts roughly 45 minutes.
- Playground with chair lift, go kart track, and scale locomotives

Admission

- Adults — € 13.-
- Children 6 to 14 years — € 10.-
- Children under 5 years — Free
- Group of 20 people — € 12.-
- IMAX & Combo tickets are extra

Hours

- Open 365 days a year
- Monday to Friday 9:00 AM to 6:00 PM
- Saturday, Sunday, & holidays 9:00 AM to 7:00 PM

Hotel Sinsheim

In der Au 25
74889 Sinsheim
Phone: +49 (0) 7261/4064
Fax: 49 (0) 7261/4064-60
E-mail: *info@hotel-sinsheim.de*
www.hotel-sinsheim.de
Hotel within walking distance

Contact Information

Auto & Technik
Museum Sinsheim e.V.
Museum Square
74889 Sinsheim
Germany

Phone: +49 (0) 7261/9299-0
Fax: +49 (0) 7161/13916
E-mail: See website
www.technik-museum.de

Speyer Technical Museum

The smaller but equally impressive Speyer Technical Museum is just a few minutes down the Autobahn A6 in the heart of the very pretty town of Speyer. This town, more known for being situated on the banks of the Rhein River, now has a new international draw. It has a Boeing 747 parked just outside of the historic downtown. Just like its sister museum in Sinsheim, this museum is a full day adventure into the transportation technologies of the last 100 years. There are airplanes, locomotives, helicopters, motorcycles, and of course cars.

History of the Speyer

The full name in German is "Das Technik Museum Speyer" and its history is shared with the history of the Auto & Technik Museum Sinsheim (See page 160). This museum opened to the public in 1992 and is sponsored by Auto & Technik Museum e.V.

Speyer Museum Today

The trademark of the museum today might be the Boeing 747 hovering over the landscape, but the real treat is the original Russian Buran Space Shuttle hidden inside. There are not as many cars here as in Sinsheim, but the museum is a bit smaller. There are only 150 cars and motorcycles here.

Quick Stats
▶ Plan on spending up to 1 day
▶ 270,000 square feet inside
▶ Over 1 million square feet of outside exhibition space
▶ Over 150 vintage cars and bikes
▶ Over 20 locomotives
▶ Over 70 airplanes & helicopters
▶ U-9 submarine

The Collection Theme
This museum is a little more balanced in terms of its transportation displays. It has a naval house, fire engines, helicopters, airplanes, and a Russian space shuttle on display.

Directions to Speyer

From **Mannheim by car:**
▶ Autobahn A6 (Mannheim-Nürnberg)
▶ Autobahn A61 (Speyer) direction Speyer
▶ Exit 64 /Hockenheim
▶ West on B39 over Rhein River
▶ Take first possible exit after crossing Rhein River/ Speyer City Center
▶ Right/north on Industriestrasse
▶ Right on Klipfelsau
▶ Right on Geibstrasse and under B39
▶ Museum is to the right

Opposite: *Lufthansa Boeing 747-230.*
Above: *1962 Chevrolet Corvette.*

Must See
▶ The Space exhibition hall is a must see. Not only is the Buran Space Shuttle on display, equipment, payloads, instruments, and space suits from ESA and NASA are also on display. There is also a walk through module of the German space laboratory SPACELAB. This is the largest space exhibit in Europe.

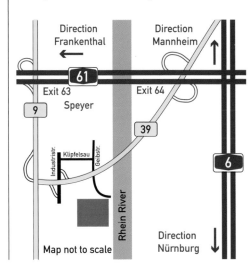

Map not to scale

The Exhibitions

The museum has two main exhibition halls and a couple smaller ones. The main building houses the IMAX theater, restaurant, gift store, and most of the displays while the other houses the space exhibition and shuttle. There are several smaller buildings at the far end of the grounds that are the marine museum and the scale model museum.

The Cars

The cars are located in both the main hall and the space exhibition hall. There are no new sports cars here, just vintage cars. Here is just a sample -

- ▶ Aston Martin DB6 Volante
- ▶ BMW Dixi DA 2
- ▶ Delahaye Fesselballonwagen
- ▶ Gaggenau LKW
- ▶ Lancia Lambda
- ▶ Mercedes-Benz 230 Cabrio A
- ▶ Mercedes-Benz 300 SL Roadster

- ▶ NSU Speed Record race car
- ▶ Opel RAK 2 rocket car
- ▶ Packard Eight

The Airplanes

Who needs supersonic jets with these aircraft? All of these aircraft are open and may be toured. Some of the staircases are steep and long. Wear appropriate shoes.

- ▶ Antonov An-22
- ▶ Antonov An-26
- ▶ Boeing 747 Lufthansa
- ▶ Dessault Mercure 100
- ▶ Douglas C-47 "Dakota"
- ▶ Fokker VFW 614
- ▶ Nord 2501 "Noratlas"

U Boats and more...

There is the largest collection of fire fighting equipment in Europe, a 1967 German submarine, wooden boats, toy trains, and various musical organs.

Amenities

- Restaurant "Hanger" is open from 9:00 AM to 6:00 PM & Biergarten during nice weather
- Children's playground with slides and electric scooters
- IMAX DOME (A dome screen that measures almost 10,000 square feet in size. It is the only one in Germany). Movies start every hour on the hour and last roughly 45 minutes.

Admission

- Adults   € 13.-
- Children 6 to 14 years   € 11.-
- Children under 5 years   Free
- Group of 20 people   € 12.-
- IMAX & Combo tickets extra

Hours

- Open 365 days a year
- Monday to Friday
  9:00 AM to 6:00 PM
- Saturday & Sunday
  9:00 AM to 7:00 PM

Hotel am Technik Museum

Am Technik Museum 1
67346 Speyer
Germany
Phone: +49 (0) 6232/6710-0
Fax: +49 (0) 6232/6710-20
E-mail:
info@hotel-am-technik-museum.de
www.hotel-am-technik-museum.de
The Hotel is within walking distance of the museum.

Contact Information

Technik Museum Speyer
Am Technik Museum
67346 Speyer
Germany

Phone: +49 (0) 6232/6708-0
Fax: +49 (0) 6232/6708-20
See website for e-mail contacts
speyer.technik-museum.de or
www.technik-museum.de

Opposite & Below: *Technical Museum Speyer.*

Toyota Museum

Oone Autobahn exit away from Austria is the largest Toyota museum outside of Japan. The museum doesn't look like much from the outside, but for anyone interested in Toyota, this is a must see museum. This museum seems a little out of place in a country full of the fast and heavy German cars, but a passion for Japanese cars is still a passion for cars. Here is one man's tribute to his love of Toyota.

History of the Toyota Museum

The museum was founded in 1999 by Peter Pichert. He was one of the first Toyota dealers in Germany (he still has a dealership in Passau).

Why Toyota? Mr. Pichert feels these early cars are great cars. He wants to show everyone, especially today's youth, the cars he sold new so many years ago. When asked what is his favorite Toyota, he replied the Toyota Corolla KE25 Coupe.

Toyota Museum Today

Neatly lined up in two rows on the ground floor of the main hall is the bulk of the collection of Toyotas. They represent all that made Toyota great during the OPEC oil crisis of the early 1970s and the drive for smaller and more efficient cars during the 1980s.

Quick Stats
- More than 120 Toyotas
- Largest Toyota museum outside of Japan
- 16,000+ square feet
- 1967 Toyota 2000 GT - the first Japanese super car

The Collection Theme
Toyota is of course the one and only theme. Even though the founder and owner runs a new car Toyota dealership in Passau, you won't see many new cars here. These are the classic Toyotas from the 1970s and 1980s.

Directions to Toyota Museum

From **Munich/Regensburg by car:**
- Autobahn A92 (München-Deggendorf)
- Merge onto Autobahn A3 (Regensburg-Passau) direction Passau
- Exit 118/Pocking
- West on B12 direction Pocking
- Exit on Hartkirchnerstrasse
- Follow as it road renames to Pockingstrasse
- Right on Obere Inntalstrasse
- Right at Julbachstrasse, museum left

Opposite: *Main exhibition hall & race track (used during their annual Toyota event).*
Above: *Sign on Obere Inntalstrasse.*

There is an authentic period garage and collection of literature that tells the visitor what Toyota was all about during the 1970s and 1980s. There is also a collection of engines on the top loft above the cars.

Must See
- 1967 Toyota 2000 GT. This particular model is not only rare (only 1 of 3 in Germany and 1 of 337 ever made) but also known for having appeared in the James Bond movie "You only Live Twice".

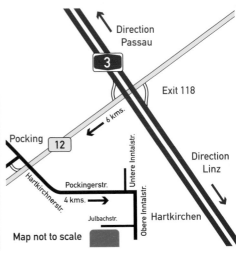

The Exhibition

The museum is housed in a single large building. There is a second floor loft that has engines, spare parts, and a period Toyota garage set up with manuals and tools. The entrance is to the museum is through the restaurant.

The Cars

The Toyotas are located in a single exhibition hall. Here is just a sample -

- 1967 Toyota 2000 GT
- 1975 Toyota 1000 KP30
- 1975 Toyota Carina TA12
- 1972 Toyota Celica Liftback TA28
- 1972 Toyota Celica Coupe TA22 LT
- 1985 Toyota Celica Supra 2.8i
- 1977 Toyota Corolla Coupe KE35
- 1978 Toyota Corolla KE30
- 1980 Toyota Corolla KE70
- 1984 Toyota Corolla Coupe AE86
- 1975 Toyota Corona Mk II RX 12
- 1977 Toyota Corona RT104
- 1975 Toyota Cressida
- 1972 Toyota Crown Coupe MS75
- Toyota JDM Sera - Rare car built only for the Japanese market from 1990 - 1996
- Toyota Land Cruiser fire truck
- Toyota MR2
- Toyota Starlet
- 1981 Toyota Tercel
- Toyota rally car/ race car

Annual Event

There is annual event worth attending. It is the "Toyota Oldtimer - Meeting at the Toyota Museum". It is a one day event held roughly every July. It is open to Toyotas manufactured prior to 2000 and limited to 80 cars. Registration is required. Please contact the museum for more information.

s'Wirtshaus am Turm Restaurant

Phone: +49 (0) 8538/912591

www.swirtshausamturm.de

- Summer Hours -
  11:30 AM to 9:30 PM
- Winter Hours -
  11:30 AM - 2:00 PM
  5:00 PM - 9:30 PM
- Closed Wednesday
- Next door to museum

Admission

- Adults   € 3.50
- Children & Seniors   € 2.-
- Groups of 10+   € 2.-

Hours

- Summer Hours -
  March to October
  11:30 AM to 6:00 PM
  (Closed Wednesday)
  Sunday and Holidays
  1:00 PM to 5:00 PM
- Winter Hours -
  November to March
  11:30 AM to 2:00 PM
  (Closed Wednesday)

Contact Information

Deutsches Toyota Museum
Obere Inntalstrasse 46
94060 Hartkirchen/Pocking
Germany

Phone: +49 (0) 851/94939-0
Fax: +49 (0) 851/94939-40
E-mail: *museum@auto-pichert.de*
www.toyotamuseum.de

Auto-Pichert
Schulbergstrasse 59 - 61
94034 Passau-Grubweg
Germany

Phone: +49 (0) 851/94939-0
Fax: +49 (0) 851/94939-40
E-mail: *info@auto-pichert.de*
www.auto-pichert.de

Opposite: *Two rows of Toyotas in the main exhibition hall.*

Above: *1967 Toyota 2000 GT. One of only 337 ever made. This is easily the rarest and most expensive car in the museum. These collectibles sell for several hundred thousand dollars.*

Zeppelin Museum

Many automobile manufacturers (such as BMW) also have a long history in aviation building engines. Maybach, as a subsidiary of Zeppelin, provided engines for the airships in the early 20th century before turning to luxury automobiles.

History of the Zeppelin Museum

The origins of this museum date back to 1869 as an art and archeology museum. In 1938 the museum moved to a new larger location with additional moves and renovations in 1956 and 1985. By 1987, the museum welcomed 100,000 visitors per year.

The current museum opened to the public in July 1996 in the renovated 1933 Friedrichshafen Hafenbahnhof (*Port Station*) in the downtown area of Friedrichshafen and sits next to the shores of the very scenic Bodensee (*Lake Constance*). The museum was renamed the "Zeppelin Museum" and now attracts more than 240,000 visitors per year.

Zeppelin Museum Today

The largest collection on the history of the airship. The museum also has a comprehensive exhibit of art from the region with collections by Otto Dix and Max Ackermann. Of course the museum has engines by Maybach and a Maybach "Zeppelin" DS 8 Sedan.

Quick Stats

- ▶ Plan on spending 2-4 hours
- ▶ 43,000 square feet
- ▶ 1998 European Museum of the year
- ▶ One of 24 museums worldwide recommended by the FAI (see *www.fai.org*)

The Collection Theme

The museum is centered around a 108 foot long life size mock-up of the LZ 129 "**Hindenburg**" Zeppelin. This display is central to the whole museum and a fascinating look into a world now gone. The themes explored

Directions to Zeppelin

From **Munich by car:**

- ▶ Autobahn A96 (München-Lindau)
- ▶ Exit 3/Sigmarszell
- ▶ West/right on B31/B308 direction Friedrichshafen
- ▶ Once in Friedrichshafen, take the exit ramp onto Lindauerstrasse direction Stadtmitte.
- ▶ Lindauerstrasse turns into Eckenerstrasse
- ▶ Left at Romanshornerplatz
- ▶ Be aware, parking is difficult

Opposite: *Entrance to the Zeppelin Museum.*
Above: *Maybach "Zeppelin" DS 8.*

are similar to other top class car museum. The technologies behind engines, power to weight ratios, and manufacturing in aluminum are all explored. The other theme in this museum is the art of Bodensee.

Must See

- ▶ The 1938/39 Maybach "Zeppelin" DS 8. This 12 cylinder road car is located on the ground floor.

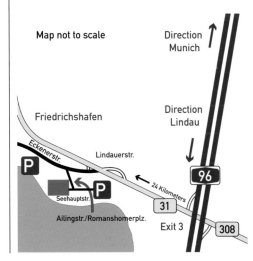

Map not to scale

The Exhibitions

The museum is divided into two different themes - technology, evolution, and lifestyle of the Zeppelin and an art collection highlighting artists from the region. The latter has nothing to do with the automobile but is interesting nonetheless.

Technology Collection
In addition to the Maybach automobile and the engines, the technology collection is further broken down into the following topics.

▶ The Physics of Flight - This area has everything from a barometric pocket altimeter to the landing instructions from the Zeppelin Airship Company.

▶ Lightweight Construction - Long before aluminum was used as a material in a car frame, there was **duralumin**, an aluminum alloy and ingredient for the countless airship girders. The displays here also explore aerodynamics and engines.

▶ Civilian and Military Uses - The history of the airship as both a passenger ship and weapon of war are explored in this collection.

▶ The History of Zeppelin - Follow the history of the Zeppelin from the birth of Count von Zeppelin in 1838 to today.

The Engines

▶ Daimler Benz DB 602 16 cylinder diesel engine. Four of these liquid cooled 1,320 hp engines powered the ill fated Hindenburg.

▶ Maybach VL2 12 cylinder engine from the "Graf Zeppelin". This 33.3 liter engine from 1930 produced 570 hp

▶ Maybach Mb IVa/IVaL in line 6 cylinder engine from 1916. This engine has roughly 240 hp.

▶ Maybach LZ 6. This was the first engine to be used by Zeppelin. It is a 6 cylinder engine and 145 hp engine equipping the LZ6 Airship.

Maybach "Zeppelin" DS 8
The sole automobile here is a 1938 Maybach Zeppelin DS 8. It's an 8 liter 60 degree V-12 engine was derived from the engines that powered the LZ 127 "Graf Zeppelin". For more information about Maybach, see page 152.

▶ 200 hp
▶ Top speed of roughly 110 mph
▶ Weighs 3.6 tons
▶ Body by Hermann Spohn in Ravensburg
▶ The name has been reborn with the new Maybach 62S Zeppelin

Art Collection

Regional artists such as Otto Dix, Max Ackermann, and Julius Bissier

Amenities

- Restaurant
- Gift store
- Media room/ theater
- Story boards in German but brochure available in English

Admission

- Adults   € 7.50
- Children 6 - 16   € 3.-
- Group of 10 people   € 6.50

Opposite: *Daimler Benz DB 602 16 Cylinder Engine.*
Below: *Maybach "Zeppelin" DS 8 sits below the "Hindenburg" display.*

Hours

- May to October - 9:00 AM to 5:00 PM (admission until 4:30 PM)
- November to April - 10:00 AM to 5:00 PM (admission until 4:30 PM)
- Closed December 24, 25, 31

Contact Information

Zeppelin Museum Friedrichshafen
Seestrasse 22
88045 Friedrichshafen
Germany

Phone: +49 (0) 7541/3801-0
Fax: +49 (0) 7541/3801-81
E-mail: *info@zeppelin-museum.de*
www.zeppelin-museum.de

Southern German Tuners, Aftermarket, & Manufacturers

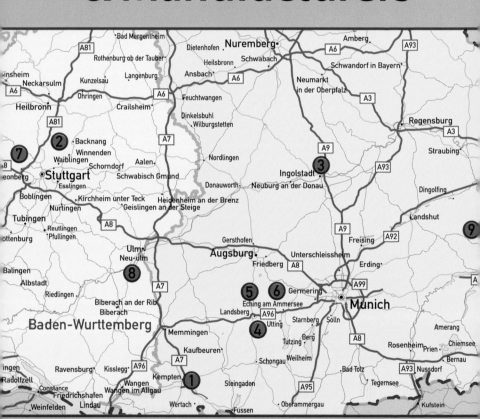

Ever notice the front badge on a car by RUF? or Lorinser?

Ever notice a Porsche modified by RUF no longer has the Porsche Crest, but rather the RUF badge instead?

As aftermarket companies rebuild cars, they are changing the technical specifications of that car and are required to re-badge that car by the German Government.

Tuners, Aftermarket, and Manufacturers

Tuner	Main Business	Also know for
1 - ABT Sportsline	Audi/VW tuning	Auto Racing
2 - Lorinser	Mercedes	Lexus
3 - MTM	Audi	Bimoto TT
4 - Novitec Rosso	Ferrari	Alfa Romeo
5 - RUF	Porsche tuning	Auto Manufacturer
6 - Alpina	BMW tuning	Racing
7 - TECHART	Porsche	2008 Tuner GP Win
8 - HAMANN	Wide range tuner	BMW Racing
9 - Rieger	Wide range tuner	Auto Sales

There is a distinction between what we call a tuner and what we call a manufacturer. A car manufacturer is a company that builds up a car from scratch. Involved in every step of the process, a manufacturer can be praised or admonished for its design, performance, and reliability. The tuner is typically a company that takes that manufactured car and improves on all those qualities. But some companies, like RUF, have gone beyond this and become their own boutique manufacturer ∎

ABT Sportsline

Not many companies today, let alone tuning companies, can boast that they were founded as a blacksmith shop over 114 years ago. But when one thinks of a blacksmith shop as a 19th century tuner, it makes sense. Since then, this family owned business has left the horse and buggy set to become a driving force in both German motor sports and in the world of tuning Audis and Volkswagens. ABT applies its knowledge learned on the race track to develop and build everything from brake and suspension systems to engine chips for customers worldwide.

History of ABT

In 1896, Johann Abt had a Kempten blacksmith shop that could be called the world first tuner. He would modify carriages so they could be used during the bitter German winters. Four generations later, Abt is still in the business.

1960 - ABT Tuning is founded.

1970 - When the VW Golf was introduced, ABT was there to tune it.

1999 - Christian Abt wins the STW (*German Supertouring Championship*).

ABT Today

This family owned business is now run by a fourth generation of brothers. Christian Abt and his brother Hans-Jürgen Abt are the two principles behind the name. There are three different divisions to ABT Sportsline. There is the motorsports department, the tuning business, and a parts business. All three are located at their headquarters in Kempten.

Directions to ABT

From **Stuttgart by car:**

- Autobahn A7 (Memmingen-Kempten)
- Exit 133 (Kempten-Leubas)
- South/right on Kaufbeurerstrasse direction Kempten
- Right on Daimlerstrasse
- ABT will be on your right side

Opposite: *ABT-Sportsline world headquarters.*

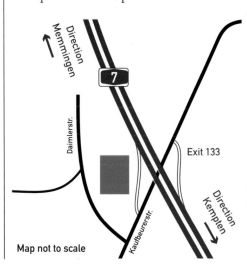

Map not to scale

ABT Sportsline

In 1991 and under the new name ABT Sportsline GmbH, the company moved into its new headquarters on Daimler Strasse in Kempten.

The Architecture

One of the first things a visitor will notice when they arrive at ABT Sportsline GmbH is the building. In fact the company name that sits a top this 9 story company headquarters can be clearly seen from the nearby Autobahn A7. The building is a modern interpretation of a twelve cylinder engine with the inside walls and halls symbolizing cylinders and pistons.

Quick Stats

▶ Founded in 1896 as blacksmith shop
▶ 120 partners around Germany
▶ ABT sells product in 70 countries around the globe
▶ 53,800 square feet

ABT Racing

ABT Motorsport actively campaigns Audis in races around Europe.

DTM

ABT Audi fields a professional team of drivers in the DTM series. Current drivers include Timo Scheider and Oliver Jarvis in Audi A4 DTMs.

ADAC GT Masters

In another mixed marque race series, ABT fields multiple ABT Audi R8 LMS.

24 Hours Nürburgring

Two ABT Audi R8 LMSs started the 2010 endurance race, but met with less than stellar results...this time.

VW Scirocco R-Cup Series

ABT Motorsport is the exclusive partner with VW in this debut season. This series is aimed at the entry level driver and ABT prepares all the cars. See *www.volkswagen-motorsport.com*

ABT Tuning

The tuning division of ABT is aimed at Audi and Volkswagen owners wishing to increase the performance of their cars. They do manufacturer products for Seat and Skoda as well.

Audi

ABT has something for just about every Audi made. Most of their products center around exhausts, wheels, aerodynamic kits, and chips to increase engine horsepower. Some models may also have brake and suspension kits available.

Volkswagen

Similar to their Audi product line, ABT has a wide range of products available for just about every Volkswagen with the Volkswagen Golf having the most extensive selection.

Tours

Customers wishing to visit the showroom or museum should call in advance of their visit. Tours of the other areas may be possible with advance notice as well. Photography of the race department is not allowed.

Opposite: *Garage for customer cars.*
Above: *Team ABT Sportsline transporter.*
Right: *Audi A4 DTM #18 Rockenfeller.*

Hours

▶ Monday to Friday
8:00 AM to 6:00 PM
▶ Saturday 9:00 AM to 4:00 PM
(only showroom open)
▶ Sunday 1:00 PM to 4:00 PM
(only showroom open)

Contact Information

ABT Sportsline GmbH
Daimlerstrasse 2
87437 Kempten
Germany

Phone: +49 (0) 831/57140-0
Fax: +49 (0) 831/72666
E-mail: *info@abt-sportline.de*
www.abt-sportline.de
www.abt-motorsport.de

ABT Partner in the U.S. -
GGI European Tuning
www.ggituning.com

ABT Museum

Up stairs on the second floor of the world headquarters of ABT Sportsline, is a surprisingly interesting little museum. The cars are the culmination of decades of racing by the motorsports division of ABT. There are a few surprises here. Ex-Formula 1 driver Ralf Schumacher's BMW Formula Junior is on display as is a Formula 1 car from Toro Rosso. Entry to the museum is free.

The Collection Theme

There are just a handful of cars in the upstairs museum, however each car is either part of the racing history of ABT Motorsports or Christian Abt the race car driver.

Must See

When we visited ABT, there was a 2006 Formula 1 car from Scuderia Toro Rosso STR 1 on the main floor. The other must see is the season winning 1999 ABT Audi A4 upstairs.

The Exhibitions

On the second floor (of nine) of the ABT building and above the show-room, is a small exhibition area. Most of the museum cars are on this floor with a few on the main floor.

The Cars

- ▶ 1984 Audi quattro - street
- ▶ 1991 Formula BMW #8
  Christian Abt
  Season winning car
- ▶ 1992 Formula 3 #51
  Christian Abt
  Season winning car (Class B)
- ▶ 1993 Formula BMW #3
  Ralf Schumacher
  This is Ralf Schumacher's first race car. He placed 2nd over all in the 1993 ADAC Formula Junior season.
- ▶ 1999 ABT Audi quattro
  Christian Abt
  This car won the 1999 STW Cup Season. (STW = *German Super Tourenwagen*)
- ▶ 2000 ABT Audi TT DTM
- ▶ 2002 ABT Audi DTM TT-R
  Championship car
- ▶ 2006 Scuderia Toro Rosso STR 1
  Formula 1
- ▶ 2008 Audi A4 DTM #18
  Mike Rockenfeller
- ▶ ADAC Volkswagen Polo Cup

Opposite: *Formula BMW of Ralf Schumacher in front of Christian Abt's Formula 3.*

Above Top: *Audi DTM pit stop.*

Above Middle: *2006 Scuderia Toro Rosso STR 1 Formula 1.*

Right: *1999 ABT Audi STW - season winner.*

Lorinser

Through out the United States, dealers and their showrooms proudly display wheels by Lorinser. For good reason too... they are stunning. Back in Germany at their world headquarters, Lorinser is divided into two different facilities. There is a glass showroom and classic center with a mini museum in Waiblingen while Winnenden houses the offices, warehouse, and workshop. The showroom in Waiblingen is open to the public and no reservations are needed. The Winnenden location has a small showroom, but call in advance if a tour is of interest.

History of Lorinser

1930 - Erwin Lorinser opens an automobile workshop in Waiblingen.

1935 - Erwin Lorinser becomes a dealer for Mercedes-Benz selling both cars and commercial vehicles.

1974 - Erwin's son Manfred assumes control of the company.

1976 - The second location in Winnenden opens.

1981 - Lorinser Sport Service opens.

2010 - The third generation of Lorinsers take over family business.

Directions to Lorinser

From **Stuttgart by car:**

▶ East on B14 direction Waiblingen/ Winnenden
▶ Follow B14 into Winnenden
▶ Right on L1140 (First possible right after entering Winnenden)
▶ Right on Forstrasse
▶ Right on Lensenhaldstrasse
▶ Lorinser is on left side

Opposite: *Mercedes-Benz Lorinser C-Class.*

Famous Customers

An impressive list of customers have shopped at Lorinser. This includes Bernie Ecclestone, Denzel Washington, and Sharon Stone.

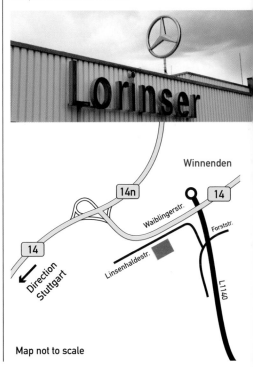

Map not to scale

Lorinser Today

Since 2010, the Lorinser family business has been run by Marcus Lorinser, the grandson of founder Erwin Lorinser. Today there are actually two distinct businesses at Lorinser. There is the tuner business "Sportservice Lorinser" and the car dealership "Autohaus Lorinser". It is the Sportservice Lorinser that manufacturers and markets the Lorinser brand wheels and body kits, while Autohaus Lorinser is a factory authorised dealer for Mercedes-Benz cars and trucks.

Quick Stats
▶ Founded in 1930
▶ Lorinser dealers in 42 countries
▶ 120 employees

Sportservice Lorinser

For customers around the world, it is Lorinser the tuner that everyone recognizes. After all their wheels are in Mercedes-Benz showrooms around North America. Lorinser isn't just about Mercedes-Benz however. Today they manufacturer upgrades for Lexus and Smart Cars.

Lorinser Mercedes-Benz
Lorinser has something for just about every Mercedes-Benz made today. This would range from the GLK-Class (see above) to the S-Class.

Lorinser Lexus
New to the Lorinser line is a Lexus LS package with body kit, exhaust, and of course wheels.

Lorinser Smart
The ever popular Smart Car has a tuner now too! There is everything from a full body kit to minor upgrades such as replacement gas and brake pedals.

Above: Mercedes-Benz GLK with Lorinser body kit and RS9 wheels.

Opposite: Lexus LS 460 with the Lorinser RS8 wheels.

Autohaus Lorinser

Not so well known is that Lorinser is also an authorized Mercedes-Benz dealer. What makes this different from all the other Mercedes-Benz dealers all across Germany is the wide range of Lorinser bodied cars and classic Mercedes-Benz for sale. The building is also pretty interesting for fans of modern architecture.

Lorinser Classic Center

One of the more unusual services offered is the rental of classic cars.

Tours

Customers wishing to tour either facility are asked to please call or e-mail well in advance of their visit. Depending on the time of year or other circumstances, a tour may not always be possible.

Hours (Sales)
▶ Monday to Friday
8:00 AM to 6:00 PM
Saturday 9:00 AM to 2:00 PM

Hours (Service)
▶ Monday to Friday
7:00 AM to 6:00 PM
Saturday 8:00 AM to 12:00 PM

Contact Information

Sportservice Lorinser
Sportliche Autoausrüstung GmbH
Linsenhalde 5
71364 Winnenden

Phone: +49 (0) 7195/181-0
Fax: +49 (0) 7195/181-200
E-mail: *info@lorinser.com*
www.lorinser.com
www.sportservice.lorinser.com

Lorinser Classic Center

Lorinser Classic Center

There are two different parts to the Lorinser Classic Center. One is the Lorinser Classics that are for sale and the other are the Mercedes-Benz on display but part of Lorinser's history and heritage.

The Exhibitions

Classic Mercedes-Benz are located on the main floor and the basement level. The Mercedes-Benz on the basement level are some of the early examples of cars tuned by Lorinser.

The Collection Theme

Classic Mercedes-Benz and the private collection of Lorinser.

Must See

Mercedes-Benz 280 SL - as it is one of the first Mercedes-Benz they tuned.

Cars

The selection is small, but nice. There is a large selection of new cars on display upstairs as well.

Above: Mercedes-Benz 300 SL & Gullwing.
Opposite Top: Mille Miglia Restaurant.
Opposite Right: Mercedes-Benz 300 D.

Mercedes-Benz 200 Cabriolet

Mercedes-Benz 300 D Adenauer

Mercedes-Benz 200 Cabriolet

Mercedes-Benz 300 SL Cabriolet

Mercedes-Benz 300 SL Gullwing

Mercedes-Benz 280 SL

Amenities
- Mille Miglia Restaurant

Contact Information

Autohaus Lorinser GmbH & Co. KG
Alte Bundesstraße 45
71332 Waiblingen

Phone: +49 (0) 7151/136-0
Fax: +49 (0) 7151/136-2880
www.lorinser.com
www.classic.lorinser.com

Hours (Sales)
- Monday to Friday
  8:00 AM to 7:00 PM
  Saturday 9:00 AM to 4:00 PM

Directions to Lorinser Showroom (Waiblingen)

From **Stuttgart by car:**
- East on B14 direction Waiblingen/Winnenden
- Follow B14 to Waiblingen
- Exit Waiblingen-Süd
- North on Schmidenerstrasse
- Right on L1193/Alte Bundesstrasse
- Lorinser is on the right side

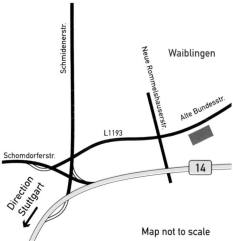

Map not to scale

MTM

Don't let the smaller size of Motoren Technik Mayer (MTM) fool you. MTM is all business, and has the records to prove it. In fact in 1992, MTM developed and built the first street legal Audi to break the 300 km/h barrier. Even the name gives a pretty clear picture of what MTM is all about. "Motors" and "Technology". Its founder Roland Mayer has made it clear that his company was founded on quality engineering and expertise. A visit to MTM is a must for any hard core Audi or Volkswagen fan. Or really anyone who appreciates function before form.

History of MTM

Roland Mayer founded the company MTM in 1985 after working for Audi AG as an engineer. He helped develop the in line 5-cylinder quattro engine.

1990 - MTM moves from Ingolstadt to Wettstetten.

1999 - Foundation of WETEC GmbH in Wettstetten (WETEC is their in house development company).

2002 - MTM wins first place at the annual Tuner Grand Prix at Hockenheimring with an MTM Audi S3.

Directions to MTM

From **Munich by car:**

▶ Autobahn A9 (München-Nürnberg)
▶ Exit 60/Lenting direction Ingolstadt
▶ Straight on St2335 when road curves
▶ At roundabout, right on Lentingerstrasse
▶ First right on to Doktor-Kurt-Schumacher-Ring
▶ MTM is on the right side

Opposite: *MTM's Audi R8 R press car in front of MTM's world headquarters.*

2003 - MTM places second at the annual Tuner Grand Prix.

2004 - MTM wins first place at Hockenheimring with a RS6 Clubsport.

2006 - *Autobild* Magazine honors MTM by naming the MTM S4 Clubsport as the "Top Car of the Year".

2007 - MTM wins again at the annual Tuner Grand Prix.

For more information about the Tuner Grand Prix, see page 210.

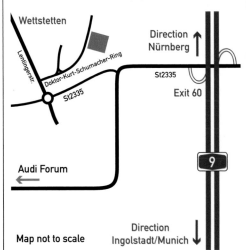

Map not to scale

MTM Today

MTM would be called one of the smaller tuning companies in Germany today. The staff is roughly twenty and their facility is tucked in a small village outside Ingolstadt. But this is a great product driven company who's vehicles out perform the competition year after year.

People who buy from MTM have two different paths they may take. One is to buy upgrade parts at their leisure or to buy a completed project which rebuilds the car to MTM's specs.

Audi Projects

The bulk of MTM's business is Audi. They offer a large number of make overs for the current Audi line up. This of course includes the R8. MTM has engineered upgrades to cover suspension, brakes, exhausts, and engines. They also offer aerodynamic packages and wheels as well.

Volkswagen Projects

Just like their Audi packages and upgrades, MTM sells parts for VW Golfs, Sciroccos, and Touaregs.

MTM-Bimoto TT

This might look like an Audi TT, but this is a whole new beast. The Bimoto has dual 1.8 liter 4 cylinder turbo charged engines. Each of the two engines has its own transmission with one driving the front axel and the other driving the rear. The car has almost 1000 hp.

Apollo

Gumpert is a German manufacturer based near Chemnitz and builder of a supercar named Apollo. What's the story behind this unknown 650 hp supercar car? MTM developed the engine, drivetrain, and gearbox of this road going race car. MTM teamed up with Nitec Engineering and Gumpert to make this car a reality.
See *www.gumpert.de*

If you get a chance to visit MTM, look for these cars hanging around -

MTM S1 quattro

This quattro is the personal car of Roland Mayer. He bought the car in 1997 and had some friends at Audi Sport help turn it into an E2 version of the famous Audi Sport quattro. It goes 0 - 100 km/h in 3.2 seconds.

KTM X-Bow Press car

Featured in a February 2009 article in *Auto Motor und Sport*. This "go kart" for the road sports a € 7,300.- engine upgrade.

Tours

MTM is worth a visit by anyone interested in Audi or Volkswagen. Their facility is close to the Audi factory in Ingolstadt. MTM does not have a showroom. Customers wishing to tour MTM are asked to please call or e-mail well in advance of their visit. Depending on the time of year or other schedules, a tour may not always be possible.

Hours

▶ Monday to Friday
  8:00 AM to
  12:00 PM
  1:00 PM to
  5:00 PM

Opposite: *Volkswagen Golf GTI.*

Above Right: *KTM X-Bow Street in front of the 530 hp MTM S1 quattro.*

Right: *MTM Audi S5 GT Supercharged.*

Contact Information

Motoren-Technik-Mayer GmbH
Dr. Kurt-Schumacher-Ring 48-50
85139 Wettstetten
Germany

Phone: +49 (0) 841/98188-0
Fax: +49 (0) 841/98188-20
E-mail: *info@mtm-online.de*
www.mtm-online.de

Novitec Rosso

Say Bavaria and Ferrari together, and it doesn't really sound quite right...at first. But here it is, a company in a quiet part the Bavarian Allgäu that specializes in tuning Ferraris. We asked Novitec Rosso what they enjoyed about their Allgäu location, and the reply we got was "It's close to a great Autobahn". Silly us. They are literally 2 minutes from the on ramp of the A-96 Autobahn. We should have known. Other than having a great locale, Novitec Rosso is at the forefront of tuning Ferraris. They are without equal in Germany, or anywhere else, for that matter.

History of Novitec

Wolfgang Hagedorn, once an employee of Porsche tuner RUF, founded Novitec Automobile GmbH in 1989. In the 1990s, Novitec Rosso became a recognized tuner of Alfa Romeos and Fiats.

2003 - Novitec presents the Ferrari 360 Modena with twin superchargers. It has 606 hp and can reach a top speed of 215 mph.

2005 - The Novitec 575M Maranello and 430 debut. The 575M is bumped up to 533 hp and the twin super-charged 430 pumps out 636 hp.

Directions to Novitec

From **Munich by car:**
- ▶ Autobahn A96 (München-Lindau/Memmingen)
- ▶ Exit 18/Stetten
- ▶ South on St2013/Hauptstrasse
- ▶ Right on Kirchstetterstrasse
- ▶ Right on Hochstrasse
- ▶ Novitec is on the left

Opposite: Novitec's 430 Scuderia 16M.

2008 - The bar is raised again when Novitec Rosso builds a Ferrari 430 with 707 hp. Developments in the intercoolers make this massive increase in horsepower possible.

2009 - Novitec Rosso builds a modified Ferrari 430 Scuderia 16M Spider with 687 hp. It too has twin superchargers. The slight loss in horsepower is due to the smaller engine compartment and smaller intercoolers.

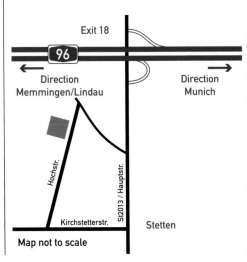

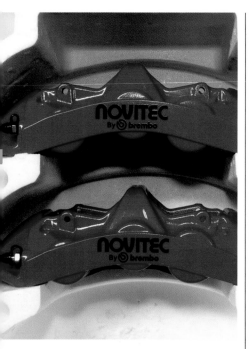

Novitec Rosso Today

Novitec Rosso is a forward looking and thinking company that strives to achieve the highest quality of workmanship and technology. They remain focused on Ferrari and other Italian sports cars.

Must See

There is a system of 3 solar paneled buildings behind the main offices. Each of the rotating solar panel showrooms generate enough electricity to be sent to the nearby town of Stetten. The sports cars inside are periodically rotated.

The Product Range

The current product range covers the new Ferrari California, 360, 430, 599, 612, Scuderia, and Enzo. It is safe to say Novitec Rosso will soon release upgrades for the new Ferrari 458 Italia.

The Wheels

One of the most popular is their NF3 wheel. They are pictured to the left.

Body Kits

Upgrades vary depending on the model. The 430 is quite popular.

Performance Upgrades

If adding an additional 150 hp with twin superchargers isn't your cup of chianti, Novitec offers just ECUs and exhaust upgrades.

Above: *Novitec /Brembo brake calipers.*
Left: *Novitec NF3 wheel.*
Opposite: *Novitec's yellow Ferrari 430 16M Scuderia Spider in the background. The Ferrari 430 Scuderia in red in the foreground.*

Ferrari 430 16M Scuderia Spider

Look for the latest twin supercharged press car. This Ferrari 430 Scuderia 16 M was featured in the February 2010 issue (#99) of the U.S. magazine *Forza*. It pumps out 687 hp using two Rotrex superchargers (stock 16M Scuderia Spider is only 510 hp).

Superchargers versus Turbos

One of the main things anyone will notice when looking at a Ferrari by Novitec is that the cars are supercharged. Porsche for years has built their 911s with turbos while Mercedes-Benz and AMG choose superchargers. Well why does Novitec go the route of superchargers when Ferrari themselves chose turbos for their 288 GTO and F40? There are a few reasons why. One is that superchargers deliver a linear power band on these high revving Ferrari engines. Another reason is turbo charging builds up too much heat in the engine bay of the newer Ferraris.

Tours and Visiting

Novitec Rosso has a small showroom open to the public. Customers wishing to visit Novitec Rosso are asked to please call or e-mail well in advance. Be advised that a tour may not always be possible.

Hours

- ▶ Monday to Thursday
  8:00 AM to 6:00 PM
  Friday until 5:00 PM

Contact Information

Novitec Rosso GmbH & Co. KG
Hochstrasse 8
87778 Stetten
Germany

Phone: +49 (0) 8261/75995-0
Fax: +49 (0) 8261/738820
E-mail: *info@novitecrosso.com*
www.novitecrosso.com or
novitec-rosso.net

RUF

History of the RUF

In 1939, Alois Ruf Sr. founded "AUTO-RUF" in Pfaffenhausen as a service garage and soon after added a gas station (Their Aral gas station is still next to RUF).

1963 - Alois Ruf buys a damaged Porsche 356. His passion begins.

1983 - RUF BTR with 374 hp crosses the 300 km/h barrier.

1987 - The 469 hp RUF Yellowbird is introduced and reaches 211 mph. RUF also becomes an approved manufacturer in the U.S. by the EPA and DOT.

1996 - RUF CTR 2 with 520 hp is released. CTR2 Sport widebody also released. Both available in the USA.

2002 - RUF 3600 S is introduced using a Porsche Boxster chassis with 345 hp 911 3.6 liter engine.

2004 - RUF Rt 12 (12th version of a RUF 911 Turbo) is presented at the Essen Motor Show with 650 hp.

2007 - Mid engine RUF CTR 3 and successor to the CTR2 is introduced with 700 hp.

2010 - Development of RUF 8 cylinder engine continues for a 2011 release. Engine produces 550 hp.

RUF Today

While RUF does tune and upgrade Porsches, they also build their own cars and are recognized in Germany as a car manufacturer. The company also offers service, maintenance, and repair for all regular Porsches as well as restoration work on classic Porsches.

The Building
In the late 1970s RUF expanded its main building. The story is that they bought a used building and the RUF staff re-assembled it at the new company headquarters piece by piece.

Tours
Generally speaking, RUF does not give tours of their facilities due to the high volume of visitor traffic they draw. Visitors may look and photograph the cars in the showroom.

Hours (Showroom)
- ▶ Monday to Friday 8:00 AM to 12:00 PM, 1:00 PM to 5:00 PM

Contact Information

Directions to RUF

From **Munich by car:**
- ▶ Autobahn A96 (München-Lindau)
- ▶ Exit 19/Mindelheim
- ▶ B16 north direction Pfaffenhausen for roughly 10 kilometers
- ▶ As you enter Pfaffenhausen, there are two RUF buildings visible from B16. The smaller one near the Aral Gas Station is the sales office.

Opposite: *Entrance to the RUF Showroom.*
Above: *RUF CTR 3.*

RUF Automobile GmbH
Mindelheimerstrasse 21
87772 Pfaffenhausen
Germany

Phone: +49 (0) 8265/911911
Fax: +49 (0) 8265/911912
E-mail: *info@ruf-automobile.de*
www.ruf-automobile.de

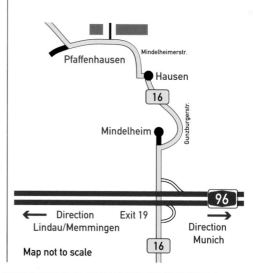

Pfaffenhausen
Mindelheimerstr.
Hausen
16
Mindelheim
Gunzburgerstr.
96
← Direction Lindau/Memmingen
Exit 19
Direction Munich →
16
Map not to scale

Alpina

For over 40 years, Alpina has been in the business of modifying and racing BMWs. They have had success in DTM and even won the 1970 24 Hours of Spa-Francorchamps. Drivers Derek Bell and Hans-Joachim Stuck have both raced Alpina BMWs. In 2008 Alpina underwent an expansion.

Visiting Alpina

Alpina has a small showroom open to the public, but there are no factory tours available. If you buy an Alpina, the car may be delivered in Buchloe. It is always recommended to call Alpina in advance if you wish to visit.

Directions

From **Munich by car:**

▶ Autobahn A96 (Lindau-München) direction Lindau
▶ Exit 23/Buchloe-Ost direction Waal
▶ West/right on Landsbergerstrasse
▶ At roundabout exit (3rd exit) onto Munchnerstrasse
▶ North/right on Alpenstrasse

Contact Information

Alpina Burkard Bovensiepen GmbH & Co. KG
Alpenstrasse 35 - 37
86807 Buchloe
Germany

Phone: +49 (0) 8241/5005-0
Fax: +49 (0) 8241/5005-115
www.alpina.de or
www.alpina-automobiles.com

TECHART

In 2008, Techart won the annual Tuner Grand Prix at Hockenheim with a 700 hp TECHART GT Street RS establishing himself as premier tuner of Porsches.

Visiting TECHART

TECHART has a showroom open to the public.

Hours

Monday to Friday
8.00 AM to 6.00 PM
Saturday
9.00 AM to 1.00 PM

Directions

From **Stuttgart by car:**

▶ Autobahn A81 (Stuttgart-Heilbronn) direction Stuttgart
▶ Exit 18/Stuttgart-Feuerbach
▶ West on B295
▶ Continue on Siemenstrasse as B295 turns west
▶ West at roundabout on Höfingerstrasse/K1689
▶ At roundabout north on Röntgenstrasse

Contact Information

TECHART Automobildesign GmbH
Röntgenstrasse 47
71229 Leonberg
Germany

Phone: +49 (0) 7152/9339-0
Fax: +49 (0) 7152/9339-33
E-mail: *info@techart.de*
www.techart.de

HAMANN

Like many other tuners, HAMANN is deeply involved in motorsports. They have run more than 700 races finishing in the top 3 over 300 times and winning 103 victories in mostly BMWs. HAMANN also won the BMW M1 Special Touring Car Trophy three times. Founded in 1986 by Richard Hamann, it has diversified into tuning just about every major manufacturer's cars from the new Ferrari 458 Italia to the new Mercedes-AMG SLS.

Visiting HAMANN

HAMANN has a showroom open to the public. We recommend you call in advance if you wish to visit them.

Directions

From **Stuttgart by car:**
▶   Autobahn A8 (Stuttgart-München) direction München
▶   Exit 62/Ulm West
▶   South on B10/B28 for 10 kms
▶   West/right on B30 for 18 kms
▶   Exit at Laupheim
▶   Straight at roundabout onto Kässbohrerstrasse

Contact Information

HAMANN GmbH
Kässbohrerstrasse 3
88471 Laupheim

Phone: +49 (0) 7392/973-20
Fax: +49 (0) 7392/973-2222
E-mail:
info@hamann-motorsport.com
www.hamann-motorsport.de

Rieger

Rieger Tuning is one of the biggest names in the business when it comes to body kits for Opels, Volkswagens, BMW 3 Series, & more. Don't expect to see Rieger Tuning win the Tuner Grand Prix, but do expect to see their body kits on cars everywhere.

Visiting Rieger

Rieger has a new showroom with at least a dozen cars on display. As always, we recommend you call Rieger if you wish to visit them.

Directions

From **Munich by car:**
▶   Autobahn A9 (München/Ingolstadt) direction Ingolstadt
▶   Exit onto Autobahn A92 direction Landshut
▶   Exit 14/Landshut-Nord
▶   South on B299 direction Neumarkt for roughly 25 kms
▶   East/left on B388 direction Eggenfelden for roughly 32 kms
▶   North/left on Weilbergstrasse

Contact Information

Rieger Tuning Kfz-Kunststoffteile Design und Tuning GmbH
Am-Rieger-Tuning-Ring
Weilbergstrasse 16
84307 Eggenfelden
Germany

Phone: +49 (0) 8721/9619-0
Fax: +49 (0) 8721/9619-30
E-mail: *info@rieger-tuning.de*
www.rieger-tuning.de

German Race Tracks

For a country that invented the automobile and now produces some of the best and fastest cars on the planet, it seems a little strange that there are so few full time race tracks. But rather than discuss the reasons why there are so few today or why the tracks of yesteryear are gone, let's say that the current full time race facilities make up for it with a host of activities. Southern Germany has only two full time facilities, so we felt it would be beneficial to list all significant race tracks in Germany ■

Above: *Sunset at the Nürburgring.* ✶ = Race tracks not covered in this guidebook.

German Race Tracks

Race Track	Website	Type of Track
1 - Hockenheimring	www.hockenheimring.de	Full time Road course/dragstrip
2 - Nürburgring - Grand Prix Track	www.nuerburgring.de	Full time Road course
3 - Nürburgring - Nordschleife	www.nuerburgring.de	Full time Road course
4 - Norisring	www.norisring.de	Part time Road course
5 - Schottenring	www.schottenring.de	Part time Road course
6 - * Eurospeedway	www.eurospeedway.de	Full time Road course/oval
7 - * Motorsports Arena Oschersleben	www.motorsportarena.com	Full time Road course
8 - * Sachsenring	www.sachsenring.de	Full time Road course
9 - * Schleizer Dreieck	www.schleizer-dreieck.de	Part time Road course

Hockenheimring

Over the past several decades, the Hockenheimring has established itself as a world class race track hosting DTM races, motorcycle races, and the FIA Formula 1 race. It is one of two full time race track facilities in Southern Germany and has a drag strip, hotel, and its own race museum. Today the Hockenheimring is a state of the art facility with easy access from both the A5 and A6 Autobahnen.

History of the Hockenheimring

1932 - The track is founded in what was a then a thick forest. The first races there were motorcycle races.

1938 - The track is redesigned to the "oval" shaped track that lasted until 2000.

1947 - Rebuilding from war damage is finished and racing resumes.

Directions to Hockenheimring

From **Nürnberg or Karlsruhe by car:**
- ▶ Autobahn A6 to Autobahn A5 (Karlsruhe-Mannheim)
- ▶ Exit 39/ Walldorf
- ▶ West on B291 direction Hockenheim
- ▶ North on L599/Reilingerstrasse
- ▶ During a race event, look for shuttle or parking signs - Non race events, right on Rathhausstrasse to track

From **Mannheim by car:**
- ▶ Autobahn A6 (Mannheim-Nürnberg)
- ▶ Exit 29/Schwetzingen
- ▶ South on B36 direction Hockenheim
- ▶ Exit onto L599/Talhausstrasse
- ▶ During a race event, look for shuttle or parking signs - Non race events, left on Rathhausstrasse to track

1960s - The facility is redesign to accommodate the new Autobahn A6.

1968 - Tragically two time (1963, 1965) world champion Jim Clark is killed on April 7 during a Formula 2 race.

2001 - The most recent major overhaul in 2001 has also been its most controversial. In a move some have called the "castrating of Hockenheim", the whole forest section was removed. Hermann Tilke, a German architect, was central to the creation of a redesigned circuit that removed the back half of the race track and shortening it from 6.2 kms to 4.57 kms.

Opposite: *Hockenheimring Mobil 1 House.*

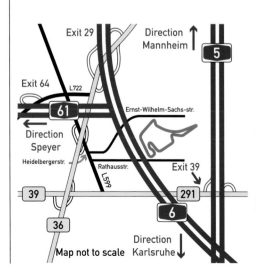

kms), and the east course is 1.92 miles (3.084 kms). The current track record is held by Kimi Räikkönen with a 1:13.780. The DTM record is 1:34.104 set by Paul di Resta in 2008 with a Mercedes-Benz. The top speed set by a Formula 1 car in the Parabolica is 205 mph.

Unlike the longer pre-2001 course, there are now grandstands situated through out the course and most passing is done just before the hairpin ...and in front of spectators.

Hockenheimring Today

The controversy of 2001 seems to be a lingering topic for those that discuss the Hockenheimring even today. But a number of good things happened during that renovation. Seating has been increased, passing is more common, and, of course, safety has improved.

Quick Stats
- ▶ 2.8 miles (4.57 kilometers)
- ▶ 17 turns (as listed by the FIA)
- ▶ Seating for 120,000
- ▶ First Formula 1 race was in 1970. That race won by Jochen Rindt in a 50 lap race.

Lap record is 1:13.780 - set by Kimi Räikkönen in 2004

The Road Course

There are 3 different configurations for the post 2001 race track. The new Grand Prix track is 2.8 miles long (4.574 kms) and has 17 turns, while the small course is 1.62 miles (2.604

The Drag Strip

Between the right hand turn of the road course and the south tribune grand stands is the starting line for Germany's best drag strip. It is a 1/4 mile track with run off extending all the way to the hairpin.

A Lap on the Hockenheimring

Thanks to Wolfgang Kaufmann, the opposite page is a turn by turn lap on the Hockenheim Grand Prix Track! Wolfgang Kaufmann is a well known German race car driver that has decades of racing under his belt - including runs at the 12 Hours of Sebring and 24 Hours of Daytona. For a lap of the Nürburgring, see "A Lap around the G.P. Track with Wolfgang Kaufmann" on page 223. Also see - *www.wolfgang-kaufmann.de*

Above: *Practice for the ADAC 500 km Motorcycle Grand Prix.*

Opposite: *Track map of the Hockenheim Circuit today.*

Lap around Hockenheimring with Wolfgang Kaufmann

Thanks to Wolfgang Kaufmann, here is a turn by turn description of a lap on the Hockenheimring! Thank you Wolfgang!

North Tribune -

A fast right after the start/finish straight. To be fast you have to use curbs as well as exit the apex especially well.

Bernie Ecclestone Curve -

Entry to Parabolica is a medium slow corner. You "destroy" a bit of the corner to make a very fast direction change to the following left and take a wide line exit to catch as much possible speed for the following Parabolica straight away.

Parabolica -

Flat out for sure. It is the fastest part of Hockenheim G.P. Circuit.

Spitzkehre -

Very hard braking, from top speed down to 1st gear and take a late apex. Use the hard curbs so that you can be as early as possible on power. This makes the car a bit unstable but to be fast, it must be. For this corner you have to be very smooth and precise.

Mercedes Tribune -

Very hard under braking. Normally in 2nd gear, short shift up to 3rd and important try to take to next right turn flat out. The advantage is that this corner opens up at exit, but it's not so easy to find the trust.

Mobil 1 Curve -

Very fast right for entry of Motodrom and important to use the curbs at the exit and the maximum width of the track.

Sachs Curve -

A good corner for overtaking under braking. Medium slow 180°corner with camber. Important to be fast at the exit and use the curbs, flat for the fast left right combination to Opel corner.

Opel Curve/South Tribune –

A bit difficult under braking because you have to trailbrake into the corner and use the maximum track width at exit to the final corner. The steering input will be more or less the same for both corners. For the final corner to the start/finish straight, the apex is very close inside, otherwise you'll get massive understeer. For the best exit, you must use all space left including curbs and rumble stripes.

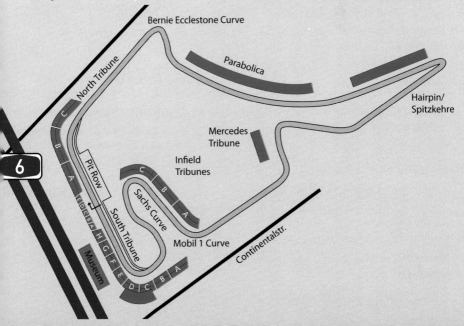

Professional Race Series

There are three professional race series that race at the Hockenheimring (we cover in another part of the book). For more info on Formula 1, DTM, or the ADAC Masters, please see "German Auto Racing" on page 304.

Major Events

Each year the Hockenheimring hosts over a dozen major annual events. Many of these have been around for decades and occur at roughly the same time every year. Here are some highlights -

Hockenheim Historic -
In Memory of Jim Clark

Every year, near the end of April, (and the anniversary of his death), a historic race is held at the Hockenheimring. This 3 day event features period Formula 1 cars, Formula 2 cars, and Le Mans race cars.
See *www.hockenheim-historic.de*

Above: *Baden-Wüttemberg Center.*
Opposite: *Sachs Curve.*

NitrOlympX

Once a year, there is one FIA sanctioned drag racing event. Started in 1986, this is one of six FIA race weekends in Europe each year. There are 3 motorcycle classes and 5 car classes including Top Fuel.
See *www.nitrolympx.com*

Tuner Grand Prix

For the last 18 years, automotive tuners have battled it out for a win at the Hockenheimring. There are 13 classes and over 100 different sports cars. MTM has won several times. (See "MTM" on page 193)

Ticket Information

Event Tickets

Tickets may be purchased online at *www.hockenheimring.net/ticketshop* or by calling +49 (0) 6205/950-222

Fancard

Discounts are available for people who buy a Fancard for € 5.- (plus postage).
See *www.hockenheimring.net/fan-card*

Renn-Taxi

Sit next to a professional in a Porsche GT3, Mercedes-Benz SLK, or Radical SR3. The price for 3 laps around the Grand Prix track is € 229.- in the closed cars and € 249.- for the Radical. Contact +49 (0) 6205/950-171 or *fahrprogramme@hockenheimring.de*

Parking

During major events people will be directed to park in the town of Hockenheim just to the west of the Autobahn A6.

Amenities

Hockenheim Hotel Motodrom

Literally behind the grandstands and start/finish line is Hockenheim's Hotel Motodrom. There are 54 rooms (including 2 suites), a hotel restaurant, and bar/racing pub. The hotel restaurant offers a daily buffet from 12:00 PM to 2:00 PM. It costs € 8.50 and is open most of the year (closed during major events). The hotel and restaurant are both closed for several weeks in winter.

Physical Address -
Hockenheim-Ring Hotel
und Gastronomie GmbH
Motodrom
68766 Hockenheim
Germany

Phone: +49 (0) 6205/2980
Fax: +49 (0) 6205/298555
E-mail:
info@hotel.hockenheimring.de
www.hockenheimring.de

Tours

Monday through Friday, the track offers guided tours. Visitors see the race track's South Tribune, winner's podium, Mercedes Tribune, the Mobil 1 House, and pit lane. The tours start at 11:00 AM and last about 1 1/2 hours. Reservations are not necessary. There are no tours during major events or on major holidays. The cost is € 9.- for adults and € 5.- for children 7 to 14 years old. The tour meets in the foyer of the Hockenheim Motor Sport Museum.

Hockenheim Motor Sport Museum

(See page 212)

Contact Information

Hockenheim-Ring GmbH
Am Motodrom
68766 Hockenheim
Germany

Postal Address -
Postfach 1106
68754 Hockenheim
Germany

Phone: +49 (0) 6205/9500
Fax: +49 (0) 6205/950299
E-mail: *info@hockenheimring.de*
www.hockenheimring.de

Hockenheimring
Motor Sport Museum

As motorists speed along the Autobahn, there are no billboards and few distractions. But when you pass the Hockenheimring on the Autobahn A6, try not to stare. One building you will see is the towering hulk of the South Tribune and another is the roof of the Motor Sport Museum. This of course is just the teaser to build to your anticipation of visiting the Hockenheimring and explore the treasures within.

History of the Hockenheimring Museum

Even though the museum was founded in 1986, the collection began much earlier. One notable acquisition was the sale of the Brandstetter motorcycle collection to Hockenheim in 1982. Today that collection and the museum is located between the Hockenheimring grandstands and the Autobahn A6.

Above: *Front entrance to foyer of museum.*
Opposite: *Benetton Ford B188 - Nannini #19 1989.*

Hockenheimring Today

Quick Stats
▶ Plan on spending 2-4 hours
▶ 23,000 square feet on display
▶ 200+ cars & motorcycles

The Collection Theme
This museum is all about racing and there are no street cars. There is also a massive motorcycle collection (motorcycles played a key role in the history of the Hockenheimring - but its history is beyond the scope of this book).

Must See
The Formula 3 car driven by 7 time Formula 1 champion **Michael Schumacher**. Prior to driving in Formula 1, Michael Schumacher started racing in Formula 3 with **Willi Weber's WTS** team in 1989. Michael Schumacher won the 1990 Formula 3 championship in this car. He started his Formula 1 career in 1991.

The Exhibitions

The main floor houses the race cars. This is a combination of Formula cars and touring cars. Most of the touring cars are DTM race cars and there is one top fuel dragster on display. Many of the cars here are a bit old in the racing world and do not reflect the current technologies in use today. The cars on display are, however, a good sample of the race cars from the 1970s through the 1990s.

The motorcycle collection is also worth mentioning. It is located on the top floor and is massive. The heart of the motorcycle exhibit is the **Walter Brandstetter Collection**. The motorcycles on display range from the 1920s to the 1970s and just about every major bike manufacturer is represented here, including bikes by Ariel, BMW, BSA, DKW, Ducati, Moto Guzzi, Norton, NSU, and several more.

Directions to Hockenheimring Motor Sport Museum

From **Hockenheim:**
▶ Follow directions to the Hockenheimring
▶ Museum is located on the south west side of the track in between the South Tribune and Autobahn A6

The Cars

The museum cars are rotated with some frequency. The pictures in the official museum brochure will not always be the same race cars on display. Here are the highlights -

The Formula 1 Cars -

- ▶ Formula 1 - ATS D5 Fahrschulen Dvf - Manfred Winkelhock #3 1982

- ▶ Formula 1 - ATS D7 BMW - Manfred Winkelhock #14 1984

- ▶ Formula 1 - Williams Renault FW12 - Riccardo Patrese #6 1988

- ▶ Formula 1 - Benetton Ford B188 Nannini #19 1989

- ▶ Formula 1 - Zakspeed 891/ Yamaha OX88 V8 East - Bernd Schneider / Aguri Suzuki #34 1989

- ▶ Formula 1 - Minardi M195B / Ford Cosworth V8 - Giancarlo Fisichella / G. Wuensch #3 1996

The Formula 3 Cars -

- ▶ Formula 3 - Reynard F 903-001 East - Michael Schumacher #5 1990
  (Season winning car - 1991)

- ▶ Formula 3 - Euroseries Dallara F303/006 - Team Rosberg Nico Rosberg #11 2004
  (He entered Formula 1 in 2006)

- ▶ Formula 3 - Klaus Trella Motorsport #3

The Touring Cars -

- ▶ DTM - BMW M3 GTR #3 Johnny Cecotto 1993

- ▶ DTM - Mercedes-Benz C Class #17 Ellen Lohr 1995

- ▶ DTM - Opel Calibra V6 Hans-Joachim Stuck #44 - Team Rosberg 1996
  (Finishing 9th for the season)

- ▶ DTM - Opel Calibra V6 J.J. Letho #43 - Team Rosberg 1996
  (Finishing 5th for the season)

- ► STW - Nissan Primera - Team Rosberg - Roland Asch #23 1998
- ► DTM - Audi Quattro Thyssengas Abt #10 - Christian Abt, Nissen, Menzel 2000
- ► DTM - Abt Audi TTR
- ► Porsche 928 ONS Pace Car/ Safety Car
- ► BMW M1 - similar to cars raced in the BMW M1 Procar Series

The Motorcycles

The museum has a world class motorcycle collection and the largest collection of race bikes in Europe. In addition to the Walter Brandstetter collection, there is also a collection from world record holder Wilhelm Herz. In 1956 he set the world speed record at the Bonneville Salt Flats as the first person to break the 200 mph barrier on a motorcycle. The highlight and must see is a very rare **1957 Gilera Quattro**.

Amenities
- ► Fan Shop Gift Store

Admission
- ► Adults   € 6.-
- ► Children 6 to 14 years   € 3.-
- ► Children under 5 years   Free
- ► Group of 10 people (per)   € 5.-

Opposite: *ATS D5 of Manfred Winkelhock in yellow, F3 from Klaus Trella in blue, Top Fuel dragster, Minardi M195B of Giancarlo Fisichella, Nico Rosberg's F3, and the Williams Renault of Riccardo Patrese.*

Above: *Michael Schumacher's season winning F3 and the ATS D7 of Manfred Winkelhock.*

Right: *Zakspeed 891 of Bernd Schneider / Aguri Suzuki.*

Hours
- ► Open daily 10:00 AM to 5:00 PM
- ► January & February open weekends only

Contact Information

Hockenheim Motor Sport Museum
Am Motodrom
68766 Hockenheim
Germany

Phone: +49 (0) 6205/6005
Fax: +49 (0) 6205/950212
E-mail: *museum@hockenheimring.de*
www.hockenheimring.net/ motor-sport-museum-action-and-fun

Nürburgring

Before any question is asked, the answer is "The Nürburgring". What is the biggest track? What is the most dangerous? What is the favorite? What is the most famous? or infamous? The answer is (*drum roll*)..well, we all already know the answer. The Nürburgring (otherwise known as "The Ring", "The Green Hell", or "Die Grüne Hölle") is comprised of two distinct tracks each with multiple layouts. (There used to be a third track known as the Südschleife. This is track is now gone.) The track known as the Nürburgring Grand Prix track is 3.23 miles long track and used during Formula 1 races, while the very famous Nordschleife is Nürburgring's 12.9 mile endurance track and open to the public as a one way toll road. Of all the tracks in Germany, or the world for that matter, this is the place by which all others are compared.

History of Nürburgring

The 1920s

The idea of the Nürburgring came from **Dr. Otto Creutz**, a councillor from the Eifel district, and supported by then Mayor of Köln (*Cologne*), **Konrad Adenauer** (who would open the first Autobahn in 1932 and become the first Chancellor of Germany in 1949). In an effort to reduce unemployment and boost tourism to the area, the project was approved and construction began in 1925.

The grand opening of the Nürburgring was on May 18, 1927 with the first race held on the weekend of June 18 and 19, 1927. The 5th annual **ADAC Eifelrennen** started with a motorcycle race and ended with a car race won by **Rudolf Caracciola** in a Mercedes-Benz.

Directions to Nürburgring

From **Koblenz by car:**
- ▶ Autobahn A48 (Koblenz-Trier)
- ▶ Exit # 6/Mayen
- ▶ North on B262 to B258
- ▶ Left/west on B258
- ▶ You will see the Nordschleife on your right.

From **Trier by car:**
- ▶ Autobahn A48 (Trier-Koblenz)
- ▶ Exit #2/Ulmen
- ▶ North on B259 to B258
- ▶ Right on B258 until you pass underneath the Nürburgring Grand Prix track.

Opposite: *In 2009, the Nürburgring Grand Prix track under went an extensive remodel. This is the new "ring°arena" and part of the new ring experience.*

The Original Specs of Nürburgring - 1927

The Nürburgring has changed both in layout and in length several times since it was first built. Here are the original specs for the track.

The Gesamtstrecke (*Whole Track*)
17.563 miles (28.265 kms)
The Gesamtstrecke was a combination of the Nordschleife, Südschleife, and Zielschleife. Depending upon who you ask, there were either 172 or 174 corners prior to the 1971 changes.

The Nordschleife (*North Loop*)
14.173 miles (22.810 kms)
reduced in 1981-1984 to
12.947 miles (20.832 kms)

The Südschleife (*South Loop*)
4.814 miles (7.747 kms)

The Zielschleife/Betonschleife
(*Finish Loop/Concrete Loop*)
1.417 miles (2.281 kms)

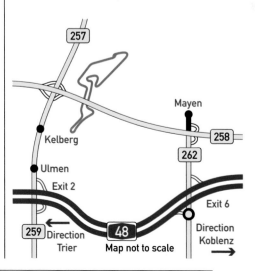

Milestones in the History of the Nürburgring

It would impossible to list all the important dates for a book such as this. Please see "Contact Information" on page 225 for links to web sites with more information.

1939 - The last time the entire track (Nordschleife and Südschleife) is used in a major race.

1945 - During World War II, the U.S. Army's 11th Armored Division uses Sherman tanks to capture the Nürburgring. They advance using the track in the wrong direction.

1947 - The repairs are finished on the Südschleife and the Eifelpokal Rennen is held that August.

1949 - The Nordschleife is repaired and is reopened for racing.

1951 - Formula 1 World Championship returns to Germany and the Nürburgring. The winner is Alberto Ascari in a Ferrari 375.

1953 - First "ADAC 1000 km of Nürburgring" is held on the Nordschleife. The winners are Alberto Ascari and Giuseppe Farina.

1970 - First year of the "ADAC 24 Hours Nürburgring". The winners are Hans-Joachim Stuck and Clemens Schickentanz.

1971 - F1 returns to the Nordschleife after a renovation of the track.

1976 - Niki Lauda's near fatal accident in a Ferrari 312 T2 is the end of Formula 1 on the Nordschleife.

"The Green Hell"

The "Green Hell", or "Grüne Hölle" in German, is a term first used by Sir Jackie Stewart to describe the Nordschleife during his 1968 Grand Prix win there. He won by more than 4 minutes in appalling conditions with rain, wind, and fog.

Above: Opening race at the Nürburgring in 1927. Schloss Nürburg can be seen on the hill in the distance.

Opposite: Nürburgring, 2009.

Südschleife

One of the interesting secrets about the Nürburgring, is the Südschleife. This little brother to the Nordschleife played a role in international racing from 1927 until the 1970s. If there was a heyday for the Südschleife, it was the 1960s. This small race track hosted Formula 2 events such as the 1964 ADAC Eifelrennen. Jim Clark won that particular race.

Today the track is long gone. It was demolished, along with the Ziel-schleife, in the 1980s to make room for the modern Grand Prix track. Unlike the Zielschleife, the Süd-schleife can still be partially driven.

The remaining portions of the Südschleife include an access road to parking lots C6a & C6b, K72 roadway, and few side streets in the town of Müllenbach. The track ran clockwise and can best be picked up as you turn off K92 on to the K72 heading south (See page 234).

Noteworthy Lap Times

Lap times are a funny thing. They are also quite controversial. Rather than discuss the track layout, type of tires, class of car, or if the given car was street legal, we are listing just a few significant Nordschleife lap times -

6:11.13 - Stefan Bellof/Porsche 956 World record holder on the 12.9 mile track (20.9 kilometers) during qualifying - 1000k Nürburgring - **1983**

6:47 - Marc Basseng Pagani Zonda R - **2010**

6:48 - Michael Vergers Radical SR8 LM - **2009**

6:58 - Niki Lauda/Ferrari 312 T2 World Record on the 14.189 mile track (22.835 Kilometers) German Grand Prix - **1976**

8:55 - Phil Hill/Ferrari 156 (first to break the 9 minute mark) German Grand Prix - **1961**

9:56 - Bernd Rosemeyer/Auto Union (first to break 10 minute mark) German Grand Prix - **1936**

Nürburgring Grand Prix Track

Underneath the asphalt of the Nürburgring Grand Prix track are the ghosts of the Südschleife and the Zielschleife. Call this the march of time, progress, or just good business, but it is only the Grand Prix track that survives today. This modern 3.23 mile long track is a high tech, FIA approved race track and facility that has taken the world of racing from the early 20th century into the 21st. While some fans of old may still be disappointed that the charm of the original layout is now long gone, two million plus visitors still come each year to see its racing today. The Grand Prix track hosts several annual and biennial international events including the very popular FIA Formula 1 Großer Preis von Deutschland (*Formula 1 German Grand Prix*).

Grand Prix Track History

Back in 1927, there was no proper Grand Prix Circuit as we know today. There was, however, a track called the **Zielschleife** (*Finish Loop*) or the **Betonschleife** (*Concrete Loop*). It was a 6 turn, 1.4 mile (2.3 kms) long warm up track that housed the pits, grandstands, and the Sporthotel. It was all closed (along with the **Südschleife**) in the early 1980s to make way for the Grand Prix track.

1981 - Due in part to the near fatal crash of Niki Lauda in 1976, approval is granted and construction begins on a new grand prix track.

1984 - The new track opens with an interesting exhibition race in identical Mercedes-Benz 190E 2.3-16's. The 24 year old **Ayrton Senna** wins that race and shows the world a taste of things to come. He beats several past world champions such as Niki Lauda, James

Opposite: The new stadium section built in 2002. The new turn 1 is in the foreground.

Hunt, Stirling Moss, Phil Hill, and Carlos Reutemann.

1985 - There was one, and only, Formula 1 race during the 1980s. This sole race was won by Michele Alboreto in a Ferrari 156/85. Formula 1 would not return until 1995.

1995 - Formula 1 returns in part due to the rise in popularity of Michael Schumacher. Additional annual races such as the "24 Hours Nürburgring" continue to use the Grand Prix track in conjunction with the Nordschleife. Other annual events such as the AvD Oldtimer Grand Prix (see page 226) continue to draw huge crowds.

2002 - The track is redesigned, upgraded, and lengthened. The major change is the removal of the "Castrol Chicane" and the addition of the Mercedes Tribune. The new layout creates a stadium section at the new turn 1. The Grand Prix track is lengthened by 592 meters.

2010 - Construction of the new ring°boulevard is complete.

"A Hotel with a View"

The Dorint Hotel

There are many places to stay around the Nürburgring, but it is the Dorint Hotel that has track side rooms set right on the main straight away looking at the Formula 1 starting grid. Prices vary by season and event.

Contact Information

Dorint Am Nürburgring
53520 Nürburg
Germany

Phone: +49 (0) 2691/309-0
Fax: +49 (0) 2691/309-189
www.dorint.com/en/location-directions-hotel-nurburgring-eifel

Above: *Track side view of the Dorint Hotel.*
Below: *Inside the Dorint Hotel.*

Grand Prix Track Today

The track and surrounding facilities that people see today are part of a 150 million Euro investment that was started in 2005 with the goal to give visitors a chance to explore "The Ring" 365 days a year.

Quick Stats

- ▶ 3.2 miles long (5.148 kilometers)
- ▶ *www.nuerburgring.de* lists 17 corners (7 left, 10 right), while *www. formula1.com* lists 15 corners (6 left, 9 right)
- ▶ Grandstand seating for 140,000
- ▶ Lap record is 1:29.468 - set by Michael Schumacher in 2004
- ▶ Almost 2 million visitors come to the Nürburgring every year.

Müllenbachschleife

(The southern portion of the Grand Prix track - used for driving schools)

- ▶ Length .925 mile (1.489 kilometer)
- ▶ Bends: 8 (3 left, 5 right)

Major Events

Oldtimer G.P. - Grand Prix Track

Every August, historic race cars take to the Grand Prix track. See <u>page 220</u>.

ADAC 24 Hours Nürburgring

This lesser known 24 hour race may be shadowed by Le Mans and Daytona, but this international showdown on the Nordschleife and Grand Prix track each spring is also open to semi-professional racers as well as professional factory teams.

A Lap around the G.P. Track with Wolfgang Kaufmann

Wolfgang Kaufmann is a well known German born race car driver who has been kind enough to help us run a lap of the Nürburgring Grand Prix track! For more info, see *www.wolfgang-kaufmann.de*

1990 - **3rd overall** with **3 wins** in German F3 Championship

1993 - **2nd place** - 24 Hours Nürburgring

1999 - **2nd place** - 12 Hours of Sebring

2001 - **2nd place** - 24 Hours of Daytona

2001 – **1st overall** - Porsche World Cup

2006 – **1st overall** - 24 Hours Bahrain

2007 – **1st place** - 24 Hours Dubai

2008 - Four **1st place** finishes in the FIA FT Championship "Citation Cup"

2010 – **1st place** - LMS Spa-Francorchamps in Formula Le Mans

Mercedes Arena – End of start/finish straight away and the slowest corner at G.P. Circuit, the Yokohama S and it's a bit difficult. Because it's a bit downhill, you brake a bit into the smooth right hand corner. It's a nice corner for overtaking out of a slipstream and under braking. Important - not so fast in and then out with a fast wide line on the left side - in preparation for the next left hand corner.

The first of the two lefts is faster. The apex should be very close to the curbs. Careful, as the corner gets a bit tight/close at exit. The second left is very slow and bit difficult as well under braking and it's easy to lock the wheels as well as understeer. It's very much important to be easy and gentle in this corner to prepare for the next right (and faster one), because then you have the straight away to Ford Curve. Mercedes Arena is very technical...

Ford Curve – The first right is much faster than second right... I personally prefer to brake and stay inside, so I can brake in straight line. The exit is very important (to carry speed) to the Dunlop corner. Important to use the curbs as much as possible exiting Ford Curve.

Right: *Wolfgang Kaufmann.*

Dunlop Curve – 180 degree corner with some negative camber. Early turn in, late apex, stay close to curbs for a long time, and exit using wide line over curbs.

Schumacher S – Very fast corner! Lift or very little braking with LMP flat. It's a very clear line and use the curbs on the right side and exit as well to the left.

Warsteiner Curve – Enter using the curbs and exit with a very wide line right over curbs. Stay mid-track in preparation for final right. Use the curbs and exit with as much possible speed. Flat out to Advan.

ADVAN-Bogen – FLAT & easy. Under heavy rain, there will be some significant aquaplaning after the right.

NGK Schikane (Chicane) – Two different options – F1 and Motorcycle Chicane. The faster one is the Motorcycle Chicane and mainly used for Oldtimer GP, 24 Hrs, and Le Mans Series. Late braking with a very clear and smooth line. Careful, in acceleration because there is a bump at the exit.

F1 Chicane - Braking point and turn in is more difficult because you don't see really the entry point.

Coca Cola Curve – Early entry and very close to curbs right side. Early exit and use the curbs on the left side to the finish line.

Checkered Flag... WIN!

(See track maps on page 228.)

"A Different Kind of Shop"

Gasthaus Döttinger Höhe

This small gas station/inn sitting along side the B258 roadway has been catering to fans of the ring since 1927. Today, the owner Hans-Joachim Retterath, is not only a purveyor of ED petrol, but also beer, food, and amazing scale models...and for all you "car paparazzi", bring your camera, and watch sports cars filling up before they hit the "Ring"!

Contact Information

An der B258 am Nürburgring
53520 Döttinger Höhe
Germany
Phone: +49 (0) 2691/923932
See page 234 for the map location and page 232 for their webcam.

The New Nürburgring

Now open 365 days a year, the new Nürburgring sports a shopping mall, a party village, and an entertainment center.

ring°boulevard

Along side the main straight away sit a string of brand new buildings. These are all part of the new ring°boulevard.

welcome°center

Start here! Sandwiched in between the ring°arena and ring°werk, this is the place to begin your journey. Book your reservations and buy tickets here.

ring°arena

Inside the new ring°arena is a number of franchise dealers and gift stores. There is Aston Martin, Brabham Racing, Ferrari, Nissan, and Radical Sportcars stores, to name a few.

ring°werk

The new ring°werk is a 160,000 square foot mini theme park. Visitors explore a 24 hour race in 4-D, a multi media theater, an interactive test center, a display of race cars that have run "Ring", and much more.

Adults	€ 19.50
Children ages 5 to 11	€ 11.-
Family card	€ 55.-

Above Left: *Scale die cast models for sale at Gasthaus Döttinger Höhe.*

Left: *Mark Webber's Red Bull #14 on display inside the ring°arena during the 2009 German Grand Prix. He won the race.*

Eifeldorf Grüne Hölle

Want to know where the "foodie" meets the race track? Located on the opposite side of the B258, this mini wood frame village has a steak house, pub, bars, biergarten, and a discotheque.

Paddock Tours

Take a one hour tour of the media center, historical paddock, pit lane, VIP terrace, and the start/finish building. Cost is € 6.- per person. Tours begin daily at 11:00 AM, 1:00 PM, and 3:00 PM. Tours meet at the welcome°center.

Historical Paddock

If you visit the Historisches Fahrerlager (*Historical Paddock*) built in 1927, look for both the statue of Wolfgang von Trips and the Rudolf Caracciola dedication plaque.

Additional Amenities

▶ Fan shops
▶ Roller coaster - "ring°racer!"
▶ Off-road Park
▶ Warsteiner Event Centre
▶ Helicopter flights

Hours

Most race track facilities are open 365 days a year. For more information contact the welcome °center.

Tickets

Ticket Hot Line (surcharges apply)
Phone: +49 (0) 1805/770750
To buy online, go to -
nuerburgring.de/en/tickets.html
For info, contact the welcome°center.

Contact Information

Nürburgring welcome°center

Ring Boulevard am Nürburgring
53520 Nürburg
Germany
Phone: +49 (0) 2691/302-630
Fax: +49 (0) 2691/302-650
E-mail: *info@nuerburgring.de*
www.nuerburgring.de

Nürburgring GmbH

Otto-Flimm-Strasse
53520 Nürburg
Germany
Phone: +49 (0) 2691/302-0
Fax: +49 (0) 2691/302-115
www.nuerburgring.de

Nordschleife Emergency Number

Phone: 08000/302112

Unofficial Information

The best enthusiast site, bar none, is the Ben Lovejoy website. Its focus is primarily on driving the Nordschleife for visitors coming from the United Kingdom.
www.nurburgring.org.uk

An additional source for tickets is the MS Event & Ticket Service.
Phone: +49 (0) 2691/809003
E-mail: *info@ringinfo.de*
www.ringinfo.de

If mountain biking is your thing, try renting a bike from Radsport Breuer in Adenau.
Phone: +49 (0) 2691/1078
E-mail: *info@radsport-breuer.de*
www.radsport-breuer.de

AvD Oldtimer Grand Prix

There is one event at the Nürburgring that stands apart from all others. It is actually more than just an event, it is an annual pilgrimage for race fans, classic car enthusiasts, car clubs, and auction junkies. While its U.S. counterpart in Monterey, California (also held in August and usually one week after the Oldtimer GP) may boast more events, it is this weekend that is a one stop over load for anything and everything a car fanatic would ever want.

Oldtimer G.P. History

Since 1973 fans have come to the Nürburgring for the annual 3 day running of the AvD Oldtimer Grand Prix. Over the years the car clubs have come too - with hundreds of street cars lining the infield paddock areas.

These classic race cars have taken to the track often by the same classic drivers that piloted them to victory years, if not decades, earlier. Regulars at the Oldtimer Grand Prix include **Nick Mason** (of Pink Floyd), **Stirling Moss**, and **Walter Rohrl**.

Oldtimer G.P. Today

Stand on the B258 on Saturday morning and just watch the event take shape, for it is an amazing site. You might see 20 Triumphs followed by a handful of Ferrari F40s with a dozen Porsche 356s not far behind. Just wait until you get inside.

Car Clubs

The 3 day Oldtimer G.P. is known for its massive club turn outs. The most prominent are the Porsches and Ferraris. But there are BMWs, Jaguars, MGs, Morgans, Triumphs, and more.

Racing

The racing is broken down into 10 races on the Grand Prix track and one endurance race on Friday on the Nordschleife. The Can-Ams and Group C cars are among the crowd favorite.

Coys Auctions

Every year, Coys Auctions set up an auction tent inside the paddock area during the Oldtimer Grand Prix. Anyone interested in attending should contact Coys directly at -
auctions@coys.co.uk
www.coys.co.uk

Schedule

Friday - 8:30 AM to 6:40 PM
Saturday - 8:30 AM to 9:30 PM
Sunday - 8:30 AM to 5:40 PM

Tickets

Adults - weekend	€ 58.-
Adults - one day	€ 38.-
Adults - Friday only	€ 18.-
Children - free with adult	

Directions

Follow the directions listed on page 217.

Contact Information

AvD-Oldtimer-Grand-Prix
Automobilclub von Deutschland e.V.
Lyonerstr. 16
60528 Frankfurt
Germany

Phone: +49 (0) 69/6606-338
Fax: +49 (0) 69/6606-253
www.avd.de/ogpracing

Opposite: *A Veritas RS leads a Porsche 356 that once belonged to Graf Berge von Trips & a Ferrari 250 Testarossa.*

Below: *A Mercedes-Benz/Sauber C-9 leads a pack of Group C race cars, while a Roush Mustang/Zakspeed over brakes a corner.*

Three different views of the Nürburgring Grand Prix Track

Map 1: Detailed view of track and surrounding parking lots.
Map 2: 3-D view of track with grandstands.
Map 3: Simple view of track and surrounding area.
Not all amenities are shown.

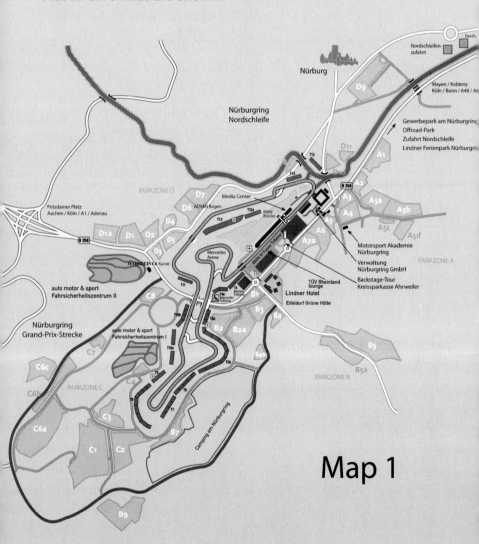

Map 1

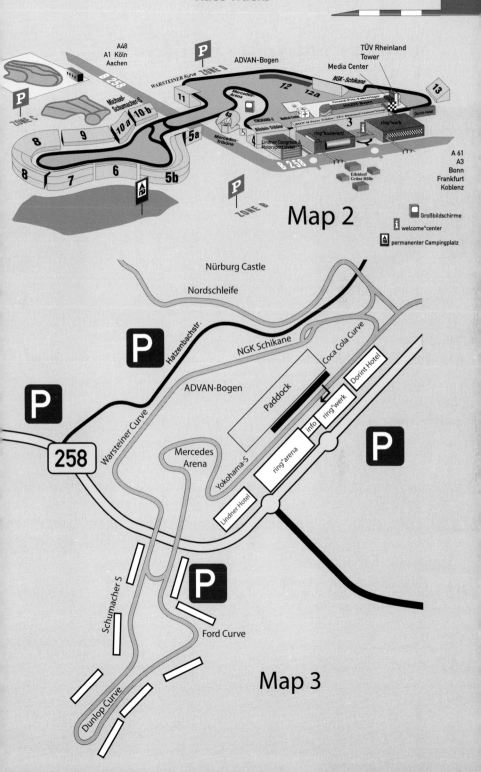

Map 2

Map 3

Nordschleife

The Nordschleife, or as many people now call it, the "Green Hell", is the ultimate challenge. Even though Sir Jackie Stewart first coined the term when describing his 1968 Grand Prix win at the Nordschleife, drivers today endearingly still use the term. Ask any factory test driver what he/she thinks of the Nordschleife and see what he says! (In case you may not know any, we do!) We asked a test driver who worked for Lancia and Fiat to describe the Nordschleife. His reply was that 8 minutes on the Nordschleife would expose problems no simulator or proving grounds could ever reveal. It is no wonder enthusiasts, amateur drivers, professionals, race teams, and manufacturers come here to test their cars and skills on the single most demanding track in the world.

Nordschleife Today

Welcome to the "Route 66" of Europe! Well, at least in spirit anyway. For anyone who follows car culture in Europe, there is really just one spiritual race track center of the world. The Nordschleife. The draw today isn't the professional races, scenery, or the new entertainment center. It is the chance to drive this track. It is matching man and machine against nature. Or perhaps against fear. Or maybe just yourself. What allows the general public the ability to drive the most notorious track on planet Earth? It's called "Touristenfahrten" or in English, "Tourist trips/Tourist outings". And it's very popular.

Directions to Nordschleife

From **Koblenz or Trier by car:**

▶ Same directions to the Nürburgring seen on page 217

Opposite: Brünnchen - a popular turn to watch the public Touristenfahrten.

What makes this possible? The Nordschleife is a public road. To be exact, it is a one way public toll road. Unless there are organized events or testing, the Nordschleife is (generally) open for Touristenfahrten.

The Use Rules

A complete list of the rules is at the track. Here are some important ones.

▶ Drivers must hold a valid drivers license, registration, and ticket.
▶ Cars with temporary/transfer plates are not permitted.
▶ Drivers of foreign registered cars must bring a valid insurance card.
▶ No slicks/racing tires or in car video cameras.

Quick Stats

▶ Length without Grand Prix track: 12.944 miles (20.832 kilometers)
▶ Corners: 73 (33 left, 40 right)
▶ Maximum slope: 17%,
▶ Maximum gradient: 11%
▶ Elevation change: 300 Meters
▶ Highest point: Hohe Acht

"Just one lap"

The first lap I ever ran on the Nordschleife was in August 1998 during the Oldtimer Grand Prix in an Audi A4 Diesel. I would like to say I put on a good show for the crowds gathered at Brünnchen, but I didn't. Turns were well marked, but I couldn't carry any speed. I had no idea what came next. Every few turns another car would pass me, and I would try to follow. No luck. Fear would set in and I would once again back off. By the end of my lap, I was covered in sweat, my nerves were shot...and I wanted to go again!

   ✒   *Ron Adams*

Touristenfahrten cont...

The Driving Rules
A complete list is at the track.

- ▶ Minimum 60 km/h speed.
- ▶ Stay left, pass on right.
- ▶ If you see an accident, slow to at least 50 km/h and do not pass.
- ▶ There is absolutely no stopping at anytime or anywhere.
- ▶ There are speed limits on the Nordschleife - specifically the entry/exit areas.

Liability and Insurance
There is a good chance your rental car is not allowed on the Nordschleife. If you take your own car, check with your provider. Accidents are expensive and the track may bill for closure, cleanup, towing, ect...

Automobile Testing
Several automobile manufacturer's have set up shop in a nondescript business park near the Nordschleife. Forget getting a tour, but keep your eyes open for prototypes being tested!

Amenities

- ▶ Grüne Hölle Restaurant - located at the Touristenfahrten entrance.

Webcams
There are two main webcams. One is at the Gasthaus Döttinger Höhe looking down on the gas station and the B258 that runs along side the Ring. *www.doettinger-hoehe.de/Webcam/webcam.html* and of course the very popular webcam showing the starting point for Touristenfahrten - *www.nurburgring.org.uk/webcams.html* or *www.nuerburgring.de/fileadmin/webcam/magnify.html*

Maybe you decided not to drive the ring after all and perhaps you're a little bored? Head to the Grüne Hölle Restaurant at the tourist entrance about the an hour before Touristenfahrten begins. This is a great place to people watch and see drivers getting ready to hit the "Ring"... and besides, you might make some friends to cheer on!

Chat with Sabine Schmitz

Sabine Schmitz isn't just any "Taxi" driver, she is a BMW "Ring Taxi" driver and two time winner of the 24 Hours Nürburgring (1996 & 1997). Via Corsa had the pleasure to ask Sabine (who has driven over 20,000 laps of the "Ring") a few questions. See her website for more *www.speedbee.de*

VIA CORSA: What is your favorite car to drive around the Nordschleife?
SABINE SCHMITZ: Racing car: Porsche GT3 R. Road car: (good for one fast lap) Nissan GTR, and for more fast laps the Porsche GT3 RS.

VC: What is the absolute slowest car (or truck/bus) have you driven around the Nordschleife?
SS: A very old Motorhome with 3 Chefs cooking a full meal for me in one lap. We've found the missing long knife in the backrest of my seat....

VC: Jackie Steward has a nickname for the Nordschleife (Grüne Hölle). What is your nickname for the track?
SS: Jackie Steward gave the nickname "Green Hell" to the Nordschleife in 1969, I just call it "The Ring".

VC: When not driving around the Nordschleife, what do you like to do around the Nürburg area?
SS: With my horses outside the track to watch tourists driving on the ring.

VC: What advice would you give to a driver about to take their first lap on the Nordschleife?
SS: Take the slowest car you can find and relax!

VC: If the Nordschleife is your favorite track, what is your second favorite? What other track best resembles the Nordschleife?
SS: Road America in Wisconsin, USA

Above: *Sabine Schmitz.*

Ring Taxis (book early!!!)
BMW Motorsports Ring-Taxi
www.bmw-motorsport.com/ms_de/ faszination/bmw_ring_taxi
€ 195.- per lap.

Sabine Schmitz Motorsport/ Porsche 997 GT3 RS - € 449.- per lap.
www.speedbee.de/13-0-Race-Taxi.html

Vintage bus - € 18.- minor /€ 24.- adult. E-mail: *info@nuerburgring.de*

Nissan GT-R - € 295.- per lap.
www.mydays.de/weitersagen.html

Touristenfahrten Hours
► Opening times vary by day and season. The normal hours are 5:45 PM to 7:30 PM during the summer. For exact times, see - *www.nuerburgring.de*

Tickets - 2010 Prices
► 1 Lap   € 22.-
► 4 Laps   € 75.-
► Annual Pass   € 1,075.-

Contact Information

See "Contact Information" on page 225.

Points of Interest

1 - Breidscheid Entrance - This is another (less used) entrance to the Nordschleife. Also a spot to see the Ex-Mühle turn.

2 - Bergwerk - Niki Lauda's near fatal crash site.

3 - Steilstrecke - An old part of the track that is no longer used. The road is accessible, but has a 27% grade and is difficult to walk/drive.

4 - Hohe Acht - Highest point of the circuit. "Hohe Acht" is also the name of a near by mountain to the north and the highest in the Eifel region measuring 2,450 feet (747 meters) above sea level.

5 - Brünnchen - Best place to watch. Located on the west side of B412

6 - Gasthaus Döttinger Höhe - Gas Station/Restaurant/Diecast Model Shop

7 - Tourist Entrance - Start/Finish line for paying customers and the Grüne Hölle Restaurant (*Green Hell Restaurant*).

8 - The Schloss Nürburg - Open to the public most days, this iconic castle sits at an elevation of 2,224 feet (678 meters).

9 - BMW M Test Center - (Closed to the public - but there is the Formula BMW Racing Experience - See <ins>page 244</ins>). The Motorsports Hotel is just a few doors away.
(See *www.motorsporthotel.de*)

10 - Südschleife - Closed in 1982 and partly destroyed. There are a few sections remaining. One section is along K72, another section are some streets inside the town of Müllenbach, and a third is the access road between parking lots C6a & C6b.

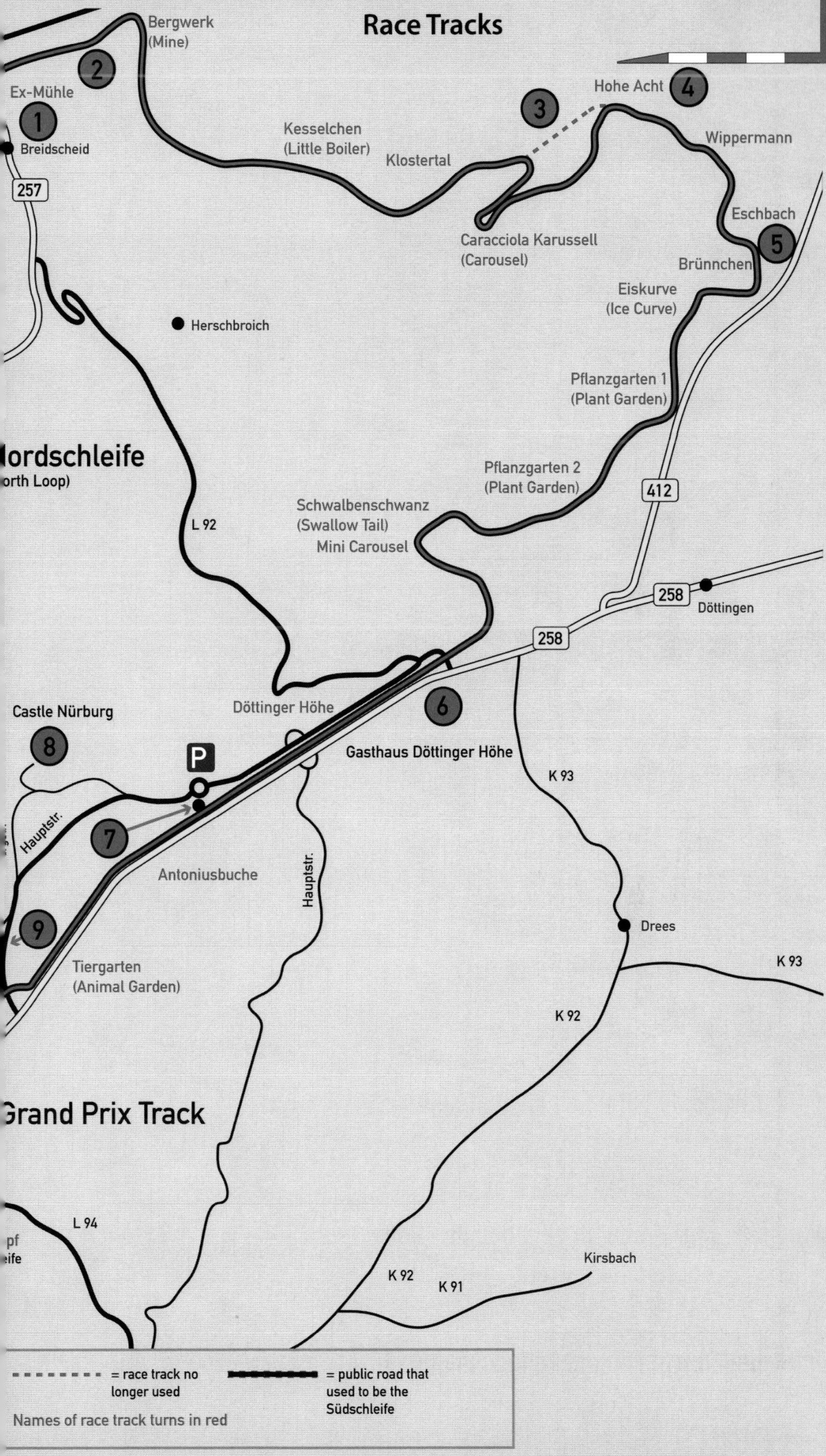

① Ex-Mühle

257

Breidscheid

② Bergwerk
(Mine)

Kesselchen
(Little Boiler)

Klostertal

③

Hohe Acht

④

Wippermann

Eschbach

⑤

Brünnchen

Caracciola Karussell
(Carousel)

Eiskurve
(Ice Curve)

Herschbroich

Pflanzgarten 1
(Plant Garden)

**Nordschleife
(North Loop)**

L 92

Pflanzgarten 2
(Plant Garden)

Schwalbenschwanz
(Swallow Tail)
Mini Carousel

412

258

Döttingen

258

Castle Nürburg

⑧

Döttinger Höhe

⑥

P

Gasthaus Döttinger Höhe

K 93

Hauptstr.

⑦

Antoniusbuche

Hauptstr.

⑨

Drees

K 93

Tiergarten
(Animal Garden)

K 92

Grand Prix Track

L 94

pf
leife

K 92

K 91

Kirsbach

- - - - - = race track no
longer used

= public road that
used to be the
Südschleife

Names of race track turns in red

Norisring

First off, The Norisring in Nürnberg (*Nuremberg* in English) should not be confused with the Nürburgring in Nürburg as they are two very different tracks. Nürburg...Nürnberg. It might be possible to confuse the two. Spelling aside, the Norisring, also called the "German Monaco", is perhaps one of the most unusual tracks with regard to history. During the Second World War, the National Socialist Party held a number of rallies on the grounds, and sitting at the Norisring start/finish line is the Zeppelintribüne (or *Zeppelin Grandstands*). A platform that was once used for the tirades of a madman are now home to the most popular of DTM races on the yearly Calendar. This would be an example of change for the better.

History of the Norisring

In 1933, the National Socialists (otherwise known as Nazis) began construction on the Albert Speer designed Reichsparteitagsgelände (*Nazi Party Rally Grounds*). The Zeppelintribüne (*Zeppelin Grandstands*) were once part of these grounds and are now the grandstands for the Norisring. The first race here was in 1947 on a 1.24 mile layout. The layout changed several times over the years with the last major change in 1971 after the death of Pedro Rodriguez.

Directions to Norisring

From **Autobahn A6 by car:**
▶ Autobahn A6 (Heilbronn-Prague)
▶ Exit 5 to Autobahn A73
▶ North on Autobahn A73
▶ Exit Nürnberg/Zollhaus
▶ North on B8
▶ Right/east on Karl-Schönleben-Str.
▶ Follow road as it curves north and enter the track at the end of turn 3

Opposite: *The inside apex of Grunding Hairpin along Beuthenerstrasse.*

Zeppelintribüne Today

All year long, the Grandstands and the surrounding sites are popular tourist sites with dozens of tour buses unloading tourists to see the what remains of this dark chapter in German history. Visitors to the Zeppelin Grandstands may walk along the main Norisring straight away and climb up into the grandstands (there is no entry fee). The Zeppelin Tribune's stone columns seen in period photos were torn down in 1967.

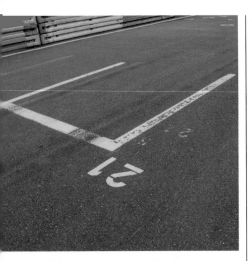

The Annual Race

There is only one race a year at the Norisring. Started in 1967 as the 200 Meilen von Nürnberg (*200 miles of Nuremberg*) it has evolved into the shortened 188.6 kilometer DTM (Deutsche Tourenwagen-Meisterschaft) race seen today. This three day race weekend held each July is popular with fans due to their proximity to the paddocks and drivers.

In addition to DTM, there are four additional race series running on the Norisring during the three day race event. There is the Volkswagen Scirocco R-Cup, Seat Leon Supercopa, Porsche Cup, and the Formula 3 Euro Series. Several of the series have races on Saturday as well as Sunday. DTM has just the single race on Sunday afternoon.

The Norisring Today

Through out the year, it is possible to drive most of the Norisring. Visitors wishing to drive the track should start on Beuthenerstrasse to the south of the Schöller S Curve and drive counterclockwise. Park after the Dutzendteich Hairpin and walk the rest. It is not possible to drive past the start/finish line. There are no proper race track facilities, but street vendors will likely be selling food and drinks. During the race weekend, the entire track is closed to automobile traffic.

Ticket Information

Tickets are available online at *www.norisring.de* or by visiting the Motor Sport Club Nürnberg inside the ADAC office listed below.

Contact Information

Motor Sport Club Nürnberg e.V. (inside the ADAC)
Äußere Sulzbacher Str. 98
90491 Nürnberg
Germany

Motor Sport Club Nürnberg
Phone: +49 (0) 911/5970-51
Fax: +49 (0) 911/5970-52
E-mail: *info@norisring.de*
www.norisring.de

Quick Stats

- ▶ 1.43 miles (2.3 kilometers)
- ▶ Referred to as the "German Monaco"
- ▶ Room for 130,000 spectators
- ▶ Lap record is 47.79 - set by Jean-Louis Schlesser with a Sauber-Mercedes C9 Group C in 1988.
- ▶ The DTM record is 48.446 set by Bruno Spengler with a Mercedes-Benz in 2008.

Pedro Rodriguez

Born in Mexico City on January 18, 1940, Pedro Rodriguez quickly climbed the ranks of the international racing scene. He raced a Ferrari 500 Testarossa at Le Mans when he was 18 years old, and entered Formula 1 in October 1963 with a Lotus-Climax. Tragically he died on July 11th, 1971 during a minor race event at the Norisring in a Ferrari 512M. On July 21, 2006, 35 years after his death, a plaque was donated by the family foundation "Scuderia Rodriguez A.C." at the site of the tragedy.

Opposite: *The starting grid along Beuthenerstrasse.*

Right: *Dedication plaque in honor of Pedro Rodriguez just before the Schöller S Curve.*

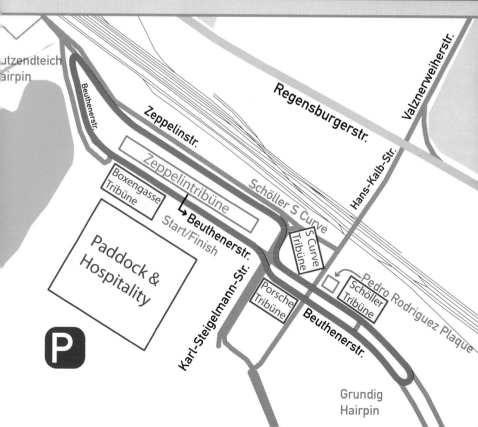

Schottenring

Tucked away in the quiet little town of Schotten, northeast of Frankfurt, is a little known, temporary street track called the Schottenring. The Schottenring, or in English, the "Scots" Ring, is actually one of Germany's oldest race tracks opening a full two years before the Nürburgring's Nordschleife. Today this little track has made a come back from obscurity with an annual motorcycle Grand Prix race and hill climb held each summer.

History of Schottenring

1925 to 1955

Schottenring opened July 25, 1925 with a 10 mile (16.08 km) temporary road course running counter clockwise from the town of Schotten through the village of Rudingshain on the L3291 and returning to Schotten on the L3139. This layout lasted until 1955 and ran mostly motorcycle races. Public concern for safety in the aftermath of the 1955 Le Mans accident involving a Mercedes-Benz 300 SLR closed this version of the track.

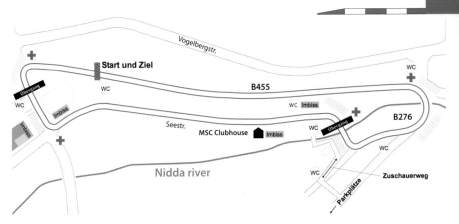

1968 to 1983

The second layout of the Schottenring was a temporary 2 mile (3.25 km) street course using a smaller portion of the original 1925 track to the east Rudingshain. Today portions of the L3291 and L3139 are named Schottenring in honor of the races that once took place there.

Schottenring Today

In 2010, the Schottenring is celebrating its 75th anniversary with a smaller .87 mile (1.4 km) street circuit

Directions to Schottenring

From **Frankfurt by car:**

▶ Autobahn A5
▶ Exit 10/Fernwald
▶ East on B457 direction Lich
▶ Left/east on L3841 direction Laubach
▶ Right/south on B276 direction Schotten
▶ Schottenring is located where B276 crosses the Nidda river

Opposite: *Gerd Schlörb at the starting line in a Formula 3 race at the Schottenring.*

Above: *Current Schottenring track layout.*

located inside the town of Schotten. The major annual event is a two day motorcycle "Classic Grand Prix" held in August. An adult two day ticket costs € 20.-.

Contact Information

Motorsportclub Rund um Schotten
Seestrasse 6
63679 Schotten
Germany

Phone: +49 (0) 6044/2083
Fax: +49 (0) 6044/2083
E-mail: *info@schottenring.de*
www.schottenring.de

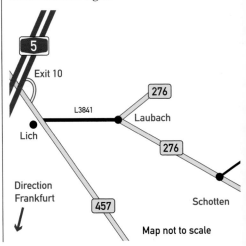

Southern German Racing Camps, Experiences, and Driving Schools

Driving Schools and Racing Schools

School	Type of Car	Race Track
Formula BMW Racing Experience	Formula BMW FB02 open wheel race car	Nürburgring
Mercedes-Benz AMG Driving Academy	Mercedes-AMG: SLS AMG, E63 AMG, C63 AMG, SL63 AMG, and SLK 55 AMG	Hockenheimring and Nürburgring
Opel Race Camp	Opel Astra OPC	Nürburgring
Hockenheimring Driving Experiences	Formula Opel-Lotus and Karts	Hockenheimring
FSZ Hockenheimring ADAC Safety Center	Personal car or Subaru Impreza WRX STI FSZ rental car	Hockenheimring
Motorsport Akademie Nürburgring	Personal car or Formula race car	Nürburgring
FSZ Nürburgring Safety Center	Personal car or FSZ rental car	Nürburgring

When the term "driving school" is thrown out to a group of car enthusiasts in conversation, most would respond with talk about threshold braking, skid pads, and lane change exercises. Not that those are bad things, it's just those activities are the norm. In Germany, there is no typical "school" experience. In fact, the enthusiast may select from a drive to a music festival, competing for a spot on a factory supported race team, or trying the skid pad...in a bus ∎

Opposite: Level #4 of Opel OPC Race Camp on the Nürburgring Grand Prix Track.

Formula BMW Racing Experience

BMW Motorsport and its partners have created the ultimate stepping stone for anyone wanting to race. The best path from a go kart to a Formula 1 ride is through the Formula BMW Racing Experience. But even if you don't have your sights set on a racing career, this is still an exhilarating experience.

BMW Experience History

The BMW Formula FB02, the spec race car behind the Formula BMW Racing Experience, was first built by BMW Motorsport in 2001. The BMW championship series, using the FB02, first ran in 2002. The Formula BMW

Racing Center held its first event in 2002 in Valencia, Spain with the goal of providing a training platform for drivers wishing to advance into professional racing. Sebastian Vettel and Nico Rosberg are two of the most famous graduates of the Formula BMW Racing Experience.

Formula BMW Racing Experience Today

Don't let the professionalism of both the car and its companion series intimidate you, the Formula BMW Racing Experience is geared to the beginner wishing to enjoy racing in a safe and fun environment.

Quick Stats

- ▶ Up to 40 students per Event
- ▶ Founded in 2002 in Spain
- ▶ 30 + event days a year
- ▶ Events at the Nürburgring Grand Prix track and the Nordschleife

The Car

Safety is number one for these race cars. The Formula BMW FB02 is made from carbon fibre/Kevlar monocoque by Mygale Racing Cars of France and the roll bar has been crash tested to withstand a 60 kN (or 6 ton) impact. The nose and rear are also carbon fibre with aluminum honey comb inlay. All BMW FB02s run with "wings and slicks".

Formula BMW FB02 Engine

- ▶ Factory sealed 4 cylinder BMW Type 124EA engine based on the BMW K 1200 RS motorcycle.
- ▶ Six speed sequential gearbox
- ▶ Max horsepower: 140 hp @ 9000 rpm
- ▶ Max torque: 128 Nm @ 6750 rpm
- ▶ 0 to 62 mph (100 km/h): under 4 seconds

Opposite: *Formula BMW FB02s waiting for action!*

Formula BMW FB02 specs

- ▶ Weight (dry): 1,023 lbs /465 kg
- ▶ Compatible with HANS Device (Head-and-Neck Support)
- ▶ Length: 156.5 inches (3,975 mm)
- ▶ Width: 68.5 inches (1,740 mm)
- ▶ Height: 38.6 inches (980 mm)

The Series

The companion series to the Formula BMW Racing Experience is the Formula BMW Race Series. There are 4 different series with one each in Europe, the United Kingdom, Asia, and the United States. It is an entry level series comparable to the Formula Ford or Formula Continental series run in North America. The European series runs from the Spring to the Fall with races in Spain, Belgium, Italy, and, of course, Germany. There are 8 three day race weekends and a total of 16 planned races for the series. Graduates of this series can move on to either the German ATS Formula 3 Cup series or the Formula 3 Euro Series.

Requirements

- ▶ Speaking German is **NOT** required, nor is prior race experience
- ▶ Valid driver's license
- ▶ 18 years old unless the minor can produce a valid karting license with karting experience
- ▶ Must be between 5 feet 3 inches (160 centimeters) to 6 feet 2 inches (188 centimeters) tall
- ▶ Weigh less than 220 lbs (100 kg)
- ▶ Wear a shoe smaller than size 13 mens (47 in Europe)

The BMW Events

The Formula BMW Racing Experience hosts events all around Europe with a total of more than 20 events.

2010 Schedule (2011 not available)
Nürburgring, Germany
April 16 - 17   € 1,290.-
Lausitzring, Germany
29 April   € 1,290.-
Lausitzring, Germany
April 30   € 1,290.-
Circuit Valencia, Spain
May 4   € 1,290.-
Zandvoort, Netherlands
June 7   € 1,290.-
Nürburgring, Germany
August 1 - 2   € 1,990.-
Nürburgring/Nordschleife   € 2,850.-
September 13
* Prices include 19% German VAT

Typical 1 Day Event
The day starts with breakfast followed by the fitting of racing suit, racing shoes, racing gloves, and helmet.

▶ Morning: Introduction to the Formula BMW FB02. Two Classroom theory sessions covering shifting, braking, and finding the racing line. Two on track practice sessions cover shifting, braking, and driving behind an instructor.

▶ Afternoon: A third theory session covering understeer and oversteer is followed by an on track free practice.

▶ To end the day, coffee, and a light snack is followed by a presentation of certificates of participation.

The Nürburgring

It should be no surprise that one of the most popular events in the Formula BMW Racing Experience calendar is on the Nordschleife at the Nürburgring. The Nürburgring also hosts more advanced level packages.

Level 1 - Nürburgring G. P. Track
1 day program   **Cost:** € 1,290.-
This is an introduction to racing.

▶ Morning: Instruction on racing line, driving etiquette, flags, safety, and physics.

▶ Tour of the Formula BMW Racing Center.

▶ Afternoon: On track instruction in shifting, braking, passing, and racing line.

Level 2 - Nürburgring G. P. Track
1 ½ day program   **Cost:** € 1,990.-
This program qualifies participants for the German National A-license as sanctioned by the DMSB.

Day 1
▶ Afternoon: Introduction followed by instruction on racing line, driving etiquette, and flags. FIA license requirements and FIA written theory test (for license applicants only).

Day 2
▶ Morning: On track instruction in shifting, braking and trail braking, passing, and racing line.

▶ Afternoon: On track instruction in passing, double clutch shifting, and race starts.

Nordschleife

1 ½ day program   **Cost:** € 2,850.-
This is the ultimate BMW Experience!
The entire Nordschleife is reserved for
just the BMW Racing Experience!

Day 1

▶ Check-in to hotel

▶ Afternoon: Introduction followed
by instruction on racing line,
driving etiquette, and flags.

▶ Tour of the Formula BMW Racing
Center followed by fitting of race
suits and cars.

▶ Dinner

Day 2

▶ Breakfast

▶ Morning: On track instruction in
shifting and driving the Nordschleife following an instructor's
car.

▶ Lunch

▶ Afternoon: Driving around the
Nordschleife.

▶ Closing briefing and presentation
of certificates.

Overview of Programs

Prices and descriptions are always
subject to change. There is a 100%
cancellation fee.

Instructors

Just a sample of the talented instruc-
tors -

▶ **Andy Priaulx** - Three-time
World Touring Car Champion

▶ **Augusto Farfus** - BMW WTCC

▶ **Jörg Müller** - Official BMW
Factory Driver

Amenities Provided

▶ Breakfast, lunch, and/or snacks
are included

▶ Certificate of completion is
awarded at the end

▶ Insurance

▶ Helmet, suit, gloves, and shoes
are provided by BMW

▶ Insurance is included with the
price of each package

▶ 1 ½ day programs include dinner
and accommodations for one
evening

Contact Information

BMW Event Hotline

If you wish to enroll into a BMW
Event or need more information, contact BMW directly (see below).

Phone: +49 (0) 89/99 92 9999
Fax: +49 (0) 89/99 92 9998
E-mail: *bmw@ra-sta.de*
*www.formula-bmw-racing-experience.
com*

The Nürburgring

For the programs unique to the
Nürburgring, you may either contact
BMW directly, or sign up directly with
the Nürburgring (see below).

Isabella Gülden
Sales Manager
Nürburgring Adventure GmbH
53520 Nürburg
Germany

Phone: + 49 (0) 2691/302 246
Fax: + 49 (0) 2691/302 101
E-mail:
isabella.guelden@nuerburgring.de

Mercedes-AMG Academy

Most of us can only dream of driving a Mercedes-AMG, let alone driving one in Germany. Thanks to the AMG Driving Academy, enthusiasts from around the world may pick from a plethora of events ranging from driving a Mercedes-AMG to a music festival on the banks of Bodensee (*Lake Constance*) to 2 ½ days of intensive on track training with a new SLS AMG.

AMG Driving Academy History

The AMG Driving Academy was founded in 2007 by Mercedes-Benz's subsidiary Mercedes-AMG GmbH. The initial programs were offered only in Europe but with a wide variety of possible events. The AMG Driving Academy came to the U.S. in 2009 and operates at Road America and Mazda Laguna Seca (see *www.amgacademy.com*). In 2010, both the European and U.S. based academies introduced the new 571 hp gullwing Mercedes-AMG SLS to event participants.

AMG Driving Academy Today

The AMG Driving Academy understands not every driver is comfortable taking a car to the limit on the race track. In an amazing display of diversity, AMG gently introduces the enthusiast to a wide range of activities starting with casual social gatherings up to exploring the limits of the latest Mercedes-Benz AMG. The AMG Driving Academy website lists all their 5 levels of programs plus a 128 page brochure for download.

The Cars

The current line up includes - SLS AMG, E63 AMG, C63 AMG, SL63 AMG, SLK55 AMG. It is possible some cars may not be available at all events.

"EMOTION-Tour"

The first level of activities gives the casual enthusiast a choice of drives along scenic routes in Germany in AMG provided cars. All events in this category are more social and do not involve driving on any race tracks. The events range from 1 to 3 days long. The 3 day touring events range in cost from € 1,290.- to € 2,850.-

"BASIC-Training"

The basics of high performance driving are explored in this 1 ½ day event. The cost of the event is € 990.- plus an additional € 250.- to € 300.- for hotel.

Opposite: A brand new Mercedes-AMG SLS is taken to the limit.

"ADVANCED-Training"

Experience braking, slalom, and cornering exercises during this 2 ½ day class held at a total of five of Europe's best race tracks. The German event is held at the **Hockenheimring**. Cost is € 2,590.- (AMG provides the car).

"PRO-Training"

If you have prior race track experience, take on the **Nordschleife**! This 2 ½ day event allows participants to use their own car or one from AMG. To use their SLS AMG costs € 5,080.-

"MASTERS Sports Trophy"

Once you have completed the "PRO-Training" event, try the ultimate and most challenging of all the 2 ½ day events! Compete against 23 other drivers in special stages to score points. Cost is € 3,790.- if you provide your own car, or € 7,130.- to rent a SLS AMG. Event held at Brno in the Czech Republic.

Requirements

Must be at least 18 years of age and hold a valid EU drivers license or International permit for US drivers. Speaking German is <u>NOT</u> required.

Contact Information

AMG Driving Academy
Phone: +49 (0) 7144/302-575
Fax: +49 (0) 7144/302-576

E-mail:
amg-driving-academy@daimler.com
www.mercedes-amg.com/
driving-academy

Opel OPC Race Camp

What happens when you give 22,000 possible race car drivers the chance to participate in one of eight spots at the ADAC/Zurich 24 Hours Nürburgring endurance race? You have an unparalleled year long driver shoot out that pits the best amateur drivers in Germany against one another to make history.

History of the Opel OPC

Since 2006, Opel's OPC (Opel Performance Center - a subsidiary of General Motors) has hosted a yearly casting call for amateur race car drivers to take on the ultimate race - the annual 24 Hours Nürburgring on the world famous Nordschleife.

Opel OPC Today

Each spring, the Opel OPC Race Camp begins its annual search for the very best amateur race car drivers. The nearly year long process then reduces the field of participants through a 12 level process to find and train the very best. Only the brave need apply.

How You Start

The good news is that the OPC Race Camp is open to anyone without prior race experience. The bad new is that you must speak German. While that most likely disqualifies most of the U.S.A., it's perhaps motivation to start those German language courses!

The Shoot Out

Headed by former Opel works driver Manuel Reuter with help from Jockel Winkelhock, the 22,000 entrants are run through a number of levels. Each level reducing the size of the participants while introducing each participate to new challenges. The first level reduces the group to 750 (German speaking) drivers battling it out on Opel's specially designed handling course at Dudenhofen.

Two months and three levels later, level 4 introduces the drivers to the Nürburgring Grand Prix Track and further eliminations.

By level 6, the field of amateurs numbers only 20. The potential 8 drivers out of the remaining candidates must endure 6 more months and 6 more levels of practice, testing, fitness camp, nutrition plans, and of course eliminations. Each level is designed to test the driver in every possible way to prepare them for the challenges of the ultimate 24 hour race.

Opposite: *Purpose built Opel Astra OPCs waiting for action.*

Right: *Level #4 drivers pushing the limits of their Opel Astras on the Nürburgring Grand Prix Track.*

The Race

Almost a full year later, the 8 remaining drivers are divided into two teams. Each team of four will be handed the keys to a fully race prepared Opel Astra OPC. The challenge is to tackle the hardest endurance race in the world. The ADAC 24 Hours Nürburgring race held each May.

How do these rookies do? In 2010, they finished 2nd and 3rd in the SP3T class and finished in the top 25 out of a total 196 cars entered. Both cars finished without even a scratch.

The Opel OPC Race Camp isn't the traditional "race school" or "high performance driving school" that amateur race car drivers in the U.S. attend. It is a uniquely German phenomenon that has no equivalent anywhere else in the world. We can all only hope Opel opens up a camp on this side of the ocean.

Contact Information

Opel OPC Race Camp
www.opel-opc.de
www.opc-racecamp.de
www.opc-blog.de

Hockenheimring

Called the "Ultimate Horsepower Kick", the Hockenheimring offers a number of brief driving schools and experiences as well as the ADAC Safety Center located in their infield area.

Track Impressions

The overall Hockenheim experience. Karting, race taxi ride, and a backstage tour of the track.

▶ Duration ½ Day, cost € 390.-

Tourist Driving

Drive your own car or motorcycle. Check for dates and prices at *www.hockenheimring.de* or by calling +49 (0) 6205/950 212

Formula Driving - First Steps

Introduction to open wheel driving. 50 to 60 kms driving distance.

▶ Duration 3 hours, cost € 579.-

Formula Driving - Basic

Second course available. 100 to 120 kms driving distance.

▶ Duration 5 hours, cost € 998.-

Formula Driving - Premium

Third course available. 200 to 240 kms driving distance. Extensive free practice at the end of session.

▶ Duration 10 hours, cost € 1,795.-

Contact Information

Hockenheim-Ring GmbH
Phone: +49 (0) 6205/950-183
Fax: +49 (0) 6205/950-163
E-mail: *fahrprogramme@hockenheimring.de*
www.hockenheimring.de

ADAC Safety Center

Located inside the Hockenheimring is the ADAC Fahrsicherheits-Zentrum. The facility covers over 11 acres and features skid pads, lane changing, and multifunction areas with water features. There are 42 different courses using motorcycles, cars, and trucks. It is one of the largest and most modern facilities of its kind in Europe.

Quick Stats

▶ Over 1.15 million square feet
▶ 55,000+ square foot skid pad
▶ 8 different and training areas
▶ U.S. drivers need an international driver's permit

The courses available at the ADAC Safety Center are not geared towards racing, but rather at the customer wishing to learn better driving techniques in adverse weather, roads, and traffic. This facility is open for all to enroll and courses in English are offered, but for whole groups only. Members of ADAC receive discounts.

Contact Information

Hockenheim-Ring GmbH ADAC FSZ
Phone: +49 (0) 1805/141-210 or +49 (0) 6205/292-515
Fax: +49 (0) 6205/292-511
E-mail: *info@fsz-hockenheimring.de*
www.fsz-hockenheimring.de

Nürburgring

The Motorsports Akademie offers a variety of courses for people wishing to hone their skills with their own car on the Nordschleife while FSZ Nürburgring offers more safety training.

Formula Training
Open for ages 14 to 20 years old.
▶ Duration 1 Day, cost on request

Touring Training - G.P. Track
Training for grade A license.
▶ Duration 1 Day, cost € 695.-

Touring Training - Nordschleife
Beginning and advance instruction.
▶ Duration 1 ½ Day, cost € 895.-

Open Track - Nordschleife
Testing for race teams.
▶ Duration ½ Day, cost € 595.-
 or 1 day for € 695.-

Contact Information

Motorsport Akademie Nürburgring
Phone: +49 (0) 2691/302246
Fax: +49 (0) 2691/933933
www.motorsport-akademie.de

Auto Motor und Sport Safety Center

Just south of the B258 are 2 paved safety centers run by the car magazine company *Auto Motor und Sport* in conjunction with the ADAC and the Nürburgring. These facilities sport numerous skid pads, water features, slalom course, and classrooms.

▶ Over 1.39 million square feet
▶ 2 different facilities
▶ Up to 8 different groups may train simultaneously
▶ Courses range in length from a few hours to two days

Like the ADAC Safety Center at the Hockenheimring, the courses here are aimed at creating safer drivers on the street rather than teaching racing techniques. Courses in English are offered, but for whole groups only.

Contact Information

Auto Motor und Sport
Fahrsicherheitszentrum Nürburgring
GmbH & Co. KG
An der B258
53520 Nürburg
Phone: +49 (0) 2691/3015-0
Fax: +49 (0) 2691/3015-10
www.fsznuerburgring.com

Left: *Motorsport Akademie Nürburgring touring cars waiting for action.*

Interesting Car Hot Spots

There really is no criteria for a "Hot Spot". Here are a few additional places we thought would make for a nice diversion from the traditional auto museum or manufacturer tour. Here are six very different "Hot Spots". Each represent a different and unique way with tying in the passion of the car to something different ■

1. Alter Wirt - Restaurant
2. a-workx - Race team
3. C.F. Mirbach - Classic car dealer
4. Herpa - Miniature car manufacturer
5. HK-Engineering Mercedes-Benz 300 SL restorations
6. Waldwirtschaft Biergarten

Opposite: A Mercedes-Benz 500 K at C.F. Mirbach looking down at sailboats on Chiemsee.

Alter Wirt

Back in 1905, Sir Hubert von Herkomer and the Bavarian Automobile Club organized "The German Auto Week 1905" rally from Frankfurt through Munich to Vienna and back to Munich . Once in Munich, a car race was held at a race track in the Forstenrieder Park. The winner of the Forstenrieder race was a Mercedes driver by the name of Willy Pöge. Sadly Forstenrieder's contribution to the world of motorsports is all but forgotten. Thanks to the Alter Wirt Restaurant, those memories are honored with their period memorabilia and news articles.

Forstenrieder

The restaurant Alter Wirt was opened 13 years ago by Michael Schulz as a restaurant with a 1930s vintage motorsports theme. With the support of Audi, there are a number of Auto Union photographs, trophies, newspaper articles, and even an Auto Union race suit and goggles.

The menu at Alter Wirt is based on traditional Bavarian cuisine. Prices are moderate with dinner in the 15 Euro range and a beer for € 3.80.

Hours
▶ Daily 10:00 AM to 1:00 AM
▶ Kitchen open from 11:00 AM to 10:00 PM

Contact Information

Fahr-Gast-Statte Alter Wirt
Forstenrieder Allee 187
81476 München
Germany

Phone: +49 (0) 89/7455460
Fax: +49 (0) 89/7455461
E-mail: *info@alterwirt-forstenried.de*
www.alterwirt-forstenried.de

Directions to Alter Wirt

From **Munich by car:**
▶ Autobahn A95 (München-Lindau)
▶ Exit 3/München-Fürstenried
▶ East on Liesl-Karlstadt-Strasse
▶ Left/north on Forstenrieder Allee
▶ Immediate right in to Alter Wirt

From **Munich by U-Bahn:**
▶ U3 direction Fürstenried West
▶ Exit Basler Strasse

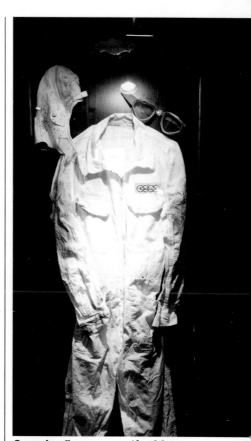

Opposite: Front entry to Alter Wirt.
Above: An original Auto Union race suit.

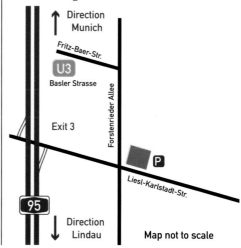

Direction Munich

Fritz-Baer-Str.

U3
Basler Strasse

Exit 3

Forstenrieder Allee

P

Liesl-Karlstadt-Str.

95

Direction Lindau

Map not to scale

a-workx

Germany is filled with a number of small race teams and workshops. Not many are as impressive as the race team a-workx. This team may not ring familiar with race fans in the United States, but their accomplishments are nothing short of heroic. Via Corsa had a "Q&A" with Florian Hebel of a-workx.

Team manager Florian Hebel was kind enough to answer a few questions about both a-workx and their racing history.

VIA CORSA: How did a-workx get involved in motorsports?

FLORIAN HEBEL: Motorsport began as a family business. It was Franz Wieth who started racing in Ferrari Challenge in the early 1990s. Later he changed to Porsche Clubsport races as soon as his elder son Niko had his drivers license. That was also

the time when the racing team "Wieth Racing" was founded - the predecessor of a-workx. The first professional race was the final round of FIA GT Championship 1999 in Zhuhai/China, where Franz & Niko Wieth won 2nd place in their class with a Porsche 993 GT2.

VC: What is the story of Wieth Racing and the development of the Ferrari F550 GTS?

Above: a-workx in the ADAC GT Masters.

FH: Franz Wieth, as a long time Ferrari enthusiast, was dreaming of a GT1-Ferrari and so we decided to use the Ferrari 550 Maranello as a basis for a GT1 racer. It was completely engineered, constructed, built up, and modified by Wieth Racing: The F550 GTS.

After a very hard start with many throwbacks, the F550 GTS became quicker and more reliable and in 2003 it was competing on the same level as the works 575. Although the big wins are missing, the company now has a priceless basis of knowledge about cars, tuning, and race cars which is invaluable knowledge for our customers who bring us their cars. They can be sure that we know what we are doing.

VC: What is a-workx doing today?

FH: 2010 marks the return to GT racing. We are one of just a few teams worldwide that have been chosen by Porsche to receive one of the brand new Porsche 911 GT3Rs to compete in the National GT Championship - "ADAC GT Masters". This also allows our drivers to take part in the same professional Porsche GT3 race series worldwide. Also, winning the inaugural race meant a perfect start for the 2010 season. Our drivers are Niclas Kentenich and Sebastian Asch (son of DTM-legend Roland Asch).

VC: What does a-workx offer the customer off the street?

Directions to a-workx

From **Munich by car:**
▶ <u>Call before visiting</u>!
▶ Autobahn A96 (München-Lindau)
▶ Exit 32 /Oberpfaffenhofen
▶ South/left on St2068/Landsbergerstr. direction Wessling
▶ South on Argelsriederstr.
▶ Left on Argelsrieder Feld

FH: Our main focus is on providing performance related tuning to our customers who own Porsche, BMW, MINI, and/or Ferrari. All of the products we are offering have been approved under racing conditions in our own cars. We offer professional set up for suspension systems, brake systems, tires, rims, KW coilover suspension systems (a-workx is "Performance & Motorsport Partner" of KW - one of only four in Germany and exclusive importer for Akrapovic Exhausts).

VC: What is the future of a-workx racing?

FH: The future in motorsports for a-workx has one clear name - Porsche. That is the brand we started with and with which we had the biggest successes. Most of our customers own Porsches and this way we can at anytime prove our experience and knowledge.

Contact Information

a-workx GmbH
Argelsrieder Feld 1A
82234 Wessling, Germany

Phone: +49 (0) 8153/984-550
Fax: +49 (0) 8153/984-511
E-mail: *info@a-workx.com*
www.a-workx.com

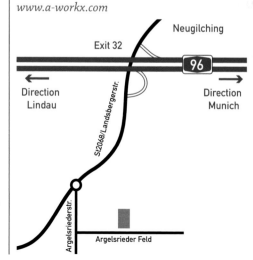

C.F. Mirbach

C.F. Mirbach was founded in 1958 as the premier dealer in vintage and classic automobiles in Germany. Today the owner, Stefan Luftschitz, carries on that tradition by offering the very best cars money can buy in one of three showrooms across Germany. Two of these showrooms are based in Bavaria. The one showroom open to the general public is their new Beuerberg dealership located in a 400 year old Bavarian farmhouse. The location photographed here are C.F. Mirbach's administration offices and showrooms reserved for private transactions.

C.F. Mirbach

There are currently 3 locations in Germany. One is in Hamburg, while 2 more are in Bavaria. Since we photographed the amazing grounds at Bernau, with its amazing views of Lake Chiemsee, C.F. Mirbach has opened a second location roughly 15 kms away. The Bernau location is available by telephone appointment only and visitors are asked to stop by their Beuerberg showroom instead.

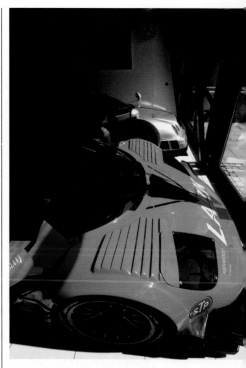

Contact Information

C.F. Mirbach South
<u>Open to the public</u>:
Beuerberg 19
83083 Beuerberg bei Riedering
Germany

<u>By appointment only (pictured here)</u>:
Hitzelsbergstraße 20
83233 Bernau am Chiemsee
Germany

Phone: +49 (0) 8036/7004
Fax: +49 (0) 8036/3972
E-mail: *post@mirbach.de*
www.mirbach.de

Directions to C.F. Mirbach

From **Munich by car to Bernau:**
▶ Autobahn A8 (München-Salzburg)
▶ Exit 106/Bernau am Chiemsee
▶ South on B305/Prienerstrasse
▶ Right/west on Aschauerstrasse
▶ Right/north on Hitzelbergstrasse

Opposite: *C.F. Mirbach Showroom in Bernau am Chiemsee.*
Above Right: *McLaren F1 GTR "Lark" and Mercedes-Benz CLK-GTR.*

Hours (Beuerberg location)
▶ Monday to Friday
   9:00 AM to 6:00 PM
▶ Saturday 10:00 AM to 2:00 PM

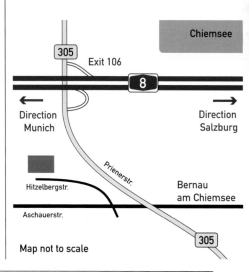

Map not to scale

Herpa Models

Herpa is a car lover's paradise in 1/87 scale. There is everything here for the enthusiast. Hundreds of Audis, BMWs, Mercedes-Benz, and Porsches. There are fire trucks, airplanes, yachts, trains, and trucks. Lots of trucks. Herpa is a world renowned toy company which builds model cars and trucks in primarily 1/87 scale and airplanes in 1/200, 1/400, and 1/500 scale. What makes Herpa different? Its dedication to quality. Collectors around the world know Herpa models are miniature works of art - exact to scale and an unparalleled level of detail.

History of Herpa

Wilhelm Hergenröther founded Herpa in Beilngries, Germany in 1949. It's name is short for "Hergenröther und Patente".

1965 - Fritz Wagner moves Herpa to Dietenhofen and focuses on the Herpa and RIWI product lines.

1978 - Herpa presents 1/87 scale cars. 1/87 scale is also known as HO scale, a popular scale in model trains.

1980 - The first 1/87th scale model truck is presented.

1986 - The new "HIGH-TECH" Herpa series debuts with the release of the Ferrari 348 and Ferrari Testarossa.

1989 - The Ferrari line expands with the addition of the Ferrari F40 in 1/87 and 1/43 scale.

1997 - The Herpa airplane line called "Wings" adds 1/200 as a new scale.

2009 - Herpa changes ownership.

Directions to Herpa

From **Nürnberg by car:**

- ▶ Autobahn A6 (Nürnberg-Heilbronn)
- ▶ Exit 54/Neuendettelsau
- ▶ North on St2410 direction Heilsbronn (not Heilbronn)
- ▶ East on B14
- ▶ North on St2410/Bürgleinerstrasse
- ▶ Stay left and merge onto Lämmerbergstrasse
- ▶ At "T" intersection, left on St2246
- ▶ Right/north on Münchzell direction Dietenhofen
- ▶ Herpa showroom and museum is on the left hand side of the road. The factory is to your right.

Opposite: *Entrance to Herpa Store and Museum.*

Herpa Today

Today, Herpa sells over 4 million models per year. The best selling lines for Herpa are actually not the cars, but rather the airplanes, or "Wings", in 1/200 and 1/500 scale. The cars and trucks manufactured by Herpa are made in 1/87, 1/160 scale, and 1/220 scale. 1/87 is still the most popular.

As Herpa looks to the future, they will continue to expand Herpa Wings and might even consider manufacturing 1/43 scale cars once more.

Quick Stats

- ▶ Founded in 1949
- ▶ Manufacturers 4 million models per year
- ▶ 1/87 scale car is 2 inches long
- ▶ Costs more to make a new Herpa model than build a house
- ▶ The final assembly of a Herpa model is not done at the factory, but by one of roughly 30 home workers living near Dietenhofen.

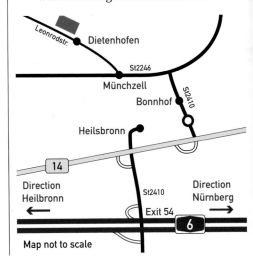

Map not to scale

The Herpa 1/87 Car

It takes up to 6 months to design a new Herpa model. The 1/87 scale Herpa BMW 7 Series has 26 parts and snaps together. There is no glue or screws used in the model. Each model run consists of 10,000 to 20,000 pieces per mold.

Your "Company Name" Here

Do you want your very own personalized model? Or one for your company? It's not only possible, it's also very popular. A large part of Herpa's business is creating custom made models for local companies, German companies, and even world wide global corporations. If by chance you would like a model made, there is a 500 piece minimum for just a decal change and 10,000 if Herpa has to create a whole new mold. If you are interested, contact Herpa directly. Customers in North American should contact the importer listed under Herpa's "Contact Information".

Herpa Museum

Herpa has a fantastic little museum. It stands in contrast to all the other museums in this book as a visitor could walk the museum from start to finish in 90 seconds. But don't do that. The history of Herpa is both interesting and fun. The one room worth just standing and staring at is the Herpa "Wings" airport.

The museum is also a walk through Herpa history with models and displays from the start of the company to present day.

Top: *The Herpa Model Shop.*
Above: *Herpa "Wings" airport display.*
Opposite: *A Herpa Museum display.*

Herpa Collector's Club

For a fairly hefty sum of € 106.- or more, overseas enthusiasts can join the Herpa Collector's Club. Yes, it sounds expensive, but there are benefits. There are the usual magazines, new product catalogs, and discounts; but also one free Herpa model. Depending on which of the 3 versions of the club you join, you get either a free model car, truck, or airplane. Then there is the factory tour...

Factory Tours

Once a summer, Herpa swings open the doors to its factory and lets the public tour the plant. Sadly it is only once a year and you must be a member of the Herpa Club to qualify.

Amenities

▶ Herpa Shop & Museum. The shop is closed Mondays.

Lobby Hours

▶ Monday to Thursday
8:00 AM to 5:00 PM
▶ Friday 8:00 AM to 2:30 PM

Museum Hours

▶ Monday to Thursday
9:00 AM to 5:00 PM
▶ Friday 9:00 AM to 2:30 PM
▶ Saturday 9:00 AM to 4:00 PM
▶ Shop and Museum are closed on public holidays

"Collecting Herpa"

Sometime between living in Germany and writing about Germany, I sold scale model cars. I sold them in all scales from dozens of manufacturers around the world. Amongst them all, Herpa always stood out. At first, it was the Herpa 1/43 scale Ferrari releases that caught my interest and later the 1/87 PC collections. While I personally have my favorite Herpa model, it was the BMW models that sold the best. It's hard to say what exactly people saw in these tiny models. It could be Herpa's level of detail, the wide range of models, the collector's lack of display space, or some unexplainable passion. I have a personal collection of several hundred Herpa models and still don't have an answer.

ᐝ *Ron Adams*

Above: *Ultra rare "Collector's Club" Models.*

Contact Information

Herpa Miniaturmodelle GmbH
Leonrodstr. 46-47
90599 Dietenhofen
Germany

Phone: +49 (0) 9824/951-00
Fax: +49 (0) 9824/951-100
E-mail: *herpa@herpa.de*
www.herpa.de

North American Herpa Distribution
www.promotex.ca

1: The process begins! Up to 12 software engineers spend up to 6 months designing a new Herpa model.

2: A mold is cut. There are up to 100 different molds created per 1/87 scale vehicle. Each mold creates about 20,000 vehicles or airplanes before being retired.

3: This copper and steel mold will be used to help cast the plastic body of a new Herpa model car.

4: Paint colors are mixed in house. All models are cast in colored plastic.

7: After the part is created inside the injection molding machine, it drops out of the mold and on to a conveyer belt. Each injection molding machine manufacturers only one part at a time.

8: Herpa's row of injection molding machines.

9: The conveyer belt drops the new part into a box of finished parts. In an 8 hour day, one machine can manufacturer 3,000 parts.

5: The injection molding process begins with a small plastic bead that is slightly smaller than a pea.

6: The heated plastic is injected into one of many injection molding machines to form a new part.

12: The drilling process above shows the cab of a fire truck being prepped for its blue emergency lights.

11: All parts are hand painted. Some of Herpa's parts are painted one at a time using special metal paint Jigs (such as the cab of this truck). Other parts are painted on a "paint tree" in large groups.

10: Once the finished parts leave the injection molding process, they are moved to the paint department.

13: The type of decals applied to each Herpa model are called "Tampon Print".

14: Finished bodies are set aside for assembly at a later time.

15: A custom machine assembles all the truck tires, wheels, and axles. There are over 200 different wheel & tire combinations for Herpa cars, but only one kind for Herpa trucks.

16: The finished truck axles rotate out of the machine to a storage bin.

Right:
The most elaborate Herpa models have dozens of unique "Tampon Prints" on them. Herpa is well known for their amazing ability to create these mini works of art.

17: The final Herpa model is NOT assembled inside the Herpa factory, but by the hands of home workers living in nearby towns and villages. These home workers then return the finished models for packaging and distribution.

HK-Engineering

G ermany is a country packed full of service shops, car dealers, and even restoration companies. That leaves the classic car enthusiast with a difficult and overwhelming choice - who to visit. However, if you want to see the very best in Germany, there is only one answer: HK-Engineering. Customers from around the world come to HK-Engineering because of its reputation for restoring one kind of car and only one kind of car, the Mercedes-Benz 300 SL. They are just one of a handful of restoration companies in the world that is exclusive to the 300 SL.

HK-Engineering History

Regensburg native Hans Kleissl's fascination with Mercedes-Benz sports cars started early in life. By the time he finished his studies, he had owned over 100 classic cars. In 1978 he purchased and then restored the Polling Kloster (*Monastery*) and later founded HK-Engineering in 1984 and placed it inside these Monastery grounds.

Directions to HK-Engineering

From **Munich by car:**
- ▶ Autobahn A95 (München-Garmisch)
- ▶ Exit 7/Seeshaupt
- ▶ West on Beuerbergerstrasse/St2064 direction Seeshaupt
- ▶ In Seeshaupt, Merge onto St2064/ Weilheimerstrasse direction Weilheim
- ▶ Once in Weilheim in Oberbayern, go past B2 and then left/south on Pollinerstrasse
- ▶ Pollinerstrasse changes name to Weilheimerstrasse
- ▶ Once in Polling, look for a sign for HK-Engineering/Polling Kloster

Opposite: *A Mercedes-Benz 300 SL Gullwing in the HK-Engineering showroom.*

HK-Engineering Today

The "H" and the "K" are the initials of its founder, but the part of the name that matters is "Engineering". Everything done at HK-Engineering is done to the highest standard possible with nothing left to compromise. The HK-Engineering headquarters inside the Polling Monastery house 25 workers and craftsmen who are involved in every step of a 300 SL full body restoration. The Monastery provides the perfect setting for the exquisite work performed inside.

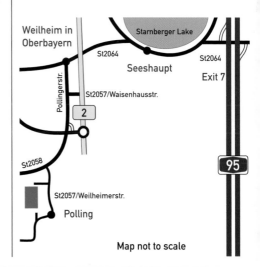

HK-Engineering Departments

Restoring a classic Mercedes-Benz is a complicated business, but HK-Engineering handles all aspects of the job on site.

Restoration
A 300 SL restoration takes 6 to 9 months. The job is never rushed and expect to see as many original parts as possible on the restored 300 SL.

Body Shop
HK-Engineering restores both aluminum and steel bodied cars.

Engine Overhauls
If a full restoration isn't needed, HK-Engineering will overhaul just an engine. This may take anywhere from 40 to 120 hours.

Service and Spare Parts
HK-Engineering Manufacturers some replacement NOS parts as well as stocks a large supply of original parts.

Racing
The HK-Rennsport Division was formed 15 years ago to help 300 SL owners run their cars on the track and in rallies. Each event HK-Engineering attends is accompanied by its classic Mercedes-Benz transporter and 170 Kombi chase car. The events are -

- ▶ Mille Miglia
- ▶ Goodwood Festival of Speed
- ▶ ADAC 1000 km Rennen
- ▶ La Carrera Panamericana
- ▶ Le Mans Classic
- ▶ Oldtimer Grand Prix at the Nürburgring

Sales
The sales floor is small, but the cars are amazing. There are usually a small selection of Mercedes-Benz 300 SLs on display in Polling..and for sale!

Polling Kloster

The buildings occupied by HK-Engineering, as well as many of the surrounding buildings, are all part of an old Augustinian Kloster (*Monastery*) that dates back to roughly the year 750, with their current buildings dating back to the 1700s. Today the complex houses a school, kindergarten, town hall, museum, mill, church, and cemetery. Visitors to HK-Engineering may want to also visit the Polling Klosterkirche on the south side of the Monastery as well as the "Tiefenbach" river running through the Monastery. See *www.polling.de*

Tours

If you are interested in a tour of HK-Engineering, please call well in advance of your visit. The showroom is open to the public.

Opposite Top Left: *A Mercedes-Benz 300 SL waiting for restoration.*

Opposite Left: *HK-Engineering's Showroom.*

Above: *Mercedes-Benz 300 SL waiting for its owner.*

Hours

▶ Monday to Friday
8:00 AM to 4:00 PM

Contact Information

HK-Engineering GmbH
Headquarters
Kirschplatz 1
82398 Polling
Germany

Phone: +49 (0) 881/925609-0
Fax: +49 (0) 881/925609-19
E-mail: *info@hk-engineering.com*
www.hk-engineering.com

Other locations -

HK-Engineering - Berlin
Phone: +49 (0) 30/34560644
Fax: +49 (0) 30/34509940
E-mail: *berlin@hk-engineering.com*

HK-Engineering - Stuttgart
Phone: +49 (0) 711/81477177
Fax: +49 (0) 711/81477178
E-mail: *stuttgart@hk-engineering.com*

Waldwirtschaft

Without a doubt "WaWi" is best known for its live jazz music, spare ribs, Auszogne (*donuts*), and chestnut trees. But here is also where the "foodie" meets "car paparazzi". For the more laid back car spotter, WaWi offers a chance to spot sports cars as well as visit the best Biergarten ever known. The biergarten is perched above the Isar River in the ritzy suburb of Solln south of downtown Munich. Here summer days move gently along to the sounds to live jazz music and the occasional tuned exhaust from a local's Porsche. Here is where we at Via Corsa go to relax.

Via Corsa Car Lover's Guide to Southern Germany

"Not Just a Biergarten"

Unfortunately the typical tourist seems to gravitate towards that tourist trap known as the "Hofbräuhaus". This is not that place. In fact the Waldwirtschaft, or "WaWi" as locals call it, is the farthest thing from that. Here, you will not see swarms of screaming tourists bouncing to "Oom-Pah" music, but instead locals relaxing to outdoor Jazz music, sipping beer, and dining on the finest spare ribs ever made. Anywhere. Oh, and the parking lot is usually filled with amazing sports cars!

୬ *Ron Adams*

Hours
▶ Biergarten open sunny summer days 11:00 AM to 11:00 PM
▶ Restaurant open all year long 11:00 AM to 10:00 PM

Contact Information
Waldwirtschaft Großhesselohe
Georg-Kalb-Straße 3
82049 Großhesselohe bei München
Germany

Phone: +49 (0) 89/74994030
Fax: +49 (0) 89/74994039
E-mail: *info@waldwirtschaft.de*
www.waldwirtschaft.de

It goes without saying that the Bavarians take their Beer seriously. But you may never know this when you see them in a biergarten. They are easy going, approachable, and sometimes outright friendly. This can be quite a marked difference than the experience most tourists will have at that other place.

Directions to WaWi

From **Munich by car:**
▶ South on B2/Wolfratshauserstrasse direction Bad Tölz
▶ Once past Solln town center, left on Melchiorstrasse (look for very small sign on B2 at the intersection)
▶ Right/south on Pullacherstrasse
▶ Left on Promenadeweg to the end of the road (parking on busy nights backs up past Pullacherstrasse)

By Train:
▶ Take the S7 train to Großhesselohe/Isartalbahnhof

Opposite: *Main entrance with VIP parking on the side. Great place to car watch!*
Right: *A sampling of their alcohol free bier.*

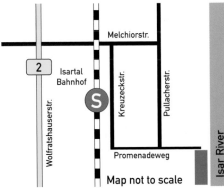

Melchiorstr.

2
Isartal
Bahnhof

S

Kreuzeckstr.

Pullacherstr.

Wolfratshauserstr.

Promenadeweg

Isar River

Map not to scale

Alpine Road

There are few reasons not to drive the Deutsche Alpenstrasse (*Alpine Road*). It has everything an enthusiast wants in a great road. The Alpine Road weaves its way by meadows, up and down mountains, next to crystal clear lakes, past historic abbeys, and through quaint Bavarian villages. Actually it's more than just a great road, it's a spectacular road. It's a shame that the Alpine Road has never become as famous and traveled as the Romantic Road. Wait...that actually might be a good thing.

"Alpine Road"

For over 2 decades, I have cruised back and forth on the Alpine Road and every time I learn, or see, something new. My last trip to Germany in 2010 was no exception. While photographing Kesselberg, Oliver Littmann and I spotted a small ADAC banner announcing the "Kesselbergrennen 2010". I would love to say our story on page 280 was planned, but sometimes the surprises are even more rewarding!

  Ron Adams

Opposite: *Alpine Road near Bernau.*
Left: *Walchensee.*

Alpine Road History

The Deutsche Alpenstrasse (*Alpine Road*), was initially developed in 1927 by **Sanitätsrat Dr. Knorz** to help promote tourism. It was further developed in the 1930s when additional roads were built near Berchtesgaden by the Bavarian State Government. However, the entire planned route was never developed. A little known fact about the Alpine Road is its roll in motorsports. Both Kesselberg and Tatzlwurm played host to hill climbs (see page 281).

Alpine Road Today

This long established theme route is now over 80 years old. It is both older and longer than the more famous Romantic Road. Like the Romantic Road, the name "Alpine Road" is a little deceiving as the road sits at the foot of the Alps and not up in them. This isn't necessarily a bad thing as often enough the Alps are the backdrop for the beautiful stops along the way. Compared to the Romantic Road, very few travel guides pay much attention to the Alpine Road. That is sad as it is far more fun to drive with equally impressive historical sites. There are a few gaps in the Alpine Road, but there are connecting roads.

Quick Stats

▶ 450 kilometers long
▶ Longest theme road in Germany
▶ 25 castles, abbeys, and palaces
▶ 20 Lakes
▶ 2 hill climb mountains
▶ Bad Tölz is the largest town

Left: *The beautiful curves of the Alpine Road on the eastern face of Tatzlwurm.*

Travel the Alpine Road

The good news is that most of the Alpine Road is in great condition. The bad news is that some sections are too far from the Alps. The best way to drive the Alpine Road is in sections. If you want to drive the entire length at once, plan on spending 2 to 3 days.

One good section to drive is from Lindau to Bad Tölz. Another section would be Berchtesgaden to Bernau. If the hill climbs are interesting, drive from Walchensee via Kesselberg to Tatzlwurm.

Major Stops

Lindau - This city on the water is also near the Swiss and Austrian borders.

Hohenschwangau/Füssen - Both towns are near the romantic Schloss Neuschwanstein (also known as the "Disney Castle").

Oberammergau - Know for the Passion Play that takes place every 10 years. This village is the stereotypical little Bavarian mountain village.

Garmisch-Partenkirchen - This large resort town was home to the 1936 Winter Olympics.

Walchensee - The deep cold alpine lake is often a beautiful shade of turquoise giving it a Mediterranean feel.

Kochel am See - This quiet lake is at the foot of Kesselberg.

Tegernsee - See page 300.

Schliersee - The very pretty lake is an alternative to visiting Tegernsee.

Tatzlwurm - See page 281.

Berchtesgaden - Tour a salt mine!
www.berchtesgaden.de/en/ salt-mine-berchtesgaden

Tourist Information

Phone: +49 (0) 89/8292180
E-mail:
deutschealpenstrasse@oberbayern.de
www.deutsche-alpenstrasse.de

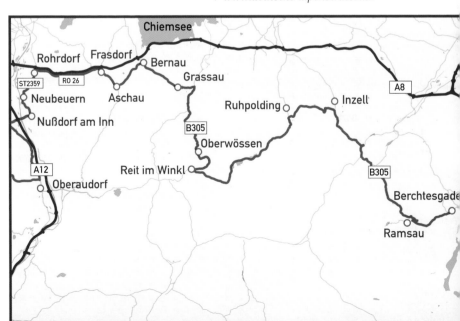

Kesselberg 75th Anniversary

Every once in a while, there is some little known event that takes us from the modern world of the 21st century back in time to the golden age of motorsports. The 2010 Kesselbergrennen *"Erinnerungsfahrt 75 Jahre Bergrekord Hans Stuck"*, or in English, the *"75th anniversary of Hans Stuck's record setting race at Kesselberg"*, was that step back into history. During this 2010 event, 89 vintage cars and motorcycles battled the 5 kilometer long hill in a steady cold rain, all in celebration of Hans Stuck's Auto Union win back in 1935. What may surprise many is that the event was casual, low-key, and not swarmed with spectators. This reunion run and car show offered more surprises; there were eight Bugattis and one Auto Union Type C!

Above: 1935 Bugatti Type 51 on a timed run at Kesselberg in 2010. In 1932 Hans Stuber raced this car on Kesselberg finishing in 2nd place behind Rudolf Caracciola in an Alfa Romeo.

History of the Kesselberg

The first annual hill climb race was held at Kesselberg on August 12, 1905 as part of the "German Auto Week 1905" with **Hubert von Herkomer** donating the trophy. The last hill climb was in 1935 with Hans Stuck taking the victory.

Kesselberg Today

Today, Kesselberg is a quiet mountain road thick with trees and scenic over looks. Most motorists would never even know that legends such as Hans Stuck and Rudolf Caracciola used to race there. If it were not for events such as this to celebrate its history, we risk forgetting it. The 2010 event was proceeded by a 2005 event to commemorate the 100th anniversary of the first race run. There is no information published as to when or if a future event may be held.

Anyone wishing to drive the Alpine Road, must drive Kesselberg. Not only is it an important part of racing history, it is also a part of Hans-Joachim Stuck's favorite drive.

Above: *1936 Auto Union Type C 16 Cylinder #5.*

A Tale of Two Mountains

Tatzlwurm and Kesselberg. Two mountains sitting on the Alpine Road. Of course, each has their own feel and personality. While Kesselberg may have a lot more history behind it, Tatzlwurm is no less the thrill. Both mountains were home to timed hill climbs and both saw many famous driver try to beat the "Berg". Kesselberg is easier to reach from Munich, while Tatzlwurm is a gem tucked away to the west of the A12. Tatzlwurm's curvy road weaves its way though open meadows while the road winding up Kesselberg is heavily shaded by thick forest. We recommend visiting both!

Contact Information

ADAC Südbayern
www.adac.de/suedbayern

Motor-Sport-Club Ohlstadt e.V. im ADAC
www.msc-ohlstadt.com

Directions

From **Munich by car:**
▶ See Hans-Joachim Stuck's favorite drive on **page 282**

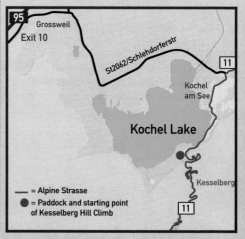

Interview with Hans-Joachim Stuck about his favorite Bavarian drive

Not only was Hans-Joachim Stuck kind enough to talk to us about racing in Germany (See "Interview with Hans-Joachim Stuck" page 48), he was also kind enough to also share with us his favorite drive in Bavaria, Germany! Thank you again Hr. Stuck!

VIA CORSA: If you were to go on a sunny Sunday morning drive in Bavaria, what kind of car would you drive and where would you go?

HANS-JOACHIM STUCK: If it's a sunny summer day, I would take my vintage car. I have a BMW 2002 TI.

HJS: I would take it from Munich to the Starnberger See (*Starnberger Lake*) and then I would drive to Kochel and then up to Kesselberg (*made famous in part by Hans Stuck's record setting runs during the 1930s in an Auto Union*). It's a famous former hill climb race track and that's where everyone goes on the weekend for scenery and the nice lake...and then I would go via the Walchensee, Mittenwald, Garmisch, and then back to Munich. It's very scenic and a nice drive.

VC: Would you go alone or with a passenger?

HJS: No doubt I would take my wife. She's very beautiful and she also loves cars and it would be the perfect occasion to spend a Sunday with her.

VC: Would you listen to music on the radio or listen to the engine?

HJS: I would say when I go in the 2002 TI, I would listen to the engine. It's a four cylinder two litre which has these inlets from the 45 Weber Carburetors. To listen to the inhaling sound is really the best music you can imagine for this kind of drive.

VC: For this kind of drive, would it be the journey or the destination?

HJS: No doubt it would be the journey.

Directions

▶ South from Munich past Starnberger See on Autobahn A95
▶ Exit 10 towards Kochel on Kochelerstrasse (St2062)
▶ Once in Kochel, right on Bundesstrasse 11 to Kesselberg
▶ Kesselberg to Walchensee
▶ Walchensee to Mittenwald
▶ Mittenwald to Garmisch on Bundesstrasse 11
▶ Return to Munich on Bundesstrasse 2 then A95

Opposite: *Route of Hans-Joachim Stuck's favorite "Bavarian Drive".*

Via Corsa: (*We heard about a funny story about something that happened in Alaska. So we just had to ask!*)

Mr. Stuck, what happened in Alaska with the Schnapps and the police?

Hans-Joachim Stuck: Oh this was a story. You call it Candid Camera in the States. We had a Fulda Challenge there, and the guy who organized it was doing all kinds of stuff for tourists and he asked me to go with him to Skagway, Alaska and do an introduction film about Skagway. I said OK, no problem. So we go.

We took a SUV with camera man and we drove towards Skagway. Going down a pass we had a big snow storm and hit a guardrail..All of a sudden the police came and made me come out of the car. They said where is your driver's license..and searched the car. They found an open bottle of Schnapps. I said it didn't belong to me, maybe the owner of the car. They said we have to take you to Skagway and we have to take you to the police station...

To make a long story short, they made me blow into the Breathalyzer and it showed 1.2! I swear I never drink!..So they had to put me in jail. Holy ****! So they took all my finger prints and put me into a cell with another guy and they let me sit there for maybe two hours. All of a sudden the door swings open and says "Welcome Mr. Stuck to Candid Camera!".

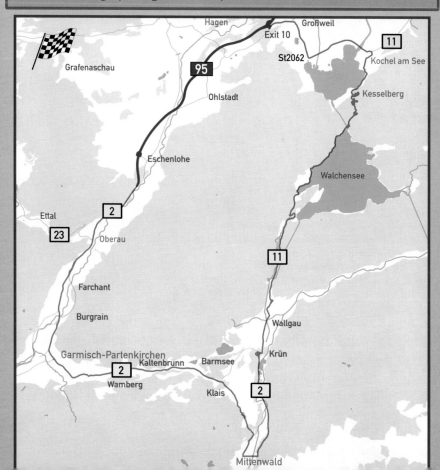

Romantic Road

The Alpine Road is where you want to go to drive, but the Romantic Road (*Romantische Strasse*) is where you want to stop. All along the Romantic Road are castles, fortresses, half timbered houses, churches, town halls, and some very impressive walled towns. Contrary to what the name implies, the Romantic Road isn't very romantic. Parts of the road are beautiful, while others are little more than a typical looking two lane industrial road full of commercial trucks. If you want to drive the Romantic Road, take your time and make the effort to stop along the way.

Romantic Road History

While many of the sites along the Romantic Road are many hundreds of years old, the route is only 60 years old. The route was created back in 1950 as a "themed" route to help promote tourism in the area.

Romantic Road Today

One of the best ways to describe the Romantic Road is to say what it isn't. The Romantic Road is not Route 66. There are no "Romantische Strasse" Gasthofs or gas stations. There isn't any memorabilia available in theme stores glorifying the name. There is another drawback for those wishing to drive the road. Several sections of the Romantic Road are choked with heavy truck traffic most of the week.

Perhaps this may sound a little disappointing for those wanting to have a spirited drive through the countryside. While the road isn't exactly romantic, it is a journey through medieval culture, history, and art. The sites along the road are exemplary examples of pristine medieval towns and architecture, several of which never experienced the destruction of any war.

Opposite: *A county Grenzsteine (border marker) near Feuchtwangen.*

Above: *Romantic Road sign in both German and Japanese.*

Quick Stats

▶ 366 kilometers long
▶ Road was created 60 years ago
▶ 3 walled towns -
  Rothenburg o.d.T., Dinkelsbühl,
  and Nördlingen
▶ Most visited theme road/ holiday
  route in Germany

Driving the Romantic Road

Because of the many possible stops, to drive the entire route will take at least 2 days at a quick pace and 3 days if you stop at most of the sites.

If driving the entire route isn't possible, there are a few alternatives. One is to focus on the southern portion south of Landsberg and visit all the sites in conjunction with a drive along the Alpine Road. The other is to drive the northern route starting at Rothenburg o.d.T. and head south to Nördlingen. This journey would cover the three ringed towns. Another possible trip would be to start at Rothenburg o.d.T. and head to Würzburg. This is especially nice in the Autumn when the vineyards are near harvest.

When driving on the Romantic Road, you will periodically see "Romantische Straße" signs along the side of the road. These signs are not directional signs posted at every turn, but rather reminders. It is possible to drive many kilometers with out spotting one. We recommend that drivers also purchase a detailed road map as well.

Top Left: *The wall surrounding Rothenburg ob der Tauber.*
Left: *Gallows Gate in Rothenburg o.d.T.*

Major Stops

These are the most significant stops along the Romantic Road. This list is from north to south and the kilometers denote distance from Würzburg.

Würzburg - 0 km - Northern most stop and known for its vineyards. That also makes late summer and autumn a good time to visit.

Tauberbischofsheim - 31 km - Visit the Türmersturm (*tower*).

Bad Mergentheim - 51 km - Visit the Deutschorden Schloss (*castle*).

Rothenburg ob der Tauber - 98 km - This medieval walled town is crowded but worth the visit. Plan to spend either a night here or at very least 4 or 5 hours. Advance hotel reservations are recommended.

Dinkelsbühl - 143 km - This walled city made history during the 30 year war (1618 - 1648) when local children pleaded with the Swedish invaders to spare the town. Every summer the city re-enacts the event. See *www.kinderzeche.de*

Nördlingen - 172 km - Visitors can walk around the entire town on its medieval walls. There is also a 15 million year old meteor crater 24 kms in diameter with Nördlingen built on the crater floor.

Augsburg - 248 km - One of Germany's oldest cities with many sites to see. One of the many is the Fuggerei - the world's oldest social housing project.

Landsberg am Lech - 294 km - Visit the Schmaltzturm (*tower*) that dates back to the 14th century.

Rothenburg ob der Tauber

Rothenburg o.d.T. is the single most popular stop along the Romantic Road. It is a walled village just west of the Autobahn A7 and south of Würzburg. Its beauty and popularity also means it is crowded, especially in the summer. The best way to visit Rothenburg is to avoid trying to see the town during the middle of the day and walk the town in the evening. If possible, spend the night!

If you do spend the night, try the night Watchman Tour (with a lantern armed tour guide!). The English tour starts at 8:00 PM and the German tour at 9:30 PM. The tour meets in the market square in front of the town hall and costs € 6.- for adults and € 4.- for students. 12 and under are free.
See *www.nightwatchman.de*

Steingaden - 343 km - The Alpine Road and Romantic Road intersect. Visit the Rococo Church "Wieskirche". See *www.wieskirche.de*

Schwangau - 362 km - Thanks to Disney, the Schloss Neuschwanstein is with out doubt the most famous and recognized landmark in Southern Germany. Hohenschwangau is also worth visiting. Best place to park is in the town of Hohenschwangau a few kilometers away.

Füssen - 366 km - Highest city in Bavaria and southern most town on the road.

Tourist Information
www.romanticroad.com
www.romanticroad.de

Tour operators
www.romanticroadcoach.de

ADAC Bavarian Historic Rally

Day 1 (Green)
Start at a Schloss Maxlrain in the town of Maxlrain and drive a loop through Rott am Inn and back to Maxlrain (Map on opposite page).

Day 2 (Red)
Start in Bad Aibling and head south through Bad Feilnbach, Kirchdorf, Grassau, and Siegsdorf. Head north to Teisendorf and through Großgmain and Grödig to the Salzburgring in Austria. Return by heading south through Hallein, Bad Reichenhall, and Inzell to Siegsdorf. From there pass the A8 to Traunstein and Seebruck

at the northern end of Lake Chiemsee. Return to Bad Aibling by driving through Rimsting.

Day 3 (Light Blue)
Start once again in Bad Aibling and head south west to Au bei Bad Aibling, Hundham and to Spitzingsee. South and into Austria driving though Bayrischzell to Hechtsee. Return to Bad Aibling via Tatzlwurm, Nußdorf, Kirchdorf, and Bad Feilnbach.

✳ This is a slightly abbreviated route of the 2010 Bavarian Rally (The full route was far more complex).

ADAC Bavaria Historic

If you own a 30 year old vintage car, try one of the many ADAC Rallies! Now in its 23rd year, the ADAC Bavarian Historic winds its way through Bavaria and a little bit of Austria in an annual 3 day summer rally with participants from Germany, Austria, Switzerland, and Italy.

There are two possible ways to drive the Bavarian Historic. One is in the timed stage rally and the other casual rally with a shorter run, longer breaks, and fewer timed stages.

At the very least, watch the website for information about the vintage car show and first day send off. The 2010 rally started at a castle in Maxlrain and drew 20,000 spectators and 3,000 vintage cars.

Opposite: *1937 Alvis 12/70 Special.*
Right: *Starting line in Maxlrain.*
Below: *Map of the 2010 Route.*

Quick Stats

▶ 150 cars
▶ 790 kilometers long
▶ Cost is € 955.-

Future dates

June 23 - 25, 2011
June 7 - 9, 2012

Contact Information

ADAC Südbayern e.V.
Ridlerstr. 35
80339 München
Germany

Phone: +49 (0) 895195-116
E-mail: *bavaria-historic@sby.adac.de*
www.bavaria-historic.de

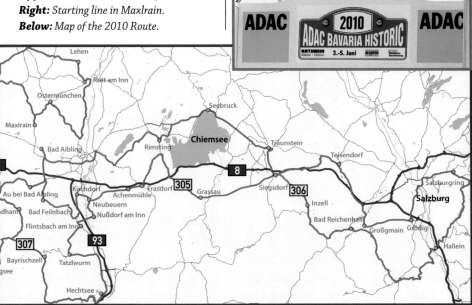

Favorite Bavarian Lake Drives

As you travel outside of the Bavarian capital of Munich, one of the many different and beautiful places to explore is the Lake District between the city and the Alps. But rather than listen to us tell you where to go, let us all follow in the foot steps (or tire tracks) of the professionals ∎

While other guidebooks just create drives and call them "*Loved*", we talked to the best source possible - a group of locals who have been in the business of sports cars for many decades. Let us proudly introduce you to "Sport und Tourenwagen, GmbH", or just "**S & T**" as they were known by both customers and friends alike.

So who was S & T? They used to be an official Munich Ferrari dealer who, until recently, sold and serviced new and used Ferraris. But what S & T offered was more than a place of business, they also offered something called the "**Stammtisch**". Literally translated, Stammtisch means *regular's table*. But to the friends of S & T, the Stammtisch was their monthly summertime drive and dinner.

Each Stammtisch would start at their Munich dealership and end at some amazing restaurant. For years, S & T collected information on drive after drive and restaurant after restaurant. For many years we here at Via Corsa were guest's of S & T, warmly welcomed by them to spend evenings in good company. Please enjoy their Stammtisch drives just as we have!

"Ausflug"

It's 5:30 AM on a summer Sunday morning, and it's is already bright. The little Porsche Boxer engine roars immediately to life...then spits a bit until the carburetor is full. The aim is the Bavarian Alps south of Munich. At this time there is no traffic and the streets are empty. When I get to the Alps, the little car drifts through the curves with each downshift. My little Speedster has forgotten nothing. No Autobahn can replace this feeling. For this is an "Ausflug".

Oliver Littmann

5 Best Stammtisch Drives

1 Ammersee

Seehaus is a small restaurant tucked on the side of the road just south of Utting. If you have 2 or more in your party, you might try reserving the dinner table at the end of the pier.

2 Chiemsee

Malerwinkel is a restaurant and hotel at the north end of Chiemsee. There is both indoor dining and outdoor dining on the deck.

3 Berg

Schloss Berg is a west facing hotel and restaurant poised perfectly for spectacular lake side sunsets over Lake Starnberger.

4 Tutzing

Tutzing is located on the eastern shore of Lake Starnberger. It is on a small peninsula that boasts both a biergarten and amazing restaurant that specializes in fresh lake fish as well as pastries and desserts.

5 Tegernsee

The views from Leeberghof are beyond spectacular. If you want that perfect romantic setting either during the day or evening, visit Leeberghof at Lake Tegernsee.

Ammersee

Ammersee

Enjoy Ammersee for either lunch or dinner!

Starting Point
Munich at the Autobahn A96 (München-Lindau)

Ending Point
Seehaus in Riederau

How long does the drive take
About one hour depending on traffic. The Autobahn A96 will experience rush hour during afternoons.

What makes this drive special
It's a nice short drive from Munich. The route is easy to follow and good for a quick lunch or dinner. The road does not follow the lake shore, but is still scenic.

Best time of day
Afternoon or evening. The patio is east facing so the sunset is behind the restaurant.

Price
Moderate. Small menu but very good seasonal dishes such as Spargel (*seasonal white asparagus*).

Directions

From **Munich by car:**

- ▶ Autobahn A96 (München-Lindau)
- ▶ Exit 29 / Greifenberg
- ▶ South on St2055 direction Greifenberg
- ▶ Follow St2055 through Schondorf and Utting
- ▶ Look for the small "Seehaus" sign. The parking lot on the east side of the St2055.
- ▶ Once parked, walk across the railroad tracks and to the right/south to the entrance of Seehaus.

Opposite: The special attraction at Seehaus is the chance to book the single table at the end of their pier. Reservations are necessary and it may be booked for parties of 2 or more.

Contact Information

Seehaus Riederau am Ammersee
Seeweg Süd 22
86911 Riederau/Diessen
Germany

Phone: +49 (0) 8807/7300
Fax: +49 (0) 8807/6810
E-mail: *info@seehaus.de*
www.seehaus.de

Hours

- ▶ Daily 12:00 PM to 10:00 PM

Special Bonus

- ▶ Ask about reserving the table at the end of the pier. The minimum is 2 people and may accommo- date up to 8.

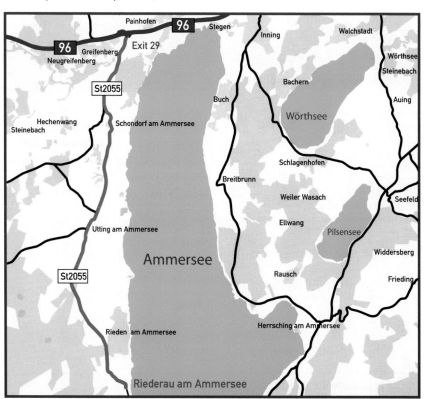

Chiemsee

Malerwinkel at Chiemsee

Tour the northern shore of Chiemsee!

Starting Point
Munich at the Autobahn A8
(München-Salzburg)

Ending Point
Malerwinkel near Seebruck

How long does the drive take
Budget one to three hours depending
on traffic, your route, and pit stops.
The A8 has heavy traffic all week long
and a daily rush hour.

What makes this drive special
This is definitely a journey to take
slowly. Once off the Autobahn, feel
free to explore the small towns dot-
ting the shores of Chiemsee. Try
taking the ferry to Herrenchiemsee to
explore the island and castle.

Best time of day
Daytime. In fact count on spending a
full day around the lake.

Price
Moderate to expensive. Set menus
range in price to almost $100.- per
person.

Directions

From **Munich by car:**

- ▶ Autobahn A8 (München-Salzburg)
- ▶ Exit 106/Bernau
- ▶ North on St2092 direction Prien
- ▶ Once north of Prien, follow signs to Rimsting, then Gstadt, and then finally in the direction of Seebruck.
- ▶ Malerwinkel is at the northern end of the lake near the intersection of St2093 and St2095. Look for the signs to the hotel.
- ▶ Here is a drive where there are several different possible routes and detours as every quaint village on Chiemsee is worth a look. Take a full day for this drive and explore!

Opposite: *The shallow shore and cold water of Chiemsee and Malerwinkel.*

Contact Information

Malerwinkel Hotel - Restaurant
83358 Seebruck-Lambach
Germany

Phone: +49 (0) 8667/8888-0
Fax: +49 (0) 8667/8880-44
E-mail: *malerwinkel@seebruck.de*
www.hotelmalerwinkel.de

Hours

- ▶ Daily 7:00 AM to 10:00 PM

Special Bonus

- ▶ There is a children's play area for guests of the hotel next to the hotel near the walking path running along side the shore of the lake.

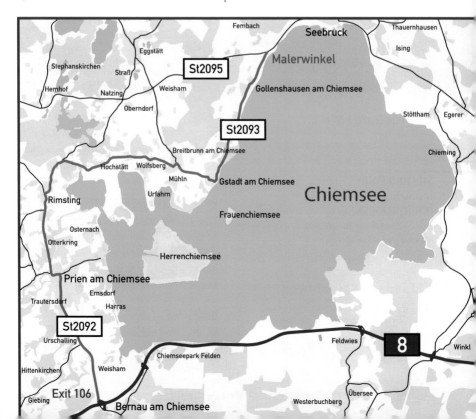

Berg on Starnberger See

Schloss Berg

Watch the sunset at Starnberger Lake!
(Both their patio and indoor restaurant seating have lake views.)

Starting Point
Munich at Autobahn A95
(München-Garmisch)

Ending Point
Schloss Berg on Starnbergser See.

How long does the drive take
About one hour. There is not a lot of traffic leaving Munich on the Autobahn A95 nor is there heavy traffic on the Autobahn A952 to Starnberg. The only exception to this would be sunny mornings on a summer weekend.

What makes this drive special
The drive itself is really short. Most of the time spent on the Autobahn is usually easy and with out traffic jams. The destination is beautiful and sunsets are spectacular.

Best time of day
Dinner and sunset is the best time. The lake view is to the west and sunsets are beautiful.

Price

Cheap to moderate. The Biergarten offers less costly fare while the restaurant offers wonderful seasonal dishes.

Directions

From **Munich by car:**

- ► Autobahn A95 (München-Garmisch)
- ► Autobahn A952 (Starnberg)
- ► Exit 2/Percha
- ► South on St2065 direction Berg
- ► Right/west on Waldstrasse
- ► Right/west on Ölschlag
- ► Parking to the left and hotel is straight ahead.

Opposite: *Overlooking Starnberger See at sunset just after a summer rain storm.*

Contact Information

Hotel Schloss Berg
Seestr. 17
82335 Berg
Germany

Phone: +49 (0) 8151/963-0
Fax: +49 (0) 8151/963-52
E-mail: *info@hotelschlossberg.de*
www.hotelschlossberg.de

Hours

- ► Daily Noon to 9:00 PM

Special Bonus

- ► The biergarten is a great bonus for sunny summer evenings!

Tutzing on Starnberger See

Tutzing Peninsula

Dine on the shores of Starnberger See!

Starting Point
Munich at Autobahn A95
(München-Garmisch)

Ending Point
Häring Wirtschaft in Tutzing

How long does the drive take
About one hour to 90 minutes. As you follow the lake, there are more than a few places to stop and take pictures, so the drive could take longer.

What makes this drive special
The windy road from the town of Starnberg to Tutzing is a quiet 2 lane country road thick with shaded trees and scenery of the lake. An alternative route is to drive on the B2 and then use one of the several side roads to reconnect to the St2063.

Best time of day
Even though the sunset is behind the restaurant, what makes Häring Wirtschaft so popular is that it is located on a small peninsula giving the visitor over a 180 degree view of the lake.

Price

Cheap to Expensive. The Biergarten offers less costly fare while the restaurant offers the very best regional fresh water fish. Ask for patio seating during clear summer evenings. Reservations are recommended.

Directions

From **Munich by car:**

- ▶ Autobahn A95 (München-Lindau)
- ▶ Autobahn A952 (Starnberg)
- ▶ B2 direction Starnberg center
- ▶ Left on Wittelsbacherstrasse
- ▶ Right on Bahnhofplatz
- ▶ Left on St2063/Possenhofenerstr.
- ▶ Follow St2063 out of Starnberg to Tutzing
- ▶ Left on Mühlfeldstrasse (in Tutzing)

Opposite: Häring Wirtschaft.

Contact Information

Häring Wirtschaft
Midgardstr. 3-5
82327 Tutzing
Germany

Phone: +49 (0) 8158/1216
Fax: +49 (0) 8158/7935
E-mail:
information@haering-wirtschaft.de
www.haering-wirtschaft.de

Hours

- ▶ Tuesday to Sunday 10:00 AM to 11:00 PM. Closed Mondays.

Special Bonus

- ▶ Known for amazing deserts and fresh fish caught daily from Starnberger See.

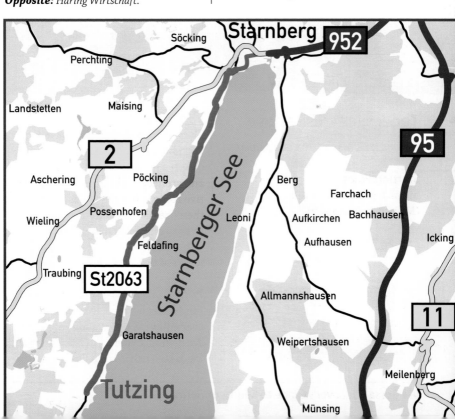

Tegernsee

Tegernsee from above

Romantic sunsets, views, and dinner!

Starting Point
Munich at the Autobahn A8
(München-Salzburg)

Ending Point
Leeberghof just south of Tegernsee.

How long does the drive take
About 1 hour to 2 hours depending on traffic and pit stops.

Above: *Spectacular views and romantic dining above Tegernsee.*

What makes this drive special
This is a very nice country drive but without a lot of lakeside scenery.

Best time of day
Afternoon and early dinner is the best time. The sunset is to the west and over the lake. Evenings outside are very romantic and guests can see the lights of distant villages and towns.

Price
Moderate to expensive. Almost everything at this restaurant is local. The jams are cooked in house and the fresh lake fish is from Tegernsee.

Directions

From **Munich by car:**

- ▶ Autobahn A8 (München-Salzburg)
- ▶ Exit 97/Holzkirchen
- ▶ South on B318 direction Lochham/ Gmund am Tegernsee
- ▶ As you approach Gmund am Tegernsee, look for B307 direction Tegernsee/Rottach
- ▶ South on B307
- ▶ Drive through the town of Tegernsee. Just after you have exited the town of Tegernsee, look for Leebergstrasse and the sign for Leeberghof pointing to the left.
- ▶ Left (and up) Leebergstrasse towards Leeberghof. The road is narrow and steep. Look for parking along the road before the restaurant.

Contact Information

Leeberghof
Restaurant - Bar - Hotel
Ellingerstr. 10
83684 Tegernsee
Germany

Phone: +49 (0) 8022/18809-0
Fax: +49 (0) 8022/18809-99
E-mail: *info@leeberghof.de*
www.leeberghof.de

Hours

- ▶ Tuesday to Sunday 12:00 PM to Midnight. Closed Mondays.

Special Bonus

- ▶ The recently renovated SASSA bar "The Most Beautiful Bar in the World" located outside the hotel.

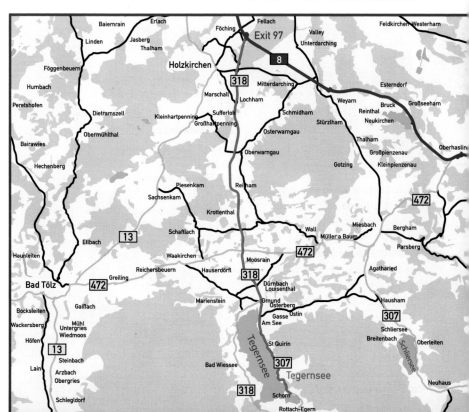

Additional Sites to see -

These sites are not covered in the main section of this guidebook. Here is a quick glimpse at some additional places to go and things to do.

Bernd Rosemeyer Memorial
The famous and talented Grand Prix driver Bernd Rosemeyer was attempting a 400 km/h high speed world record run on January 28, 1938 in an Auto Union Streamliner. He lost control and perished in the accident. The Autobahn A5 where he perished is still used today. If you head south on Autobahn A5 from Frankfurt towards Darmstadt, there is an Autobahn rest stop/memorial on the west side just south of exit 24 Langen/Moerfelden. Park at this rest stop and follow the signs to the memorial.

Solitude Rennen Track Building
Visitors can see the Schloss Solitude and the old timing and scoring building on the side of the road on L1187/Mahdentalstrasse between Glemseck and Mahdental. This ghost race track is slowly making a return to racing. Both are to the west of Stuttgart.
www.solitude-rennen.de

Above: *The Porsche Weissach Test Track west of Stuttgart.*

Alemannenring
From 1991 to 1995, the DTM series raced on a 1.7 mile temporary street circuit in the town of Singen. Efforts are underway to revive this race. *www.alemannenring.de*

Feldbergring
Outside of Frankfurt there is a ghost track by the name of Feldbergring. The track was in use from the 1920s through the 1950s and ran on what is now public roads. Anyone wishing to find the track should look for the town of Oberreifenberg. The start/finish line was on Siegfriedstrasse and ran through the Hoch-Taunus Nature Park.
www.feldbergrennen.de

Schleizer Dreieck
Since 1923, the race track Schleizer Dreieck (*triangle*) has held races ranging from Formula 3 to the current fare of motorcycle races. The track is still used periodically.
www.schleizer-dreieck.de

Weissach Research Facility
About 25 kilometers west of Stuttgart is the secret and famous Weissach Research and Development Center. Porsche opened the center back in 1971 as a state of the art facility and test track. It has been central to the development of new Porsches ever since. In subsequent years, the center has undergone expansions and updates. There are ways to visit Weissach, but it isn't easy. Start by asking your local Porsche Dealer if a tour is possible or by joining a Porsche Club (as a few sometimes arrange trips).

Wiesmann

Sadly some cars never make it to North America and Wiesmann is one of them. This northern German manufacturer has been in the business of manufacturing sport cars since 1985. Their top of the line car is the BMW powered Wiesmann GT MF5. This model has the same 507 hp V10 from the BMW M5. Want to see a Wiesmann? There are sales centers in Stuttgart and Munich. For Stuttgart, contact Wiesmann Meilenwerk Stuttgart at *www.merz-pabst.com*. For Munich contact C&C Premium Cars. *www.wiesmann-muenchen.de*

Wiesmann offers a factory tour at their plant north of Dortmund. For information about the manufacturer or the factory tour, see their website. *www.wiesmann.com*

Nürnberg Industrial Museum

We simply ran out of room to include this otherwise fine museum. Its exhibition halls are filled with historic cars, motorcycles, industrial machines, and even vintage computers. *museums.nuremberg.de/industrial-culture/index.html*

Above: *Wiesmann Jubiläumsmodell Roadster MF 3 CSL.*

Munich Toy Museum

This wonderful little toy museum is hidden in Munich's Alten Rathaus just off the Marienplatz. There aren't a lot of toy cars, but there are teddy bears, robots, and dolls. This is a nice (and quick) family stop during the usual tour of the downtown Munich pedestrian zone. *www.spielzeugmuseum-muenchen.de*

Opel Factory Tour

Opel is, by all accounts, a major automotive manufacturer and well respected all over Europe. The problem is Opels are not sold in the United States. If you find yourself in Rüsselsheim (a city to the south west of Frankfurt) stop by the Opel Forum. The factory tours of Opel are run twice a day Monday through Friday at 11:00 AM and 3:00 PM There is currently no listing for an English tour.

Admission

Adults	€ 4.50
Children under 12 years	€ 2.50
Groups of 10 persons (per person)	€ 3.50
Disabled	€ 2.50

Opel Forum
Bahnhofplatz
65428 Rüsselsheim
Germany

Phone: +49 (0) 6142/765600
Fax: +49 (0) 6142 /765619
E-mail: *diewerkstour@de.opel.com*
www.opel-diewerkstour.de

www.opel.de/experience/werkstour/index.act

German Auto Racing

Race Series

Formula 3 Euro Series
www.f3euroseries.com

ATS Formula 3 Cup
www.formel3.de

GP2 Series
www.gp2series.com

FIA GT3 European Championship
www.gt3europe.com

NitrOlympX Drag racing
www.nitrolympx.com

VLN - Nürburgring
www.vln.de

Deutsche Tourenwagen Meisterschaft (DTM)
www.dtm.com

ADAC GT Masters
www.gtmasters.org

Porsche Sportscup
www.porsche.com

Porsche Carrera Cup Germany
www.porsche.com

Single Event Races

FIA Formula 1 - Run once a year at either the Hockenheimring or Nürburgring. See *www.formula1.com*

Hockenheim Historic - In Memory of Jim Clark
www.hockenheim-historic.de

1000 KM Rennen
www.1000km-hockenheim.de

ADAC 24 Hours Nürburgring
This is the only 24 hour race in Germany and it is raced on the Nordschleife.
adac.24h-rennen.de (no www.)

FIA GT1 WM
International series that visits Germany once a year.
See *www.gt1world.com*

ADAC Eifel Classic
This annual event is a revival race based on the race started in 1922.
www.adac-eifelrennen.de

AvD Oldtimer Grand Prix
Please see page 226.

German Born Drivers

Christian Abt, Sebastian Asch, Michael Bartels, Marc Basseng, HH Frentzen, Timo Glock, Nick Heidfeld, Claudia Hürtgen, Wolfgang Kaufmann, Walter Röhrl, Nico Rosberg, Bernd Schneider, Michael Schumacher, Ralf Schumacher, Sabine Schmitz, Hans-Joachim Stuck, Adrian Sutil, Marcel Tiemann, and the Winkelhock family.

Opposite: Formula 1 at Hockenheim in 2008. Lewis Hamilton starts the race in pole position, finishes in the race in first place, and takes the 2008 driver championship.

Top: DTM - Hockenheimring October 2005. Bernd Schneider in a Vodafone AMG-Mercedes scores his 39th win in his 200th race.

Above: The start of the 2010 Porsche Carrera Cup race at the Norisring in Nürnberg. Nicolas Armindo took pole position and won the race in his 450 hp Porsche GT3 Cup car.

Tickets

www.nuerburgring.de
www.hockenheimring.de
www.formula1.com
www.gpticketshop.com
www.grandprix-tickets.com

Calendar of Events

Our list of events covers all of Germany. While most events here are run every year, some are not. Some annual events take place the same weekend each year while others may occur in the spring one year and then the fall the next. Please check with the organizers for up to date information.

February

Trade Show: Spielwarenmesse - International Toy Fair Nürnberg
www.spielwarenmesse.de

Trade Show: Automobil Expo Freiburg (Biennial)
www.fwtm.freiburg.de

Trade Show: Auto Salon Metropolregion Nürnberg
www.freizeitmesse-nuernberg.de

Trade Show: Bremen Classic Motorshow
www.classicmotorshow.de

March

Show: Retro Classics Stuttgart
www.retropromotion.de

April

Market: Veterama Ludwigshafen
www.veterama.de

Race: Hockenheim Historic - In Memory of Jim Clark
www.hockenheimring.de

Rally: Langenburg Historic
www.langenburg-historic.de

Trade Show: Techno Classica Essen
www.siha.de

May

Market: Technorama Ulm
www.technorama.de

Race: Tuner Grand Prix at Hockenheimring
www.hockenheimring.de

Race: ADAC Masters Weekend at Hockenheimring
www.hockenheimring.de

Race: Jim Clark Revival
www.jimclark-revival.com

Rally: ZF Sachs Franken Classic
www.sachs-franken-classic.de

Rally: ADAC Rallye Wurttemberg
www.rallye-wuerttemberg-historic.de

Trade Show: Car + Sound in Friedrichshafen
www.carandsound.com

Trade Show: Tuning World in Friedrichshafen
www.tuningworldbodensee.de

Retro Classics

Event Coordinators

RETRO Promotion GmbH
Postfach 1321
71266 Renningen

Phone: +49 (0) 7159/9278-09
Fax: +49 (0) 7159/172-08
E-mail: *info@retropromotion.de*
www.retroclassics.de
www.messe-stuttgart.de

Directions to Messe Stuttgart

From **Stuttgart by car:**
▸   Autobahn A8 (Stuttgart-Ulm)
▸   Exit 53a / Stuttgart-Flughafen/ Messe
▸   West on L1192n
▸   Messe is located on south side

Above: *Retro Classics in Stuttgart.*

This 4 day long show in early spring attracts over 60,000 visitors, 1,100 exhibitors, and 3,000 vehicles. The large majority on display are classic cars. 2011 marks the 12th annual event.

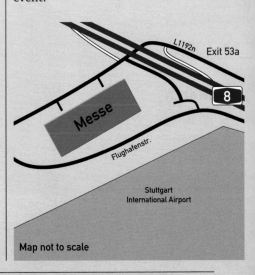

Klassikwelt Bodensee

Experience an event celebrating land, air, and water. This annual 4 day event fills all 12 exhibition halls of the Messe Friedrichshafen and thrills the public with a temporary race track and parade.

Event Coordinators

Klassikwelt Bodensee
60327 Friedrichshafen
Germany

Phone: +49 (0) 69/7575-0
www.klassikwelt-bodensee.de
www.messe-friedrichshafen.de

Directions to Messe Friedrichshafen

From **Munich by car:**

▶ Autobahn A96 (München-Lindau)
▶ Exit 3/Sigmarszell
▶ Right/west on B31/B308 direction Friedrichshafen
▶ Right on Allmannsweilerstrasse
▶ Convention Center is located on the right side of the road

Above: *Klassikwelt Bodensee.*

June

Concours: Retro Classics meets Barock
www.retro-classics-meets-barock.de

Market: Oldtimer Markt Bockhorn
www.oldtimermarkt-bockhorn.com

Race: 24 Hours Nürburgring
adac.24h-rennen.de

Race: ADAC Eifelrennen 2010
www.adac-eifelrennen.de

Rally: ADAC Deutschland Klassik
www.adac.de/oldtimer

Rally: Württembergische Classic
www.wuerttembergische-classic.de

Rally: ADAC Bavarian Historic
www.bavaria-historic.de

Rally: Donau Classic in Ingolstadt
www.donau-classic.de

Rally: 2000 km durch Deutschland
www.2000km.com

Rally: ADAC-MSRT-Breisgau
www.msrt-freiamt.de

Rally: ADAC Sachs Franken Classic
www.sachs-franken-classic.de

Rally: Bosch Boxberg Classical
www.bosch-boxberg-klassik.de

Rally: ADAC Sudelfeld Classic
www.amc-miesbach.de

Show: Klassik Welt Bodensee
www.klassikwelt-bodensee.de

July

Concours: Oldtimer Meeting Baden Baden
www.oldtimer-meeting.de

Concours: Classic Days Schloss Dyck
www.schloss-dyck-classic-days.de

Race: FIA Formula 1 Race
www.formula1.com

Race: DTM - Norisring
www.norisring.de

Race: Solitude Revival
www.solitude-revival.org

Rally: Heidelberg Historic
www.heidelberg-historic.de

Rally: ADAC Rallye Heidelberg Historic
www.msc-ziegelhausen.de

Show: Freiburg Schauinsland-Klassik
www.schauinsland-klassik.de

August

Open Track: Public Race Days at Hockenheimring
www.hockenheimring.de

Race: AvD Oldtimer Grand Prix at the Nürburgring
www.ogpracing.de

Race: Schottenring Grand Prix
www.schottenring.de

Race: NitrOlympX
www.nitrolympx.com

September

Concours: Schloss Bensberg Classics
www.sbc2010.com

Concours: Classic-Gala Schwetzingen
www.oldtimergala.de

Hill Climb: Automobile Club Hersbruck ADAC Hill Climb of Happurg
www.ac-heb.de

Party: Oktoberfest
www.oktoberfest.de

Race: ADAC 1000 km
www.fhr-langstreckencup.de

Rally: Eifel Classic
www.motor-klassik.de

Rally: MTC Meeting and Rally
www.mtc-bobenheim.de

Rally: "Lap of Celler Castle"
www.msc-celle.de

Show: DKW Club Nürnberg
www.dkw-club.org

Show: Oldtimer Days Fürstenfeld
www.oldtimertage-fuerstenfeld.de

Trade Show: Automechanika Frankfurt (Biennial)
automechanika.messefrankfurt.com

October

Market: Oldtimer-Teilemarkt Freiamt
www.msrt-freiamt.de

Market: Veterama Mannheim
www.veterama.de

Trade Show: Frankfurt Book Fair
www.buchmesse.de

November

Trade Show: Professional MotorSport World Expo
www.professionalmotorsport-expo.com

Trade Show: Essen Motor Show
www.essen-motorshow.de

December

Holiday: Christkindlmarkt/ Christmas Markets. See each respective city tourist web site for info -
www.muenchen-tourist.de
www.stuttgart-tourist.de

All events are subject to change or cancellation. Please contact the event organizers for up to date information.

Above: Isdera "Autobahnkurier" prototype at the 2010 Classic-Gala Schwetzingen International Concours D'Elegance.
Opposite: IAA Show in Frankfurt in 2009. The 2010 show was in Hannover with the 2011 show returning to Frankfurt.

IAA
Frankfurt Auto Show

Event Coordinators

IAA Frankfurt
Ludwig-Erhard-Anlage 1
60327 Frankfurt am Main
Germany

Phone: +49 (0) 69/7575-0
www.iaa.de
www.messefrankfurt.com

Directions to Messe Frankfurt

From **Frankfurt by car:**
▶ Autobahn A5 (Mannheim-Frankfurt)
▶ Exit on A-648 direction Frankfurt and follow until Autobahn ends
▶ Follow the signs for "Messe Frankfurt"

Every two years this annual new car show comes to Frankfurt. This is the world's largest automotive fair and a show many manufacturers use to debut new model releases.

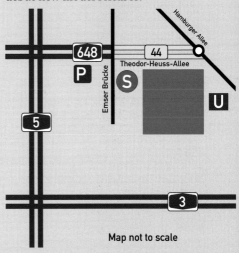

Map not to scale

Driving Essentials

Start Driving!

As soon as you arrive in Germany, one of the first things you will be doing is picking up the rental car (or European Delivery car). But before you start the engine, there are many things to know about driving in Germany safely. Here is our list of the most important German traffic laws.

Driver's License

You must have a valid driver's license. While rental car agencies recognise U.S. issued licenses, we recommend obtaining an international permit as well (some driving schools require one). International permits may be obtained from the AAA - *www.aaa.com/vacation/idpf.html*

Speeding

The German police are very efficient at nabbing speeders by constantly developing new technologies derived to slow down motorists. There are fixed cameras, temporary cameras, cameras on road signs, cameras in the bushes, and cameras in tunnels. In fact unless you are practically standing next to a photo radar box, the tricky ones are all but invisible.

Above: *One of many types of photo radar in Germany.*

Speeding Tickets

So what happens when you are caught speeding? One of two things happen. Either there is a police car or motorcycle waiting down the road to pull you over, or the ticket is mailed to you later. If you are pulled over, you must pay on the spot. If you are sent a ticket in the mail to your U.S. address, you may find that your rental car company has charged your credit card and forwarded your name to the German authorities.

Speed Limits

- ▶ City - 50 km/h on city streets
- ▶ Secondary roads - 80 km/h
- ▶ Dual Carriage - 100 km/h
- ▶ Autobahn - 130 km/h is the recommended speed limit. There are speed limit signs posted on the Autobahn if a limit applies.

Safety Belts

- ▶ Belts are mandatory for all passengers - both front and rear.
- ▶ Car seats are mandatory for children under 12 years old or shorter than 4 foot 11 inches.
- ▶ Children under 10 years of age may not ride in the front seat.

Rude signs

It is illegal to offend another motorist. This includes the middle finger or tapping your forehead with your index finger.

Alcohol Limits & DUIs

The legal limit is 30 mg/100 ml or 0.3 (which can be as little as one beer). The penalty can be as high as 5 years in jail with fines in the thousands of Euros. To make things simple, don't drink and drive. Use public transportation.

Parking

Parking is a nightmare in the best of times. Instead of parking meters, Germany uses a system of prepaid vouchers and parking discs.

Parkshein

Buy the voucher at a nearby ticket dispenser. They usually take coins, notes, and credit cards. Place the ticket inside your car on top of your dash.

Parkscheibe

Rotate your Parkscheibe (see **page 319**) to your arrival time. If you get caught fudging the time, you could get a ticket.

Park Garage

A parking garage is usually underground, dark, difficult to navigate, and full of parking spaces made for 3/4 scale cars. Take your ticket with you and pay at either a cashier or ticket machine when you are about to leave the garage.

Yielding

The general rule of thumb is everything and everyone has the right of way over you. There are massive fines for failing to yield the right of way.

Bikes & Pedestrians

If you brave driving around a city center, there will be people and bikes everywhere and they always have the right of way. Be very careful when turning right on green.

Emergency Vehicles

Yield to fire trucks, ambulance, police, or anything else with a flashing blue light.

Trams & Buses & Trains

Yield to Buses and Strassenbahn (*Trams*) as they leave a station or stop. Buses can be somewhat aggressive when they leave a stop and often makes other motorists ponder if they actually look before pulling out.

Miscellaneous

Mobile Phones

Drivers are banned from using a cell phone without a hands free device. So are bicyclists, for that matter.

Stop Lights

Of course in Germany it is illegal to run a red light. You must stop at red lights and if you run one, the fine could be as high as € 360.-. There is no right turn on red in Germany - except in some instances. In some parts of Germany, if you come to a red light intersection and see a small metal sign (not illuminated) with a green arrow pointing to the right, you may make a right on red. In order to do so legally, you must come to a complete stop first, then make your right.

Top: *Parkscheinautomat (or automatic parking voucher machine).*

Above: *A bike path running through automobile traffic.*

Autobahn Driving Essentials

Types of Highways

A - Autobahn (*German Highway*)
B - Bundes Landstrasse (*Federal Road*) -
Some of these roads are divided highways
while others look like a country road.

Autobahn Rules

▶ No passing in the right lane (there
   are 2 exceptions - entry /exit ramp
   lanes and passing in traffic jams). No
   passing on a hard shoulder.

▶ If you are not passing another car, do
   NOT stay in the fast lane. Not only
   can you be ticketed and fined up to
   € 80.-. It is dangerous, so stay right.

▶ No stopping or U-turns on the
   Autobahn.

▶ No backing up on the Autobahn.
   Ever. The site of reverse lights at
   night look like the head lights of an
   on coming car and may be mistaken
   for what every Autobahn driver fears
   most, a Geisterfahrer (*Ghost driver*).
   In fact backing up or driving against
   Autobahn traffic is punishable with a
   jail term up to 5 years.

▶ Keep a safe distance from the car
   in front of you at all times. There
   are massive fines (up to € 400.-) for
   tailgating.

▶ Drivers in the fast lane might flash
   their headlights or use their left turn
   signal (rare these days) to signal
   slower drivers to move right. Techni-
   cally this is illegal, but it is done.

▶ When you enter a tunnel during the
   day, turn on your low beams. Once
   out, turn them back off.

▶ If there is a traffic jam in front of
   you, briefly turn on warning hazards
   to warn the people behind you.

▶ Truck traffic is mostly banned on
   Sundays. This is by far the best day of
   the week to drive the Autobahn.

▶ *www.autobahnpolizei.de*

Accidents /Emergency Stopping

Turn on hazards and place your warning
triangle roughly 100 yards behind your
car (the warning triangle, first aid kit, and
safety vest are all mandatory to be in your
car at all times) and call the police.

Speeding Fines

Contrary to popular belief, many parts of
the Autobahn system have a speed limit
(and a lot of speed cameras). The first fine
is for speeding outside built up areas and
the second fine is for speeding inside a
town or city. Anyone caught speeding in
excess of 31 km/h in a town or 41 km/h
outside will have their license revoked for
a minimum of 1 month. So be careful!

▶ Up to 10 km/h - € 10.- / € 15.-

▶ 11 to 15 km/h - € 20.- / € 25.-

▶ 16 to 20 km/h - € 30.- / € 35.-

▶ 21 to 25 km/h - € 70.- / € 80.-

▶ 26 to 30 km/h - € 80.- / € 100.-

▶ 31 to 40 km/h - € 120.- / € 160.-

▶ 41 to 50 km/h - € 160.- / € 200.-

▶ 51 to 60 km/h - € 240.- / € 280.-

▶ 61 to 70 km/h - € 440.- / € 480.-

▶ Over 70 km/h - € 600.- / € 680.-

Above: *The open Autobahn and in the*
passing lane at almost 200 km/h.

Brief Autobahn Listing

- ► A3 - More crowded than the A92 or A93, but can be nice on a Sunday.
- ► A5 - Hit and miss here. Can be crowded, but nicer in the south.
- ► A6 around Nürnberg - Crowded with construction. A lot of truck traffic from Eastern Europe.
- ► A7 Würzburg - Memmingen - Easy and light traffic.
- ► **Autobahn A8** - (see below)
  - • A8 Stuttgart - Ulm (2-3 lanes) - heavy traffic and the Autobahn narrows, slows to 80 km/h, and bottlenecks in the Schwäbische Alb between exits 59 and 60.
  - • A8 Ulm - München (2-3 lanes with 120 km/h limits) - heavy construction and traffic make this a terrible and unpleasant drive.
  - • A8 München - Salzburg (2-3 lanes) - If there is no traffic, which is unlikely, this can be a nice drive and scenic as well.
- ► A48 near Nürburgring - Light traffic and fun.
- ► A81 - Crowded around Stuttgart.
- ► A92 to Deggendorf - very good with only a few speed limit zones.
- ► A95 München - Garmisch (2 lanes) - best Autobahn there is. Scenic on a clear day heading south.
- ► A96 - nice with a little construction.

Speed Conversions

- ► 50 km/h = 31 mph
- ► 80 km/h = 50 mph
- ► 100 km/h = 62 mph
- ► 130 km/h = 81 mph
- ► 200 km/h = 124 mph
- ► 250 km/h = 155 mph

Roadside Assistance

ADAC Phone: +49 (0) 180/2222222
www.adac.de
AvD Phone: +49 (0) 69/6606600
www.avd.de

Autobahn Service Station

There are 2 types of gas stations along the Autobahn, the **Rasthof** and **Autohof**. The Rasthof has its own dedicated exit along side the Autobahn, while the Autohof requires a little more effort to reach by exiting the Autobahn and perhaps driving a few hundred meters. The Autohof has better food and usually cheaper gas. Toilets just about everywhere cost 50 cents just to enter. When you stop at a gas station, just start pumping your gas. There is no need to prepay or swipe a credit card prior to pumping. When you are done, head into the Kasse (*Cashier*) to pay.

Gas Type (1 gallon = 3.78 liters)

- ► 91 Bleifrei (*Unleaded*)
- ► 95 Normal
- ► 98 Superbleifrei (*Super Unleaded*)
- ► Diesel
- ► Erdgas (*Natural Gas*)

Payments

- ► Pay after you pump
- ► Say "Tankstelle Eins" for "Pump 1"
- ► Regular unleaded gas costs roughly € 1.50 a liter, or about $7.94 / gallon

Hours

- ► Autobahn stations are open 24 hours and accept credit cards
- ► Inside cities - closed Sunday

Above: *Typical Tankstelle at an Autohof just off the Autobahn in Germany.*

German Road Signs

Autobahn Signs

Left: The start or entrance to an Autobahn. This does NOT mean there is no speed limit at this point. This sign usually appears at an on-ramp or as you exit a city.

Left: Autobahn exit or the Autobahn ends. Signs are posted at Autobahn exits or as the Autobahn enters a city or is reduced from a divided highway to a lesser road.

Left: "Ausfahrt" - literally translated as "out driving" or to "drive out". This is an Autobahn exit sign.

Left: This is it. The sign of legends. This is official permission to go as fast as you can. Provided you do this on the Autobahn and in a safe and prudent manner. If you see this on a road other than the Autobahn, this is NOT carte blanche to speed, but rather a removal of previous speed restrictions.

Above: *Where two Autobahnen meet. This is traveling on the Autobahn A-96 approaching the Autobahn A-7.*

Opposite: *Temporary speed limits imposed on traffic on the Autobahn. These signs change without notice.*

Autobahn Signs

Above: Autobahn exit distance markers. Each of the 3 signs appear from left to right each 100 meters prior to a marked exit.

Speed Limit Signs

 Left: Maximum speed allowed in a given zone. Usually seen in a town.

Right: Removal of the speed restriction for that zone. You can return to the prior posted speed limit.

 Left: Maximum speed allowed.
Right: Removal of that speed restriction.

 Left: Advised speed limit. You will see this sign on the Autobahn recommending a speed of 130 km/h.

Right: Removal of speed limit recommendation.

 Left: Minimum speed limit.
Right: Removal of the minimum speed limit.

Numbered Road Signs

Above Left: Autobahn sign. They are always blue with white letters.

Above Right: "Bundesstraße" or "Bundesstrasse". The English translation is "Federal Street" or "Federal Highway".

 Left: This is the international highway number given to Autobahnen entering other countries.

Warning Triangles

 Left: Danger or caution ahead.

 Left: Road narrows ahead on both sides road/ street.

 Left: Two way traffic ahead.

 Left: Approaching a junction or crossroad where the traffic to the right has priority.

 Left: The universal yield sign.

 Left: Rough road ahead.

 Left: Train crossing ahead where there is a full or half barrier or gate.

Traffic Flow Signs

 Left: Far right arrow indicates a shoulder traffic lane.

 Right Top: Shoulder lane is closed to through traffic.

 Right Bottom: Shoulder lane merges with traffic.

 Left: Roundabout. Yield to traffic in roundabout. Traffic travels counterclockwise.

Directional Signs

 **Left:** If you want to go left, you will find yourself turning right.

 **Left:** One way street - go right.

 **Left:** Detour begins.

 Left: Go straight.

 Right: One way street.

Below: Various directional signs.

Yield Signs

 These two signs are always seen together as a pair. One is posted for traffic traveling in each direction. The most common place they are seen are at single lane roads in smaller towns and villages.

Above: Yield to on coming traffic.

 Right: You have right of way. On coming traffic must yield.

 Left: You have right of way. Traffic at intersections and side streets must yield. These are seen all over residential neighborhoods.

Right: Right of way ends.

Important Note - If you approach an intersection that has **NO** indication or sign to who has right away, do not assume that this is a four way stop or four way yield. The cross traffic could have a "right of way" sign that is out of your field of view. It is a good rule to yield at any unmarked intersection.

 Left: Right of way at the next intersection only. Side street traffic must yield. The right of way could be different at the intersection past this particular one.

 Left: Right of way through a turn. Side street traffic indicated on sign must yield. This sign particular sign indicates a left turn.

 Left: Stop sign for Buses and Strassenbahn (*Trams*) only.

Parking

Parking is a headache in Germany no matter where you go. Even quiet residential streets will have restrictions and limits. To park in any timed zone, you will need this **Parkscheibe** (*Parking Disc*). Place it inside your vehicle atop your dash and set the dial to your arrival time.

Right: Parkscheibe (*Parking Disc*)

Left: Parking sign that requires a Parkscheibe. This is parking sign allows 2 hours of parking.

Left: Parking to the left of sign.
Right: Parking to the right of sign.

Left: No stopping or parking to the left of sign.
Right: No stopping or parking to the right of sign.

Left: No stopping or parking at all.
Right: No stopping or parking to either side of sign.

Left: No parking. This sign may be seen in all the "no stopping or parking" sign variations shown above.

Miscellaneous

Left: "Wet Surface" speed limit. This sign is always placed just below a speed limit sign.
Right: Turn-out lane ahead.

Left: No Passing.
Right: Passing allowed.

Left: No passing by vehicles over 3.5 tons. For example trucks with trailers.
Right: Passing allowed.

Left: Vehicles forbidden/ No entry.

Right: Only residents are allowed.

Left: Dead end street ahead.

Right: Detour off the Autobahn. This sign starts at an Autobahn exit indicating a detour. Signs follow side streets to rejoin the Autobahn at the next possible exit.

* Please note that we have **NOT** included every possible German Road sign. There are roughly 280 different signs listed by the ADAC and they are all important to driving in Germany. Please visit the ADAC (*www.adac.de*) for a complete list.

German License Plates

The German "Kennzeichen", or licence plate, is known around the world as an icon for automotive freedom. Retailers sell copies to enthusiasts to adorn their garages, offices, or even (in some states) the front license plate frame of their favorite car. Here is a breakdown of the license plate of choice by car enthusiasts everywhere!

The Fonts - DIN 1451

All German license plates and road signs used the font DIN 1451 Mittelschrift (Deutsche Industrie Norm or *German Industrial Standard*). Around the year 2000 there was a redesign and Germany switched all license plates to a new font called FE-Schrift (Fälschungserschwerende Schrift or *False-hindering script*).

This new font isn't popular with the motoring purists and widely criticized as being ugly. However, this much maligned new font is supposed to prevent errors in photo radar and make it more difficult for people to change or manipulate letters and numbers with black paint or tape.

Top: *A collection of German license plates using both the old and new font styles.*

Right: *The current German plate using the new FE-Schrift font and the blue sidebar.*

Format

Every German license plate on a private vehicle starts with a city letter (or letters). There are some exceptions for the army and diplomats (see below). For the examples below, **X** = letters and **0** = numbers.

City versus Suburbs
- **M-XX 000 or M-XX 0000** = City of Munich.
- **M-XX 00 or M-X 0000** = Outlaying areas/suburbs of Munich.

Temporary plates
- M-06000 = Car dealer plate.
- M-07000 = Private individuals for cars 20 years and older.
- **M-XX 0000 03/11** = Registration valid from only March until November.
- **S-496 U 96/06** = Older export plate (as seen in the photo to the left). Current export plates end with a "Z" for "Zoll" (*customs*).

Government
- **M-00000** = Government/Police.
- **THW-00000** = Technisches Hilfswerk (*German Technical Relief*).
- **Y-00000** = Bundeswehr (*Army*).

Miscellaneous
- M-XX 000 = Tax free (Farmers for example).
- **M-XX 000 H** = Historic vehicles (over 30 years old).
- **0** = Diplomatic plates for governments and embassies.

Major City Codes

As a rule of thumb, the larger the city, the fewer letters. Hamburg (**HH**) is one notable exception.
Major city letters -
- **M-XX 0000** = München - One letter is for a large city.
- **IN-XX 0000** = Ingolstadt - Two letters is usually for a medium sized city.
- **STA-XX 0000** = Starnberg - small town or rural area.

- **A - Augsburg**
- **B - Berlin**
- **D - Düsseldorf**
- **E - Essen**
- **F - Frankfurt**
- **H - Hannover**
- **IN - Ingolstadt**
- **K - Köln (Cologne)**
- **L - Leipzig**
- **M - München (Munich)**
- **N - Nürnberg (Nuremberg)**
- **O - Diplomatic Vehicles**
- **R - Regensburg**
- **S - Stuttgart**

Buy a German plate!

If you want to buy a German license plate, head to the nearest Kfz-Zulassung (*Motor Vehicle Department*). Look for small nearby shops that advertise "Kfz-Kennzeichen". We paid € 15.- per plate from Goßler & Riedl on Ludwighafenerstr. 1 in Munich.

Left to Right: *The registration seal from Stuttgart, registration seal from the state of Hessen, and the TÜV safety sticker (now only on rear plate).*

German Driver's License

FÜHRERSCHEIN

The German "Führerschein", or driver's license, is available for any German resident once they reach the age of 18. The process is long and complicated and many students fail their first attempt. The outcome is a country that has some of the best educated motorists in the world. Foreigners, especially the ones from outside the European Union, can only watch and wonder how it is all done. Here is a brief glimpse.

The Fahrschule

In order for a German resident to obtain a "Class B/BE" German driver's license, the future driver must start with a school. The "Fahrschule", or driving school, is mandatory for any first time driver wishing to obtain a license. A German driving school is pricey. The cost is about € 1,000.- to € 1,500.- and that doesn't count in the factor a lot of people must repeat portions.

Here is a brief list (by no means complete) of what German students will learn in a Fahrschule -

▶ Minimum of 10 hours driving plus driving at night and on the Autobahn.
▶ Students may try to pass 3 times.
▶ If a student cannot pass after 3 attempts, they must have a psychological test.

Above: *The old style German driver's license.*
Opposite: *A typical Fahrschule vehicle.*

Living in Germany

U.S. Drivers

There are very specific rules if you are a U.S. citizen living in Germany as a full time resident.

▶ You are legally allowed to drive in Germany for the first 6 months of your residency on just a U.S. license. This can be extended up to 12 months.

▶ If a German license is not acquired within 3 years of establishing residency, you will have to start learning from the beginning as a first time driver.

▶ Usually the foreign license is collected, but because a U.S. license also serves as identification, the U.S. driver's license is exempt.

▶ There are 26 states that have reciprocity with Germany. In other words, you can walk right into a Führerscheinstelle and get a license without taking any tests.

To obtain a German license from one of the 26 states listed below, here is what you need -

▶ Signed and filled out application form from the German "Führerscheinstelle", or Driver License Office.

▶ One passport photo.

▶ Eye test.

▶ Official identification (Passport).

▶ U.S. License plus a translation into German.

▶ Anmeldebestätigung (*Proof of German residency*)

▶ Statement by applicant giving valid dates of their U.S. license.

States that have only partial reciprocity or no reciprocity will require varying degrees of testing.

European Union

Anyone holding a license from another European Union country can just use their home license.

Visiting Germany

If you are just visiting Germany, a U.S. license is sufficient. Some people may opt for an International Driving Permit (IDP) as some driving schools require one, but normally it is not necessary. See *www.aaa.com/vacation/idpf.html* for more information.

U.S. States with full driver's license reciprocity

Alabama	Illinois	New Mexico	Texas
Arizona	Iowa	Ohio	Utah
Arkansas	Kansas	Oklahoma	Virginia
Colorado	Kentucky	Pennsylvania	West Virginia
Delaware	Louisiana	South Carolina	Washington (state)
Idaho	Massachusetts	South Dakota	Wisconsin
	Michigan		Wyoming

German Travel Information

When to Visit

The easy answer is summer. Several of the museums listed here are either closed or have reduced hours during the winter. Roads are covered with dirt, snow, and ice during the colder months and rental cars are running winter tires. Don't be discouraged if your travel plans are during winter. Many automotive conventions are in the winter and all the large museums and factory tours are open for business.

Currency

Transactions are done by Euros. Each Euro has 100 cents. Currently 1 Euro costs roughly 1.40 U.S. dollars and 1 U.S. dollar buys .72 Euro cents. The symbol for the Euro is - €

Customs/Entry

U.S. Citizens must present a valid U.S. passport when entering Germany. When entering as a tourist, you may stay up to three months.

Time

Greenwich Mean Time (GMT) plus 1 hour. Germany uses a 24 hour time clock. In other words, 1:00 PM is written as 13:00.

Travel with kids

Germany has a lot to offer children. In fact a large portion of the museums covered in this book have sections and displays made specifically for children. The only place that children are not allowed are on a number of factory tours. In addition to the museums listed in this book, there are a number of great zoos around Southern Germany. Even though the name may not suggest, a biergarten is a fantastic place to take children and our favorite, Waldwirtschaft outside Munich, has a children's play area.

Electricity

Voltage in Germany is 220V/240V
- ▶ Germany uses a 2 prong plug. A voltage adapter is needed however most lap tops and cell phone chargers have a built in adapter.

Television

- ▶ Germany uses PAL B/G versus NTSC in the United States
- ▶ Major stations are ARD & ZDF with sports and Formula 1 broadcast on RTL and Sky Sport.

Weights and Measures

- ▶ 1 Kilometer = .62 miles
- ▶ 1 Meter = 39.37 inches
- ▶ 1 Liter = 2.11 pints
- ▶ 1 Gallon = 3.78 liters
- ▶ 1 Kilogram = 2.2 pounds

Public Holidays

- ▶ January 1 - All Germany
- ▶ January 6 - Bavaria & Baden-Württemberg only
- ▶ Good Friday - All Germany
- ▶ Easter Sunday- All Germany
- ▶ May 1 - All Germany
- ▶ August 15 - Bavaria only
- ▶ October 3 - German Unity
- ▶ November 1 - All Germany
- ▶ December 24 - 26 - All Germany
- ▶ December 31 - All Germany

Business hours

- ▶ Banks - Monday to Friday
  8:30 AM to 1:00 PM
  2:30 PM to 4:00 PM
  (5:00/6:00 PM on Thursdays)
- ▶ Retail stores - city centers
  9:00 AM to 8:00 PM
  Monday to Friday
  8:30 AM to 4:00 PM Saturday
  Closed Sundays

Phones

Cell Phones - Germany uses the GSM900/1800 network. iPhones that use AT&T are compatible. iPhone tip: turn "Data Roaming" off while overseas. It is possible to rent or buy prepaid cell phones that use a German network. *www.blau.de* is one such provider.

Calling to/in Germany -

+011-49-89 = Dialing Munich from U.S.

+0049-89 = Dialing Munich from inside the EU, but outside Germany.

+089 = Dialing Munich from inside Germany.

Calling from Germany

+001 - U.S.A. & Canada

+0044 - United Kingdom

+0041 - Switzerland

Travel inside a large city

Sometimes it is better to just leave your car and use German public transportation such as the **S-Bahn** or **U-Bahn**. The system is easy to understand, punctual, and mostly clean. The German authorities trust people to buy their tickets, validate them, and not cheat the system. Schwarzfahrer (*people who purposefully don't have tickets*) are fined € 60.- on the spot when caught (by plain clothes inspectors).

ATMs/Credit Cards

Credit cards are still not as widely accepted in Germany as they are in the United States and some gas stations may still not take credit cards. Visa and Mastercard are most widely accepted while American Express and Discover are not.

Tipping

Restaurants - Rounding the bill up by two or three Euros is polite. Tipping 15% to 20% in addition to the bill is not normal and a good way to shock a server.

Taxis - Taxi drivers will add a fee for baggage. Tips are generally a Euro or two.

VAT (sales tax)

Sales tax is 19% - a portion can be refunded using sales tax forms when leaving the EU. They are redeemed at the airport at time of departure.

Tourism Websites

www.baden-wuerttemberg.de
www.bayern.de
www.cometogermany.com
www.deutschland.de
www.germany-tourism.de
www.germany-tourism.co.uk
www.muenchen-tourist.de
www.stuttgart-tourist.de

Consulates in Munich

British Consulate-General

Möhlstr. 5
81675 München
Germany
Phone: +49 (0) 89/211090
Fax: +49 (0) 89/21109 144
ukingermany.fco.gov.uk

Consulate of Canada - Munich

Talstr. 29
80331 München
Germany
Phone: +49 (0) 89/2199570
Fax: +49 8(0) 89/21995757
E-mail: *munic@international.gc.ca*
www.canadainternational.gc.ca

US Consulate General in Munich

Koeniginstr. 5
80539 München
Germany

Phone: +49 (0) 89/28880
E-mail: *ConsMunich@state.gov*
munich.usconsulate.gov/munich/offices.html

Airports

Frankfurt Airport
www.frankfurt-airport.de

Munich Airport
www.munich-airport.de

Stuttgart Airport
www.flughafen-stuttgart.de

Airlines

Air Canada
Phone: +49 (0) 69/275115-111
www.aircanada.com

American Airlines
Phone: +49 (0) 180/511 3709
www.aa.com

British Airways
Phone: +49 (0) 180/526 6522
www.britishairways.com

Delta
Phone: +49 (0) 180/333 7880
www.delta.com

Lufthansa
Phone: +49 (0) 180/580 5805
www.lufthansa.com

United
Phone: +49 (0) 69/5007 0387
www.united.com

Race Cars Rental Car Companies

RSR Nürburg
Phone: +49 (0) 2691/931666
www.rsrnurburg.com

Rent a Race Car
Phone: +49 (0) 2691/931770
www.rentracecar.de

Normal Rental Car Companies

Avis
Phone: +49 (0) 1805/217702
www.avis.de

Budget
Phone: +49 (0) 69/710 445596
www.budget.com

Dollar
Phone: +49 (0) 89/2035230 51
www.dollar.com

Enterprise
Phone: +49 (0) 800/368 3777
www.enterprise.com

Europcar
Phone: +49 (0) 180/58000
www.europcar.com

Hertz
Phone: +49 (0) 180/533 3535
www.hertz.de

National Car
Phone: +49 (0) 800/464 7336
www.nationalcar.com

Sixt
Phone: +49 (0) 180/525 2525
www.sixt.de

Insurance

If you drive a car in Germany (rental or otherwise), you will be required to obtain third party liability insurance. The major car rental companies provide this insurance as well as offer full coverage as an additional option.

Please read your policy BEFORE driving on the Nordschleife (or any race track). There is a very good chance your rental policy forbids it! Look for wording such as rules against driving on a "One Way Toll Road".

Traffic Alerts

Traffic alerts on the car radio are called *Verkehrsrundfunkbereich*. These announcements in German are alerting motorists to traffic jams, accidents, and even photo radar. If you know some German, it should be enough to understand if your Autobahn is mentioned.

Emergency Services
▶ Police - dial 110
▶ Fire - dial 112
▶ Medical - dial 112

Radio Stations
Some are good, some are bad, and a few are just ugly. Listen to at your own risk!

Bayerischer Rundfunk (*Bavarian Radio*) covering all of Bavaria. Stations are - BRD1, BRD2, BRD3, BR-Klassik, B5 aktuell

Munich Radio Stations
89.0 - Radio2Day - *Funk/soul/rock*
92.4 - Radio Feierwerk - *alternative*
93.3 - Energy Munich - *Top 40 music*
95.5 - Radio Charivari (Bavaria) - *Pop*
96.3 - Radio Gong - *Top 40/main stream*
101.3 - Antenna - *Top 40 music*
104.0 - egoFM - *Dance/electric*
106.4 - TopFM - *Top 40 music*

Nürnberg
92.9 - Radio N1 - *Rap/dance*
97.1 - Gong - *Top 40 music/main stream*
98.6 - Charivari - *Pop*
99.0 - Star FM - *Rock*
103.6 - egoFM - *Dance/electric*
106.9 - Radio Energy - *Top 40 music*
105.1 - Klassik - *Classical music*

Südwestrundfunk (*Southwest Radio*) covering Rheinland-Pfalz and Baden-Württemberg. Stations are - SWR1, SWR2, SWR3, SWR4

Mannheim
98.7 or 104.6 - AFN (U.S. Armed Forces)
100.9 - Welle - *Rock*
103.3 - Radio BoB - *Rock/pop*
106.1 - Sunshine - *Electric*
106.7 - Big FM - *Rock/pop/rock*
107.9 - Rockland - *Rock*

Stuttgart
89.5 - Big FM - *Rock*
99.2 - Freies Radio
100.7 - Radio Energy - *Top 40 music*
101.3 - Hit Radio Antenna
102.3 - AFN (U.S. Armed Forces)
107.7 - Die Neu 107 - *Rock/pop*

Understanding Country Codes
Look closely at the license plates around Germany. You may notice that each plate has a blue bar with a letter or two written inside. These letters identify the country of registration for that vehicle.

▶ A - Austria
▶ B - Belgium
▶ CH - Switzerland
▶ CZ - Czech Republic
▶ D - Germany
▶ DK - Denmark
▶ F - France
▶ NL - Netherlands/Holland
▶ PL - Poland

Car Magazines
There are several great German car magazines worth buying -
▶ *Auto Motor und Sport*
▶ *Auto Bild*
▶ *Auto Bild Sports Cars*
▶ *Auto Bild Klassik*
▶ *Motor Klassik*
▶ *Markt Sport Auto*
▶ *Auto Zeitung*

Car Shows
If you get a chance to watch some German TV, here are some shows to look out for -
▶ *Alarm für Cobra 11* (TV series with good action, stunts, and cars)
▶ *Grip das Motormagazin* (on RTL2)
▶ *Auto Mobil* (on VOX)
▶ Motorsports are on Sport 1 and DMAX.

Hotel Chains and Brief Hotel List

These chains are based in Europe and often have hotels near airports and city centers. They are not the prettiest places and are often marketed towards the business traveller.

Kempinski Hotels
www.kempinski.com

Lindner Hotels & Resorts
www.lindner.de

Mövenpick Hotels
www.moevenpick-hotels.com

Alps /Alpine Road

Seehotel / Grauer Café & Restaurant
Mittenwalderstr. 82-86
82431 Kochel am See
Germany
Phone: +49 (0) 8851/9250-0
www.grauer-baer.de
(Articles and photos about the Kesselbergrennen are on display in the restaurant)

Munich

Schlosshotel Grünwald (Our favorite)
Zeillerstrasse 1
82031 Grünwald
Germany
Phone: +49 (0) 89/649626-0
Fax: +49 (0) 89/649626-36
E-mail: *info@schlosshotelgruenwald.de*
www.schlosshotelgruenwald.de

Hotel Bayerischer Hof (expensive)
Promenadeplatz 2-6
80333 München
Germany
Phone: +49 (0) 89/2120-0
Fax: +49 (0) 89/2120-906
E-mail: *info@bayerischerhof.de*
www.bayerischerhof.de

Nürburgring

Dorint Am Nürburgring Hocheifel
An der Grand-Prix-Strecke
53520 Nürburg
Germany
Phone: +49 (0) 2691/309-0
Fax: +49 (0) 2691/309-189
www.dorint.com

Lindner Hotel Nürburgring
Stefan Bellof Strasse
53520 Nürburg
Germany
Phone: +49 (0) 2691/3025-000
Fax: +49 (0) 2691/3025-655
E-mail: *info.nuerburgring@lindner.de*
www.lindner.de

Motorsporthotel
Hauptstr. 34
53520 Nürburg
Germany
Phone: +49 (0) 2691/92000
Fax: +49 (0) 2691/920099
www.motorsporthotel.de

Speyer/Hockenheimring

Hotel Grafs Garni
Johannesstr. 13
67346 Speyer
Germany
Phone: +49 (0) 6232/6222870
Fax: +49 (0) 6232/6222875
E-mail: *info@grafs-garni-hotel.de*
www.grafs-garni-hotel.de

Stuttgart

Hilton Garden Stuttgart NeckarPark
Mercedesstr. 75
70372 Stuttgart
Germany
Phone: +49 (0) 711/90055-0
Fax: +49 (0) 711/90055-100

Acknowledgements

AMG Driving Academy
Audi Forums
BMW Motorsport
Yvonne Brandstätter
Stephanie Bourassa
Anka Busch
Greg Clark
Daimler Archives
Birgit Eccard
Katharina Engelbrecht
Ariane Fiedler
Tony Fouladpour
David Hamprecht
Corinna Handrich
Florian Hebel
Marlies Herrscher
Stefanie Hohn
Stefan Hopfinger
Jackie Jones
Karla Kanz
Rainer Klink
Julia Kopaunik
Jessica Landen
Astrid Lübke
Mercedes-Benz USA
Dirk Moersdorf
Susanne Mickan
Michael Mühlberger
Claudia Müller
Kerstin Nieradt
Sabine Ochaba
Susi Peschke
Porsche Cars N.A. & Porsche Media
Oliver Runschke
Peter Schack
Andrea Schindler
Christoph Seiler
Daniel Stiegler
Stephanie Voit
Bernhard Weidemann
Nico Wieth
Miriam Weiss

Thanks for the Interviews!

Derek Bell
Wolfgang Kaufmann
Sabine Schmitz
Susie Stoddart
Hans-Joachim Stuck

Special Thanks

Jim Milavec for that first trip to Germany.
The pretty German girl who unknowingly helped me fall in love with Germany.
Alexander Bachner for two amazing tours.
Everyone at S & T who hosted 2 decades of Ferrari Stammtischs and other fun!

Photo Credits - All photos taken by Ron Adams except -

Daimler AG - Daimler Archives - pages 28, 29, 30, 31, 70, 218, top - 305
Hans-Joachim Stuck - page 49
Hoch-Zwei - page 82, 83, 2x 304
Derek Bell - page 94
AMF Museum - page 98
Maybach Museum - page 152
MTM - pages 194, bottom 195
Wolfgang Kaufmann - page 223
Schottenring - page 240, 241
Sabine Schmitz - page 233
AMG Driving Academy - page 248
a-workx - page 258
Porsche Media - bottom page 305
Florian Kunkel - page 307
Oliver Littmann - pages 18, 88, 89, 90, 2x 91, 226, 227, 288, 289, 308, 310, 311, 323

Map Credits

Hockenheimring - page 209
Nürburgring Automotive GmbH - page 228, top of 229
Following maps based on Map Resources German map - page 10 - 13, 34, 96, 144, 178, 205, 255, 285
Following maps based on an Open Street Map base layer - pages 14 - 17, 146, 234-235, 239, 276-279, 281, 283, 289, 293, 295, 297, 299, 301

German Words & Phrases

Driving

Abschleppwagen - *tow truck*
Anlieger frei - *residents only*
Ausfahrt - *exit*
Autohof - *gas station outside the Autobahn*
Autobahnkapelle - *Autobahn church*
Autobahnkreuz - *cloverleaf*
Baustelle - *construction zone*
Bundesstrasse - *Federal Highway*
Bundeswehr - *military*
Einbahn Strasse - *one way street*
Einfahrt - *entrance*
Feuerwehr - *fire truck*
Geschwindigkeit - *speed*
Geisterfahrer or Falschfahrer - *ghost driver or wrong way driver*
Halt - *stop*
Hilfe - *help*
Höchstgeschwindigkeit - *top speed*
Krankenwagen - *ambulance*
Linksabbieger - *turn left*
LKW - *truck*
Maut - *toll*
Motorrad - *motorcycle*
Notfall - *emergency*
Notruf - *emergency call*
Pannenhilfe - *roadside assistance*
Parkhaus - *parking garage*
Parkschein - *parking voucher*
Parkscheibe - *parking plaque/disk*
PKW - *car*

Polizei - *Police*
Radfahrer - *bicyclist*
Radweg - *bike path*
Rasthof - *gas station inside the Autobahn system*
Rollsplitt - *gravel*
Straßenbahn - *trolly*
Strassen dienst - *road service*
Stau - *traffic jam*
Umleitung - *detour*
Unfall - *accident*
Verkehr - *traffic*
Weg - *path*
Zentrum - *city center*
Zufahrt - *entrance*

License & Registration

Brief - *title*
Kennzeichnung - *license plate*
Zulassung - *registration*
Führerschein - *drivers license*
Fahrschule - *driving school*
Landeshauptstadt - *city*
Teilkaskoversicherung - *liability only/3rd party insurance*
Vollkaskoversicherung - *full/comprehensive insurance*

Direction

Links - *left*
Rechts - *right*
Nord - *north*
Ost - *east*
Süd - *south*
West - *west*
Geradeaus - *straight ahead*

Gas Station

Angabe - *liters pumped*
Benzin - *gasoline*
Betrag - *total cost*
Bleifrei - *unleaded gas*
Erdgas - *natural gas*
Kasse - *cashier*
Motorenöl - *oil*
Tankstelle - *gas station*
Tank Platz - *gas pump*

Car Parts

Abblendlicht - *low beams*
Antrieb - *gearbox*
Allrad - *all wheel drive*
Auspuff - *exhaust*
Baujahr - *year built*
Bremsen - *brakes*
Bremssättel - *calipers*
Bremsscheiben - *rotors*
Felgen - *wheels*
Fernlicht - *high beams*
Getriebe - *Gearbox*
Gewicht - *weight*
Hubraum - *displacement*
Klimaanlage - *air conditioning*
Leistung - *engine performance*
Lenkrad - *steering wheel*
Nebelscheinwerfer - *fog lights*
PS - *HP (Horsepower)*
Reifen - *tires*
Rücklicht - *tail lights*
Scheinwerfer - *head lights*
Schlüssel - *key*
Stoßstange - *bumper*
Teppich - *carpeting*
Ventile - *valve*

Factory Tours

Auslieferung - *delivery*
Besucher - *visitor*
Ersatzteile - *spare parts*
Fahrzeug - *car*
Karosseriebau - *body shop*
Kunde - *customer*
Kundendienst - *customer service*
Lackierung - *paint shop*
Mitarbeiter - *employee*
Presswerk - *press shop*
Sicherheit - *safety*
Sonderausstattung - *car options*
Technische Abnahme - *technical inspection*
Teile - *parts department*
Treffpunkt - *meeting place*
Verkauf - *sales area*
Warenanlieferung - *delivery area*
Werksbesichtigung - *factory visit*
Werkführung - *factory tour*
Werks Tor - *factory entry gate*
Zubehör - *accessories*

Museums

Anfang - *start*
Ausgang - *exit*
Ausstellung - *display*
Eingang - *entrance*
Empfang - *reception*
Eintrittspreise - *entry fee*
Erwachsene - *adult*
Geschlossen - *closed*
Quittung - *receipt*
Maßstab - *scale*
Nicht Berühren - *do not touch*
Öffnungszeiten - *hours opened*
Ruhetag - *day off*

City & Country Words

Altstadt - *old city*
Berg - *mountain*
Burg or Schloss - *castle*
Fußgängerzone - *pedestrian zone*
Hauptbahnhof - *main train station*
Stadtmitte - *city center*

Numbers

Eins - 1
Zwei - 2
Drei - 3
Vier - 4
Fünf - 5
Sechs - 6
Sieben - 7
Acht - 8
Neun - 9
Zehn - 10

Days of Week

Montag - *Monday*
Dienstag - *Tuesday*
Mittwoche - *Wednesday*
Donnerstag - *Thursday*
Freitag - *Friday*
Samstag - *Saturday*
Sonntag - *Sunday*

Restaurant/Biergarten

Bier - *beer*
Damen - *ladies*
Guten Appetit
Helles - *export beer*
Herren - *men*
Kaffee - *coffee*
Nachtisch - *desert*
Prost! - *Cheers!*
Rotwein - *red wine*
Speisekarte - *menu*
Sekt - *sparkling wine*
Weisbier - *white beer*

General Conversation

Ja - *yes*
Nein - *no*
Grüß Gott - *hello (only in Bavaria)*
Bitte - *please*
Danke - *thank you*
Es tut mir leid - *I am sorry*
Guten Morgen - *good morning*
Guten Tag - *good day*
Guten Abend - *good night*
Haben Sie ..? - *Do you have..?*
Ist der Tisch frei? - *Is this table free?*
Ich bräuchte ... - *I need ...*
Ich hätte gern ein Bier - *I would like a beer*
Ich heiße... - *My name is...*
Was kostet das? - *What does that cost?*
Was ist das? - *What is that?*
Wo ist..? - *Where is..?*
Wie geht's? - *How are you?*
Sprechen Sie English? - *Do you speak English?*
Ich sreche kein Deutsch - *I don't speak German*
Bezahlung Bitte - *check please*
Auf Wiedersehen - *good bye*

Alphabet and Umlauts

The "ß" is called a scharfes S and = "ss". For example the word "Strasse" may also be written as "Straße".

The two dots over a vowel are called Umlauts. Words such as Nürburgring may also be written as Nuerburgring.

ä = ae
ö = oe
ü = ue

Now Available!

Via Corsa Car Lover's Guide to Arizona is all about Arizona and the love of the car!

This 256 page four color book features stories about the Barrett-Jackson Auction, Phoenix International Raceway, Penske Museum, Scottsdale Automobile Museum, NASCAR, Copperstate 1000, Route 66, and much much more!!!
ISBN-13: 978-0982571002

Exclusive Interviews with **Alice Cooper**, **Craig Jackson,** and **Arie Luyendyk**. Plus an exclusive sneak peak at the top secret Ford Motor Company Arizona Proving Grounds!

Available online at *www.amazon.com*, *www.barnesandnoble.com*, and *www. motorbooks.com*. You may also order by calling (800) 458-0454.

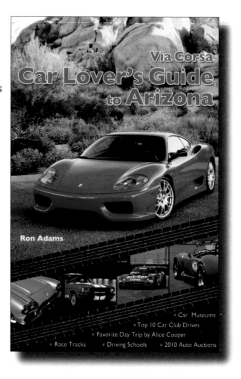